BUILDING CULTURE

BUILDING CULTURE

Studies in the Intellectual History
of Industrializing America,
1867–1910

RICHARD F. TEICHGRAEBER III

The University of South Carolina Press

Published by the University of South Carolina Press
Columbia, South Carolina 29208

www.sc.edu/uscpress

Manufactured in the United States of America

19 18 17 16 15 14 13 12 11 10
10 9 8 7 6 5 4 3 2 1

Library of Congress Cataloging-in-Publication Data
Teichgraeber, Richard F.
  Building culture : studies in the intellectual history of
industrializing America, 1867–1910 / Richard F. Teichgraeber III.
      p. cm.
  Includes bibliographical references and index.
  ISBN 978-1-57003-925-6 (cloth : alk. paper)
  1. United States—Intellectual life—1865–1918. 2. United States—
Civilization—1865–1918. 3. Industrialization—Social aspects—United
States—History. 4. Emerson, Ralph Waldo, 1803–1882—Influence.
5. Education, Higher—United States—History. 6. Universities and
colleges—United States—History. 7. Racism in education—United
States—History. 8. African Americans—Education—History. I. Title.
  E169.1.T39 2010
  973.8—dc22

                                        2010008127

The author wishes to thank the Tulane Murphy
Foundation for its support.

This book was printed on Glatfelter Natures, a recycled paper with
30 percent postconsumer waste content.

To Thomas Bender and Thomas L. Haskell

CONTENTS

ILLUSTRATIONS

PREFACE AND
ACKNOWLEDGMENTS

The studies collected here are intended as contributions to the intellectual history of modern America. They invite readers to explore how and why an unprecedented wave of interest in building cultural institutions swept through America during the era of industrialization. Twenty-five years ago most historians took the words "culture" (a hierarchical, privileged, mostly Europhilic domain of social refinement, aesthetic sensibility, and polished manners) and "industrialization" (the triumph of corporate capitalism) as unproblematic starting points. Their discussions centered on showing how and why "culture" became a new rallying cry of increasingly wealthy, native-born elites and of what these elites did in culture's name to alter or control what disturbed them about industrializing America. The prevailing mode of explanation acknowledged that at a time when America's institutional landscape was relatively barren, monied and privileged champions of culture were vital agents of the future of the nation, putting in place what remain among our key official institutions: municipal museums, opera houses and concert halls, immense central public libraries, municipal parks, and large private research universities. But twenty-five years ago most historians also downplayed (or simply ignored) the possibility that a normative concept of culture exists as a distinct category of analysis or substantial sphere of experience. Assuming such an approach would screen out the realities of unequal social and economic power, the consensus was that the architects of America's first national cultural institutions understood "culture" in ways that made it difficult for them to see the turmoil and divisions that accompanied industrial incorporation, let alone see them critically.[1]

This view of the relationship between industrialization and culture has been called into question in recent decades, and for various reasons. Most economic and labor historians no longer believe that during the late nineteenth century big business had the economic, political, and cultural authority conventionally ascribed to it. Declines in prices, profits, per capita output, and labor productivity, combined with the ability of skilled workers to enforce—both by strikes and in contracts—social norms that sanctioned their continuing control of machine production, now suggest that the late nineteenth century was in fact a time of economic, political, and cultural stalemate.[2] More recently feminist and other revisionist historians have highlighted the multiplicity of attitudes and interests displayed by men and women intent on building new cultural institutions. Indeed, the more closely historians examine the full range of first efforts made to build a national culture during the industrial era, the more elusive and fraught with contradiction the enterprise has become. It no longer makes good sense to say simply that the industrialization of the American economy prompted a single-minded parallel effort to build a hierarchical national culture.[3] Likewise, to continue to think in terms of "high" and "low" levels of American culture is to imagine a much clearer pattern of stratification than actually was achieved by the turn of the century. And so the social control interpretation, for the time being, has given way to a more pluralistic approach.[4]

Part of the purpose of *Building Culture* is to add weight to the new pluralist approach by drawing attention to some important but still poorly mapped aspects of American intellectual and cultural history during the industrial era. Three of these receive extended and sometimes linked discussions. The first is the concept of "culture" itself. The second has to do with Emerson's central place in the story of how Americans have gone about the work of building new cultural institutions. The third is the modern American university, undoubtedly the most distinctive and significant of many late-nineteenth-century institutions spawned by the new determination to build a national culture.

Yet in exploring these issues, *Building Culture* also attempts to lay the groundwork for overcoming a new inhibition displayed (to varying degrees) in recent pluralist approaches to the study of American culture during the industrial era. Curiously enough, this inhibition grows out of widespread acceptance of one of the most important truths highlighted by the approach—namely, that in industrializing America, the normative ideal of culture had diverse and not obviously compatible uses. The fear here is that historians who attempt to make sense of the many-sidedness of America's first great effort to build national cultural institutions will never be able to provide a framework in which all its facets somehow fit. The studies in this volume suggest there are several ways of overcoming this historiographic inhibition.

Among the most important is bringing greater chronological specificity to what I consider two central but inadequately mapped developments in the intellectual and cultural history of late-nineteenth- and early-twentieth-century America. The first is the many-sided, and ultimately successful, effort to secure Emerson a central place in American thought and culture; the second is the institutional growth and consolidation of modern American academic culture. History of course is not chronology. But if we are ever to understand how widespread talk about "culture" was accompanied by the prodigious expansion of American cultural institutions during the industrial era we certainly need a more refined temporal articulation of these two developments.

More careful attention to context also prompts new and more carefully focused questions about what some historians now believe was once a distinctively American understanding of culture. We know that talk and thinking about culture was as protean as it was persistent during the era of industrialization. But what do we make of the several adjectival couplings—"liberal culture," "scientific culture," "literary culture," "ethical culture," "Christian culture," "physical culture"—that characterized this discourse? And of whom ought we to speak when we attempt to identify its primary spokesmen? Walt Whitman and W. E. B. DuBois certainly mustered as much passion in its defense as did Charles Eliot Norton and Andrew Carnegie. And what of the institutional provenance of culture in late-nineteenth- and early-twentieth-century America? In his 1871 inaugural address, James Angell said that the state of Michigan had created its new university to put "a means of obtaining generous culture within the reach of the humblest and poorest child on its soil." Fifteen years later the Johns Hopkins economist Richard T. Ely argued that the Knights of Labor served much the same purpose for America's new working class.

Because such questions presuppose a single, unitary account of a diverse cast of characters who thought "culture" was a prize worth fighting for, it is not surprising that pluralist historians have scarcely considered them. The first essay in *Building Culture* addresses them directly. It argues that during the industrial era "culture" was understood as an inclusive ideal by most educated Americans, partly because it continued to carry its antebellum meaning of "self-culture"—that is, individual self-development or self-construction. "Culture" was also considered an inclusive ideal because there were as yet so few accepted symbols (either individual or institutional) of distinctively American achievement. And in these circumstances it is not surprising that talk about culture frequently pushed beyond the perceived constrictions of a European vision of culture by holding that in America culture not only lay in the future but promised to define and sustain the purposes of a society of unprecedented heterogeneity.

Building Culture also includes two studies that together make what I take to be a new case for according Emerson a special degree of attention in understanding the institutional workings of American cultural and intellectual life during the industrial era. Emerson never claimed the title of founder of his nation's culture, and these studies do not thrust representative status upon him. Rather, they aim to reconstruct specific historical developments—many of which Emerson neither anticipated nor lived to witness—that allowed him to remain a continuous presence in the life of a society undergoing fundamental economic and social transformation. At the same time they explore ways in which various individuals and groups enlisted Emerson to establish new, as well as secure old, cultural institutions and practices. Put another way, the growth and development of Emerson's reputation during the industrial era is more important for what it tells us about the new and changing cultural needs he was recruited to serve than it does about some "real" yet poorly understood figure who somehow existed separately from those needs.[5]

Building Culture also reflects some significant changes that have substantially broadened the domain of intellectual history in recent years. Among the most important of these—especially evident in my two final chapters—is the carefully contextualized study of academic intellectuals as active and self-conscious participants in American culture at large. Most contemporary intellectual historians remain wedded (as I am) to the notion that analysis of the discourse of intellectuals defines a central part of our domain. But quite a few of us now seek to gain access to that discourse by mapping different and changing institutional settings within which texts written by intellectuals appear and gain meaning. New questions have come to the fore. How does the discourse of intellectuals find its way to audiences of interested readers and interpreters? How do certain intellectuals and their texts happen to gain and maintain great cultural value? What roles do cultural and economic institutions play in shaping the production and reception of texts written by intellectuals? For whom and to whom do intellectuals speak? Such questions have given rise to a new kind of intellectual history—evident to varying degrees in all the studies in this volume—that moves back and forth between close readings of texts and careful reconstruction of their cultural and economic contexts.

In the case of American intellectual history, these questions have also invited more careful scrutiny of the commanding role the university has come to play among the institutions that give cultural authority to the discourse of intellectuals. To go back to the American university during the industrial era is to revisit an era when university presidents and professors first proclaimed that the American university system would be the arena within which sustained reflection on the cultural and intellectual life of the nation would now largely take place. The final two chapters in *Building Culture* probe the meaning of that promise, and how and why it gained almost immediate credibility. Put somewhat schematically, my argument is that the architects of the American university system were not only deeply concerned with defining their relationship with those who lived outside its walls but also remarkably successful in gaining their attention and approval. The growth and consolidation of modern American academic culture played itself out before many audiences and in multiple sites. And the upshot was that America's new universities and new professional academic associations created and occupied a new social space that I call the "academic public sphere." Mass-marketed books, mass-circulation magazines, and local and national newspapers were among the instruments that made it possible. So too were the complex career paths followed by leading university administrators and academic intellectuals, as well as the adult education movement in its various forms.

The final chapter, which begins by recounting the now largely forgotten story of the founding of the American Political Science Association (APSA) in New Orleans in late December 1903, continues this discussion. And it does so by focusing closely on another development that played an important role in the institutional growth and consolidation of modern American academic culture: racism. It is perhaps relatively well known, but even so still depressing, that America's first generation of academic intellectuals was almost uniformly racist and so had no quarrel with the Jim Crow South. Less well known is a fact I draw attention to in the last chapter: the new institutions they built were consciously designed to include the segregated South and therefore represented something more than a passive accommodation of racism. Chapter 5 shows that the founding of the APSA turned out to be one of a series of linked events that took place in 1903 that help us understand more fully how racism facilitated the national growth and consolidation of American academic culture.

A few other things about this book. By "America," I mean not the North American continent or the Americas but the United States. Like the normative concept of "culture," "America" too is a period term, one that virtually everyone used to describe the nation until the 1930s, when the country became better known as the United States. (There is in fact no country called America; we live in the United States *of America*, and have appropriated the adjective "American" even though we cannot claim exclusive title to it.) I also have avoided two commonly used terms in periodizing American history during the late nineteenth and early twentieth century—the "Gilded Age" and "Progressive Era"—mostly because they tend to lock us into two separate and conventional stories about the era of industrialization, making it difficult to draw attention to what I believe was actually a flexible continuity of ideas and interests. I would note, too, that I understand the intellectual history of the industrial era to be an addition, not an alternative, to its social and economic history. I also believe it would be a mistake to view it as a removable ornament. Removing it would hardly end discussion of the industrial era, but we would no longer be discussing the same thing. Intellectual history exists, as Wolf Lepenies insists, to remind us that "human societies are characterized not just by what people do, but also by what people say and think they are doing. History is not only about what is happening, history is also about making sense."[6]

Finally, part of my answer to the question of what attracted countless men and women to the pursuit of culture during the industrial era is evident in this book's title. In the late nineteenth and early twentieth centuries, Americans were encouraged to think of culture as an active and unfinished process rather than a thing in itself. Yet culture in America was not simply a work in progress, it was work open to a broad array of individuals and groups, not just people affluent enough to enroll in universities, attend operas, or practice a profession. The concept's inclusiveness, in other words, proved to be a centrally important part of its appeal, allowing it to apply across lines of class, gender, and race.

This collection is made up of articles and lectures initially produced for separate occasions. All have made earlier but also differently shaped appearances in print. Chapters 1, 3, 4, and 5 have been substantially expanded and revised for publication here; chapter 2 has been edited down somewhat. Each essay now also includes contemporary photographs of some of the figures I discuss, as well as illustrations and images taken from late-nineteenth- and early-twentieth-century books, magazines, and newspapers, all designed to enrich some of the stories I tell or to add weight to points I make along the way. Since these chapters do not constitute a completed map of the historical landscape, each piece can be read independently. But I also have prefaced each chapter with a headnote that not only indicates the essay's chief concerns but also clarifies its ties to the other studies collected here. None of the earlier versions of these chapters, it may be worth adding, is available online.

Building Culture is dedicated to the two intellectual historians who in recent years have taught me the most about the appeals and challenges of writing American intellectual history.

I am grateful to those who during the last decade provided me with the forums in which the studies in this book first came to life. They include Charles Capper, Conrad E. Wright, and the Center for the Study of New England History at the Massachusetts Historical Society; David Throsby and Michael Hutter and the Rockefeller Study and Conference Center in Bellagio, Italy; Helmbrecht Brening and the Bavarian American

Academy in Munich, Germany; Greg Cooper, Ted DeLaney, Bob Strong, and Tom Williams and Washington and Lee University; and Martyn Thompson and the Conference for the Study of Political Thought. I also want to acknowledge warmly the criticism and support of former and current colleauges on the Tulane University faculty from whom I learned important things while writing this book. At the top of a long list stand Geoffrey Harpham, Wilfred McClay, and Teresa Toulouse, who have been carefully reading my work and providing valuable advice for longer than I care to remember. I am also grateful for the collegial stimulation of Gerald Gaus, John Howard, Meg Keenan Tom Langston, Doug Nelson, Dan Purrington, Ben Reiss, Jonathan Riley, Judith Kelleher Schafer, and Michael Zimmerman. Beyond Tulane I have profited greatly from the critical suggestions of Casey Blake, Howard Brick, Charles Capper, Stefan Collini, Robert Gross, Jackson Lears, James Livingston, and Dorothy Ross. Readers are, as am I, also indebted to Frederick Bradley for his assistance in the initial editing of the manuscript and Bonnie Hanks for her indexing. I am deeply grateful for the example of their work, even more for their unfailingly helpful critical responses to my forays into this field.

I was fortunate that the University of South Carolina Press found two readers—one who prefers to remain anonymous; the other, Lewis Perry—who offered very thoughtful comments on the original manuscript of *Building Culture*. Their suggestions have aided my effort to merge originally separate studies into a unified and coherent argument. I also wish to thank Bill Adams at the University of South Carolina and the copy editor, Karin Kaufman, for working with me during the production process to improve the manuscript. My able research assistant during the summer of 2008, Nancy B. Stockton, helped to gather this book's photographs and illustrations. My thanks go to Molly Rothenberg for suggesting the title. I also am deeply and happily indebted to Ruth A. Carter, who assisted in the production of this book from start to finish.

ONE

"The word of the modern"

"Culture" in Industrializing America

Why did countless American men and women who lived during the era of industrialization believe "culture" was prize worth fighting for? And what exactly was the prize? In recent decades, many specialists in intellectual and cultural history have recognized the importance of these questions. But they have not been able to give them straightforward answers, and with good reason. Because the concept of culture enjoyed a prominence in late-nineteenth-century and early-twentieth-century American society it had never known before, we cannot avoid thinking of culture as an influential force. Yet precisely because at one time or another the concept embraced so much of what surface during the industrial era—science, literature, ethics, music, the university movement, the women's club movement, struggles for racial and social justice, even health and fitness consciousness— historians have been reluctant to view culture as an internally coherent force. The best we can do, it seems, is to adopt a pluralist approach that emphasizes the multiplicity of interests displayed by its many advocates and promoters during the era of industrialization.

This chapter adds weight to the new pluralist approach by drawing attention to several important but still poorly mapped developments that enriched and sustained American discourse about culture. But it also addresses the question of where the pluralist approach should be leading us. Stressing the malleability of the American concept of culture has allowed historians in the pluralist camp to see that those who believed in its individually and socially redemptive power did so for a variety of reasons we only trivialize by trying to reduce them to a single agenda. But there is an important difference between acknowledging the limits of interpretation caused by the abundance of historical evidence and failing to provide a coherent account of that evidence. Or put more strongly, I believe the new pluralist approach, while commendably concerned with avoiding the charge of reductionism, runs the risk of antiquarianism as it gathers more and more facts that threaten to become a burden to memory. I end the chapter with a discussion of three steps that may help historians in the pluralist camp avoid this trap.

I

"The writers of a time hint the mottoes of its gods. The word of the modern, say these voices, is the word Culture." No discussion of the history of American talk and thinking about culture during the industrial era can proceed very far without quoting several sentences from Walt Whitman's *Democratic Vistas* (1871), an essay that contains, among other things, one of the most powerful statements of an understanding of culture that is democratic and inclusive rather than hierarchical and elitist. More specifically, it is Whitman who gave expression to the hope that the pursuit of culture in postbellum America would entail "a radical change of category," a new program "drawn out, not for a single class alone, or for the parlors or lecture rooms, but with an eye to practical life, the west, the workingmen, the facts of farm and jackplanes and engineers, and of the broad range of women also of the middle and working strata." He also believed that talk of culture was just beginning to gain widespread circulation in American society, and he depicted this development as an opportunity to "include the widest human area" and "have for its spinal meaning the formation of a typical personality of character, eligible to the uses of the high average man—and *not* restricted by conditions ineligible to the masses."

In directly associating the concept of culture with the promising future of American democracy, however, Whitman also worried he had put himself "abruptly in close quarters with the enemy." For while "culture" was "the word of the modern," it disturbed him that "as now taught, accepted, and carried out," it also seemed to have become a new mark of social privilege in America, defining a new preserve of "mainly educated classes" who found the masses an "affront" and understood culture as an activity to be administered to them from above, as if from a celestial source. In these remarks Whitman did not make use of the word "genteel" to describe his "enemy," but it probably captures what he had in mind.[1]

Approached by way of the received account of the industrial era, which typically proposes the story of American cultural development in the late nineteenth century as one of exclusion and sacralization, Whitman's brief chronicle of a *Kulturkampf* taking shape in the immediate postwar years has a plausible ring. In fact, nothing remains more frequently cited in *Democratic Vistas* than Whitman's nervous anticipation

Fig. 1.1. Walt Whitman, 1871. Division of Photography and
Prints, Library of Congress

of the triumph of a genteel concept of culture that will serve to distinguish a new American elite rather than unify its ordinary people, as if he were almost conceding in advance that efforts to develop institutions and practices rooted in a democratic and inclusive understanding of culture are bound to fail. Yet there are various other strands of this story, which, when pulled, require us to construct a more complicated narrative in which Whitman's uneasiness about associating the word "culture" with the cause of democracy seems either premature or simply misplaced.

I begin by pulling on just three. First, at the time *Democratic Vistas* appeared—Whitman's legendary pamphlet of 1871 had its origins in two essays that first appeared in the late 1860s in the New York–based magazine the *Galaxy* (1866–78) — the word "culture" was considerably less "modern" than he believed (or cared to acknowledge).[2] Derived from the Latin root *cultura* (meaning "tending" or "cultivation"), culture had first come into English in the sixteenth century, when it was linked primarily to natural processes of tending and preservation. While that usage remained commonplace in late-nineteenth-century America, "culture" had long since been extended to include human nurture and development. Advocates of "self-culture," in particular, believed that human souls were living things not unlike plants or animals, and that with careful cultivation human souls too could be nurtured to develop their full capacities.

Throughout the nineteenth century, dictionary definitions typically included examples of both usages. But use of the word "culture" to describe the development of individual human capacities also grew increasingly complicated, with distinctions now drawn among the moral, mental, physical, and spiritual aspects of individual self-development.[3] It is true that during the late 1860s some sophisticated British and American writers such as Matthew Arnold had begun to say that culture meant "the best that has been thought and said," yet it is extremely difficult to pinpoint exactly when the sense of culture as literary and artistic masterpieces gained widespread currency in American life. (Frederick Jackson Turner's several references to culture in his famous 1893 essay on "The Significance of the Frontier in American History," for example, were all synonyms for cultivation and tillage.) Arnold's haughty personal manner and his dismissal of postwar America as a society of Philistines did little for his American reputation, which fluctuated in the 1870s and 1880s before fading in the 1890s. It also is worth noting that many American cultural historians have overlooked the fact that the wording of one of Arnold's other, now less-well-known definitions of culture — "a harmonious expansion of all the powers which make the beauty and worth of human nature" — echoed conventional nineteenth-century usage.[4]

Also quite forgotten in most discussions of *Democratic Vistas,* and perhaps more important, is the fact that during the late 1860s and early 1870s talk of culture was accompanied by an unprecedented wave of interest in creating new cultural institutions. Amid confident pronouncements that a vast intellectual and spiritual renewal would sweep through American society — after all, if the Civil War had settled the supremacy of national political institutions, why should it not also have cleared the road for building national cultural institutions? — a remarkable variety of new developments claimed the name of culture in the immediate postwar years.

After decades of what seemed fruitless agitation, the university movement began abruptly with the opening of Cornell under Andrew White in 1868 and the election of Charles William Eliot as Harvard's president in 1869. About the same time that architects of the modern American university began to brake the grip of religious sectarianism and reorganize higher education to serve the needs of a more professionally conscious society, other reformers undertook initiatives designed to expand educational opportunities for women and African Americans. The first of the great private women's colleges were established: Vassar in 1865, Smith and Wellesley in 1875, and Bryn Mawr in 1880. Midwestern states that received land-grant funds from the 1862 Morrill Act either began to admit women to their universities or founded new state universities that admitted women from the start. In the South the first African American institutions of higher education—Atlanta University (1865), Fisk University (1867), Howard University (1867), and Talladega College (1870)—also date from the immediate postwar years.

Yet cultural reform was by no means limited to, or even focused primarily on, formal education in schools. In the period of economic expansion immediately following the war, Ohio, Wisconsin, Connecticut, Iowa, Indiana, Illinois, and Texas followed the lead of four New England states in passing laws enabling municipalities to tax their residence for the support of free libraries. The growth and intellectual vitality of the natural sciences also attracted considerable attention among educated Americans, who read accounts of technological innovations and new research in the "scientific columns" or "scientific departments" of magazines and newspapers as well as in new general science magazines such as *Popular Science Monthly* and *Science.* The woman's club movement also dates from the late 1860s, with the establishment of Sorosis in New York and the New England Women's Club in Boston. Eventually drawing women from all social groups in postbellum America, the club movement not only gave women a new place beyond parlors and schools to pursue self-development but also allowed them to redefine the concept of culture to include their own human interactions.[5]

By any reasonable standard, these developments signaled the onset of changes that by the turn of the century would serve to transform America nearly beyond recognition. But how could so many different developments claim the name of "culture," and what meaning was the word meant to convey? We can make a start at answering these questions simply by reminding ourselves that during the immediate postwar decades the concept of culture for most Americans remained roughly synonymous with self-culture. Hence its pursuit did not logically entail any particular place of activity so much as a particular manner of being in the world that invited an intense moral and intellectual preoccupation with one's self. Or put another way, because culture continued to carry its antebellum meaning of individual self-development or self-construction, various individuals and groups could (and did) apply it—with no inconsistency—to a wide variety of new activities and institutions.

Three examples from the late 1860s and 1870s will suffice here. Although we usually think of the work of building American universities as marked by a new and growing stress on professional credentialing and scientific research, Eliot and the other architects of the modern university did not have to abandon the rhetoric of culture in pressing their reforms, and initially, at least, none of them did.[6] Precisely because they remained wedded to an understanding of culture as the practice of self-construction and self-development, they saw no inconsistency between promoting new possibilities for vocational training and research in higher education and imagining the university as an institution within which a student would also be free to make choices, exercise his will, and thereby begin the work of creating a life for himself. "Liberal culture" was Eliot's label for a new educational ideal that gave university students freedom to choose their own courses at the same time as it encouraged them to feel at home in every field of knowledge. The rhetoric of culture also offered itself to him as a reassuring polemical resource. At the outset of Eliot's famous 1869 inaugural address, it allowed him to cut through what he saw as pointless internal controversy over the primary purpose of a university education. Because Harvard was committed the ideal of "liberal culture," Eliot said, it recognized no real antagonism between literature and science and "consents to no such narrow alternatives as mathematics or classics, science or metaphysics. We would have them all, and at their best." Later he also used the rhetoric of culture to announce his alternative to the antebellum collegiate ideal of the classically trained and generally educated Christian gentleman. Knowing his nonsectarianism pitted him directly against still-powerful forces of religious orthodoxy, Eliot anticipated their criticism with the succinctly confident proclamation that Harvard now considered "the worthy fruit of academic culture" to be "an open mind."[7]

Schematic as these and countless other similar formulations seem from afar, it clearly mattered to Eliot and other university presidents of his generation that Americans view university reform as a matter of creating institutions in which the pursuit of culture (understood as an ongoing process of individual self-development), professional training, and scientific training would be conterminous activities. In his 1876 inaugural address, for example, Daniel Coit Gilman announced that Johns Hopkins University had been created to promote both "the liberal and special culture of advanced students." Its faculty, he said, would pursue their particular academic interests "on the foundation of a broad and liberal culture," thereby developing "character" in their students and in turn making them men "who would be wise, thoughtful, and progressive guides to whatever department of work or thought they may be engaged in."[8]

Similarly, between 1866 and 1870 the notion of culture as a process of individual self-development helped to underpin J. W. Alvord's efforts to refute the idea of Negro inferiority. In his semiannual reports as the general superintendent of Freedmen's Bureau schools, Alvord addressed himself to almost every major theory of racial inferiority then current, challenging the idea that some races were naturally so inferior that, in competition with superior races, they inevitably must succumb or perish. He argued in reply: "We have a better theory. The human race, though diverse in characteristics, is progressive in culture, with opportunities and right conditions for improvement overcoming every deficiency." "Equal endowments substantially, with equal culture," he wrote, "will produce that equality in all mankind." True enough, Alvord may not have perceived the irony in trumpeting an individualistic ideal of self-construction in the name of a people whose very survival as slaves had depended on mutual assistance. In the late 1860s, however, there can be little question that throughout the South freed slaves embraced the promise of "culture" offered by bureau schools, trusting that education would equip them to take full advantage of citizenship and provide the skills and knowledge needed to succeed as free laborers. More specifically the "opportunities and right conditions for improvement" Freedmen's Bureau had been established to coordinate were new educational efforts launched by both freed slaves and northern missionary and benevolent associations in the South. As early as the summer of 1867, some 3,695 new schools enrolling 238,342 students were reporting to Alvord. With assistance from the bureau, northern societies also founded and staffed the first black colleges in the South, from which emerged members of the first generation of a professional class of African American teachers, ministers, businessmen, and doctors. These were also the black men and women "emancipated by training and culture" for whom, as we shall see, DuBois presented himself as spokesman in the late 1890s.[9]

Finally, we can learn something more of the welter of new circumstances in which the rhetoric of culture was employed in the late 1860s and 1870s by taking a brief look at the magazine in which Whitman originally sketched his nervous vision of democratic culture. Although published only between 1866 and 1878, the *Galaxy* was one of the more important magazines of the immediate postwar period. Conceived by its editors as a national publication in which "the current of thought in every sector could find expression as thoroughly as New England" did in the Boston-based *Atlantic Monthly*, the journal melded an egalitarian and nationalist cultural ethos with a loathing for an elite ideal of culture that at the time of its founding was perhaps most clearly represented by the vogue in America of England's leading critical monthly, the *Saturday Review*. Although the *Galaxy* published some of Whitman's postwar poetry and prose, and for a brief time counted Mark Twain and Henry James among its contributors, it did relatively little to promote the new class of "native authors" Whitman believed was needed to prepare the way for America's democratic culture. In practice its embrace of an egalitarian cultural ethos took shape instead as an editorial commitment to explore a variety of serious social issues, among the most significant of which was its effort to grasp the growth and intellectual vitality of the natural sciences. For the editors of the *Galaxy*, the "culture" postbellum America needed included "scientific culture," and with that end in mind they published a steady stream of articles and notices on a broad range of scientific subjects ranging from public health problems to contemporary research in the natural sciences.[10]

It also is worth noting here that the *Galaxy*'s widely read and imitated monthly feature "Scientific Miscellany"—which began to appear in 1871, the same year Whitman published *Democratic Vistas*—was introduced and, for the next three years, edited by E. L. Youmans. Now remembered mostly as the founder of *Popular Science Monthly*, and one of the great popularizers of scientific ideas in the late nineteenth century, Youmans grounded his career in his belief that scientific education lay at the heart of what, as early as 1867, he had called "the culture demanded by modern life." While promoting a democratic concept of the use of science, he also argued that those engaged in the work of "self-instruction in science" were pursuing "a new type of culture" that was not only different from an "older literary ideal of culture" but also "in essential respects superior to it."[11]

II

Other examples of efforts to adapt and expand the antebellum ideal of self-culture are not difficult to find in books, magazines, and newspapers published during the last three decades of the nineteenth century and the first decade of the twentieth. James Freeman Clarke's *Self-Culture: Physical, Intellectual, Moral, and Spiritual* (1880), which had its origins in a popular national lecture series of the mid-1870s, was a contemporary book that in itself perhaps summarized the ideal of self-construction as generally understood by most Americans in the last three decades of the nineteenth century. Published at a time when Clarke was viewed as an intellectual equal of Emerson, *Self-Culture* went through at least twenty-one editions by the end of the century.[12] Beginning in the mid-1870s, architects of the American Library Association and the Chautauqua movement joined with the leaders of the woman's club organizations to establish voluntary adult education—"culture study" some would call it—as one of the primary means by which Americans set out to develop their faculties and talents. At the founding of the American Library Association in 1876, one observer commented that while leaders of European industrializing societies exercised their power over an illiterate majority, it fell to the United States to demonstrate that "real culture is possible to a class or to an individual in society only when all members of it are cultured."[13]

A similar sort of language was used again and again to promote the various undertaking of the Chautauqua movement, perhaps most visibly in the pages of the *Chautauquan* (1880–1914), a monthly magazine for home study that was devoted to, as its subtitle proclaimed, the "Promotion of True Culture." Steady growth in the number of institutions for voluntary popular adult education also introduced new elements into the story of what self-culture meant in America. Virtually nonexistent before the Civil War, by the turn of the century free public libraries became almost as much a part of America as churches and school houses. The Chautauqua Literary and Scientific Circle (CLSC) was the first major experiment in education by mail in the United States. Between 1878 and 1894, some 225,000 students signed up for CLSC courses, subscribed to the *Chautauquan,* and purchased textbooks distributed through the CLSC, which in many cases were written specifically for the ten thousand local Chautauquan circles that came into existence by the end of the nineteenth century.[14]

It is true that architects of the public library movement and of the various subdivisions of the Chautauqua Assembly often spoke of culture in Arnoldian terms and conceived of their work as a matter of developing popular taste for great writers and thinkers. It is also true, however, that we will never satisfactorily decide how much their identification of "culture" with "good reading" helped to build constituencies for their institutions. In tracing the ways in which the ideal of culture served as an organizing motif for voluntary popular education movements during the 1870s and 1880s, Joseph F. Kett has shown that the growth in popular demand for programs of "culture study" was in fact driven by a variety of religious, philosophical, and vocational concerns. For example, the cofounders of the Chautauqua Assembly, Methodist bishop John H. Vincent and Methodist manufacturer Lewis Miller, aimed to break the grip of evangelical Protestantism by promoting a nondenominational view of spirituality that equated it with the growth of knowledge. Yet they also moved quickly to establish educational programs that spread the reputation of the main assembly at Lake Chautauqua well beyond the confines of a Sunday school reform movement. Among the most successful of these were summer "scientific congresses," the first of which Vincent organized in 1876 as a rival attraction to the prospective Centennial Exhibition in Philadelphia. Vincent also catered to the popular taste for scientific culture with a steady supply of articles in the *Chautauquan* on technology and scientific research that came equipped with sundry aids for study, including tables of questions and answers. Local branches of the CLSC, which developed initially along the path taken by women's clubs by organizing programs that included readings from great writers and group question-and-answer exercises, also came to serve more immediately practical purposes. Beginning in the mid-1880s, as a growing number of states required prospective teachers to secure formal educational certificates, many Chautauqua circles did double duty as teachers' reading circles. And in this setting, both the *Chautauquan* and textbooks commissioned and distributed by CLSC were used as aides to study for examinations.

"Liberal culture," "ethical culture," "literary culture," "scientific culture," "Christian culture": multiplicity of purpose notwithstanding, there was persistent agreement in many circles on two important points regarding how the pursuit of culture ought to be understood. The first was the belief that "culture" was synonymous with "self-culture" and thus connoted a process of individual self-construction that aimed at the full development of a variety of human capacities. Or as E. L. Youmans put it, "The aim of culture is to give such perfection to human nature as it is capable of—to develop not one set of faculties only, but all faculties."[15] The other was that to speak of culture in America was to speak of an inclusive ideal that aimed to open rather than close doors. Explaining what the idea of culture had come to mean in America at the turn of the century, Charles Eliot said in a 1903 speech to the National Education Association that "all authorities" now agreed that "true culture" was not "exclusive, sectarian, or partisan, but the opposite." American teachers must recognize, he concluded, that "no single element or kind of culture" was essential but that "the best fruits of real culture" were "an open mind, broad sympathies, and respect for all the diverse achievements of the human intellect at whatever stage of development they may actually be."[16]

III

It is clear, at least in retrospect, that during the last three decades of the nineteenth century belief in an individualistic and inclusive conception of culture was sustained by the existence of remarkably loose institutional boundary lines between the different levels of education within American society. With their book-buying and reading clubs, summer assemblies and scientific congresses, lyceums, seminaries, women' clubs, academies, and municipal free libraries, most American men and women did not yet equate higher education with degree-granting universities and colleges. In fact, at its height in 1887, enrollment in the Chautauqua Literary and Scientific Circle exceeded that of the nation's largest universities. A total of 4,468 men and women received diplomas for completing CLSC's four-year program of study, 18,000 were enrolled in the program, and untold tens of thousands more unreported (non-dues-paying) members participated as ex officio circle members or casual readers.[17] In this context it is not surprising that many late-nineteenth-century Americans were proud autodidacts who believed that the pursuit of culture entailed a variety of activities and institutions. The spread of programs to promote voluntary adult education, however, was not the only development that sustained belief in an individualistic and inclusive concept of culture. It was also the consequence of at least two other less widely recognized developments, which I approach in the final sections of this essay by concentrating on two texts.

The first is the young Johns Hopkins political economist Richard T. Ely's *Labor Movement in America* (1886), which appeared at the high point of academic and political radicalism during the industrial era. Ely's book aimed to show that the American labor movement was playing an important yet largely misunderstood role in transforming the existing framework of industrial society. Rather than promoting class warfare, Ely argued, the Knights of Labor, then America's largest and most encompassing labor organization (it numbered more than three-quarters of a million members by 1886), was in fact preparing the way for a moral and cultural regeneration with which both academics and middle-class reformers could identify. *The Labor Movement in America* not only emphasized the diverse occupational groups—including Confederate and Union Civil War veterans and freed slaves—integrated within the Knights' ranks but also proclaimed that labor organizations in general were "among the foremost of our education agencies, ranking next to our churches and public schools in their influence upon the culture of the masses." By "culture," Ely explained, he did not mean simply what could be learned out of books or acquired at school: "I mean what the Germans might perhaps express as *Bildung,*—the entire development of a man in all his relations, social, individual, religious, ethical, and political" (120–1).[18]

In chapter 5 of *The Labor Movement in America,* Ely gathered a variety of anecdotal evidence that, in his view, suggested laborers themselves viewed their organizations as agencies of culture. From the earliest period of their existence, he explained, both British and American trade unions and labor organizations had aimed to provide workingmen with means of mental and moral improvement. As an example he cited an 1832 address to workingmen by the New England Association of Farmers, Mechanics, and other Workingmen that explained the evils the organization had been created to remedy as follows: "An illiberal opinion of the worth and rights of the laboring classes; an unjust estimation of their moral, intellectual, and physical powers; an unwise misapprehension of the effect which would result from the cultivation of their minds and the improvement of their condition." Ely also mentioned that during the antebellum period supporters of workingmen had been active in education movements. The most important of these, in his view, had been William Ellery Channing, whose still-celebrated essays on social topics—"Self-Culture" and "On the Elevation of the Laboring Classes"— had proclaimed that the American laborer was to be "a student, a thinker, an intellectual man, as well as a laborer" (121–22).

Direct testimony from contemporary American workers provided Ely with additional and more concrete evidence of the culture-bearing services provided by the American labor movement. "Glad to give the exact words of the workingmen," Ely reprinted passages taken from the first *Report of the Massachusetts Bureau of Labor Statistics,* which he presented as evidence showing that trade unions and labor organizations were, in part, "popular schools of oratory in which workingmen learn to express their thoughts and to address a public audience, while their press furnishes opportunity for the development of any literary talent among them" (127). Ely also praised the Knights and other labor organizations for beginning to turn their attention to the establishment of libraries for their members. Other examples of what the American labor movement was doing to "encourage social and moral culture," he concluded, could be multiplied *ad libitum* (130).

Appearing in three editions before 1890, and remaining a standard work on American labor history for the next three decades, *The Labor Movement in America* was the book that established Ely's reputation as the most influential academic reformer of his generation. His bid for the language of culture, however, has been largely forgotten, partly because it is not without its problems. Writing as he did at the height of the power of the Knights of Labor, Ely of course could not have anticipated the labor organization's sudden decline, and with it an explanatory reproach that attributed the decay of the Knights to "the undue elevation as well as the superabundance of their ideals"—the very features Ely believed had contributed so directly to their success.[19] In reading chapter 5 of *The Labor Movement in America,* one also never gets the impression that Ely recognized that in the mid-1880s the concept of culture was beginning to operate in a new register of meaning, now just beginning service as one of the new ideals that late-nineteenth-century capitalists would use to constitute themselves as a social class.[20] From Ely we hear nothing of the establishment and endowment of new urban institutions—museums, research libraries, orchestras, and exhibitions—that not only identified the high arts and artifacts of Europe as the inheritance of modern American capitalists but also promoted them as the primary agents of a missing American culture. In Ely's account it is as if the primary institutional locations of culture had yet to be determined and the egalitarian political implications of the concept still could be taken for granted.[21]

This is not the place for an extended discussion of the role and influence of culture in the American labor movement during the era of industrialization. For my purposes here, however, there are two points about the character of that movement at the time Ely came to write his book that bear emphasizing. The first is a simple one and probably would not be denied even by historians doubtful of his claim that the ideal of self-culture formed part of the native tongue of the American working class. During the immediate postbellum decades, leaders and advocates of workers organizations were, for the most part, figures who had come of age during the 1840s and 1850s and whose attitudes on social issues embodied an amalgam of values derived from various sources. Neither proletarian nor members of the middle class, they more resembled, as Leon Fink as described them, "worker-intellectuals" who championed equality and independence, mutuality and social obligation, and collective political action to correct injustice. Their popular and cross-class republican vision of American worker-citizens, however, was coupled with an equally powerful, if less well noticed, preoccupation with the inner life of ordinary working men and women. Prominent labor leaders such as Ira Steward (1831–83), William Sylvis (1828–69), George McNeil (1837–1906), and Terence Powderly (1849–1924) took the ideals of individual self-improvement and self-education as seriously as citizenship. They also encouraged rank-and-file workers to do the same by establishing their own libraries, reading rooms, and lecture programs in local union halls and assemblies throughout the country. In fact, the keystone of organized labor during the years that marked the immediate onset of industrialization—the campaign for an eight-hour day—was routinely justified as a reform that would not only spread work and lessen unemployment but also give workers more free time for education and other cultural pursuits.[22]

Exactly how widespread the embrace of culture was among rank-and-file workers is of course hard to say. By the mid-1880s urban working-class neighborhoods had long since divided between the "rough" and the "respectable," with the roughs—especially men—setting little premium on education, ignoring the dictates of respectability, and continuing to spend their leisure time in saloons and other social centers. Yet the rough and the respectable lived side by side, and respectable workers were attracted to and active in local labor organizations precisely because, as Ely was among the first to point out, they played a decisive part in efforts to educate as well as to represent the working class. Any reader of Francis G. Couvares's account of the role and influence of the Knights of Labor in Pittsburgh during the 1870s and 1880s, for example, will be impressed by the fact that within working-class neighborhoods it was ordinary workers themselves who first established various organizations dedicated to cultural self-improvement: libraries and schools for adult education, book-buying and reading clubs, art galleries and brass brands. True enough, many of these organizations were also conceived as alternatives to the saloons, which had done much to nurture the labor movement but which respectable labor leaders such Powderly now believed were threatening its progress. Couvares demonstrates persuasively, however, that while the Knights' ambitious national reform program aimed to discipline and unify all spheres of working-class life, to a remarkable degree the organization's program closely corresponded to the existing cultural and social realities of Pittsburgh in the immediate postbellum decades. The citizen-worker idealized by the Knights of Labor, in other words, referred not simply to a local worker set in motion; he was, as Ely had recognized, a new man of culture as well: sober, self-educated, and cosmopolitan, rooted in the new world of the urban working class but also intent upon remaking it.[23]

IV

In the late 1890s, the inclusive notion of culture Ely believed had been given new life by the Knights of Labor was employed again as a key element in a criticism of the outlook and style of Booker T. Washington, a former member of the Knights whose sudden ascendancy as national

Fig. 1.2. W. E. B. DuBois, 1907. Special Collection at University Archives,
W. E. B. DuBois Library, University of Massachusetts

spokesman for African Americans and accommodation with racism stim-
ulated several chapters in the final text I review here, DuBois's *The Souls
of Black Folk* (1903). In the opening chapter of this book, which first
appeared in August 1897 as an essay in the *Atlantic Monthly,* DuBois
proclaimed that while "the history of the American Negro" remained a
story of two as yet unreconciled strivings—"to be both a Negro and an
American"—the end of this struggle was clear: "to be a co-worker in the
kingdom of culture, to escape both death and isolation, to husband and
use his best powers and his latent genius" (3). Criticizing Washington's
call in 1895 for political retreat and the exclusive cultivation of manual
skills, DuBois demanded for African Americans access to the same economic opportunities, intellectual activities, and political advantages open

to whites. "Work, culture, liberty,—all these we need," he wrote, "not singly but together, not successively but together, each growing and aiding each, and all striving toward that vaster ideal that swims before the Negro people, the ideal of human brotherhood" (8).[24]

In understanding DuBois's repeated invocations of "culture" in *The Souls of Black Folks,* it is, I think, almost impossible to overestimate the importance of his complex appraisal of Washington. Some contemporary interpreters who, on political grounds, find DuBois's bid for the language of culture not to their taste have suggested that the accommodation he denounced in Washington's case was reinstated when DuBois came to celebrate cultural ideals and practices more or less identical with those of late-nineteenth-century educated white elites. But in fact it was not, as is often said, Washington's accommodationist stance so much as his anti-intellectualism and his extraordinary power as a machine boss that disturbed DuBois. Close examination of the various ways in which he appealed to the ideal of culture in *The Souls of Black Folks* to challenge that power also suggests that his criticism of Washington is better understood as a delicate balancing act rather than an outright denunciation.

In presenting himself as a spokesman for "educated and thoughtful colored men in all parts of the land," DuBois made it clear he believed that in America culture was an inclusive ideal that spoke of a desire for individual "self-assertion and self-development" (35) shared by all its people, white and black alike. Behind this argument lay the belief that if culture as a normative standard existed to draw attention to the greatest achievements of the human spirit, black Americans had already staked out important claims in this domain that Washington and his supporters had ignored. "We are that people," DuBois proclaimed, "whose subtle sense of song has given America its only American music, its only American fairy tales, its only touch of pathos and humor amid its mad money-getting plutocracy."[25]

On the other hand, DuBois also made it clear he believed a small class of "leaders of thought and missionaries of culture" had a particularly urgent role to play within the African American community at the turn of the century. Indeed, he argued in chapter 6 of *The Souls of Black Folks* that the best chance for the social regeneration of the African Americans lay neither in their music nor in their oral traditions but in making the existing structure of Negro colleges and universities solid and permanent. For these were institutions, DuBois believed, that promised to produce exceptional men and women who would embody and promote "a loftier respect for the sovereign human soul that seeks to know itself and the world about it; that seeks freedom and self-development."

This last message, essentially a call for African Americans to recognize it was incumbent on them to develop more of their own "missionaries of culture," was first presented in an address on "The Conservation of the Races" on March 5, 1897, DuBois had presented at the founding meeting of the American Negro Academy in Washington, D.C. There too he proclaimed that "the eight million people of Negro blood in the United States of America" were a nation "stored with wonderful possibilities of culture." Yet he had stressed as well that the principal danger African Americans faced was not race prejudice so much as the prospect of being led to believe their destiny was "a servile imitation of Anglo-Saxon culture." "Let us not deceive ourselves at our situation in this country," DuBois warned. "Weighted with a heritage of moral iniquity from our past history, hard pressed in the economic world by foreign immigrants and native prejudice, hated here, despised there and pitied everywhere; our one haven of refuge is ourselves, and but one means of advance, our own belief in our great destiny, our own implicit trust in our ability and worth." From this diagnosis sprang not simply justification for the new Negro Academy but also a broader prescription to strive for "race regimentation" and "race solidarity." To realize "that broader humanity which freely recognizes differences in men, but sternly deprecates inequality in their opportunities," DuBois concluded, African Americans had to build and maintain more of their own separate "race organizations"—not simply Negro colleges and universities but also "Negro newspapers, Negro business organizations, a Negro school of literature and art, and an intellectual clearing house, for all these products of the Negro mind, which we may call a Negro Academy." All these organizations, he added, were needed not simply for positive advances but also because they were "absolutely essential for negative defense."[26]

Analyzing DuBois use of the rhetoric of culture in this way suggests that by the turn of the century he was employing it to pursue a campaign with two different but related fronts. Clearly he wanted to raise the tone and the stakes in efforts to solve the problem of educating African Americans by breaking open the anti-intellectual blockhouse in which Washington and his supporters had taken refuge. Yet DuBois at the same time plainly wanted to build an alliance with what he labeled the "Tuskegee machine" on a platform of racial separation. Indeed, if we focus primarily on chapters 1, 2, 5, and 6 of *The Souls of Black Folks*, it seems clear that DuBois's immediate practical purpose in publishing the book was to bring new support to Negro universities and colleges in the South by identifying them as the chief sources of teachers for Negro trade and manual training schools. Pointing out that "neither Negro common-schools, nor Tuskegee itself, could remain open a day were it not for teachers trained in Negro colleges, or trained by their graduates," DuBois apparently hoped that together he and Washington might usher in an era of "loving, reverent comradeship between the black lowly and the black men emancipated by training and culture" (75). He had no quarrel with Washington's view that for the immediate future "the Negro must strive and strive mightily to help himself." Yet he was also convinced, as we will see in more detail in chapter 5, that without the presence of a distinct class of educated African American professionals, this striving would never see any great success.

Perhaps no figure who came of age in late-nineteenth-century America ever spoke and wrote more passionately of the redemptive power of culture. As with Ely's earlier effort, however, DuBois's bid for the language of culture, while by no means forgotten, is not without its problems. Because a very small class of African American "men of training and culture" are the acknowledged heroes of *The Souls of Black Folks*— "the talented tenth," he would famously (yet also misleadingly) label them—DuBois has been reproached more than once for adopting an elitist attitude.[27] And there is some justice in this view. It is worth noting again that when he made his case for the importance of an educated black leadership in chapter 6 of *The Souls of Black Folks*, DuBois did not argue for assimilation. He also appeared to accept the racist premise that postwar African Americans needed cultural leadership more than other contemporary groups because they had no customs, traditions, and family ties of their own. In fact, as he had done at the end of his address "The Conservation of Races," in chapter 6 DuBois appealed to white Americans to support his argument less for the sake of the Negro than because it made good economic and social sense for themselves. And here, once again, he seemed to identify himself as both a supporter and a potential ally of the Tuskegee machine. The "question of the future," DuBois wrote, was how best to keep "the nine millions of Negroes in this nation" from "brooding over the wrongs of the past and the difficulties of the present, so that all their energies may be bent toward a cheerful striving and cooperation with their white neighbors toward a larger, juster and fuller future." Certainly one method for doing this was by means of the common schools and trade schools that aimed at closely knitting the Negro to "the great industrial possibilities of the South." These efforts, however, needed to be supplemented and reinforced by black colleges and universities, institutions where the "foundations of knowledge in this race, as in others" were sure to find "a solid, permanent structure" (75).

As an interpretation of the central message of *The Souls of Black Folks*, however, too much can made of DuBois's commitment to the concept of a saving "cultured" elite. Robert Stepto has aptly described the chapters that form the final third of the book as "a cultural immersion ritual" that had DuBois, the one-time New England black, finding and reconstructing his cultural identity anew in the southern Black Belt. Here DuBois's attention shifted from providing a blueprint for the duties of college-educated Negro leadership at the turn of the century to accounting for the transforming power, from antebellum slave culture through the post-Reconstruction period, of what he now presented as the central expressive form of African Americans, the "sorrow songs." In the five chapters he wrote specifically for *The Souls of Black Folks,* DuBois substantially connected himself for the first time with the vast majority of African Americans he recognized had little in common with the "thinking classes of American Negroes" (39). And what came of this connection was, in part, a now well-known effort to gain for slave spirituals recognition as a central contribution to American culture. As Eric Sundquist has argued persuasively, however, the last five chapters also substantially tempered DuBois's commitment to an understanding of culture that was too easily identified both with his own personal taste for past European achievements and with his belief in the importance of a black "talented tenth" whose future achievements, he had argued in earlier chapters, promised to raise up the uneducated black masses below them. In putting the spirituals at the center of *The Souls of Black Folks,* in other words, DuBois not only identified their slave creators as the foundational voice of African American culture but also signaled his refusal to accept as necessary a supposed contradiction between elite and folk.[28]

V

Where should historians' efforts to deepen and complicate our awareness of the many-sidedness of American talk and thinking about culture during the industrial era be leading us? In at least three directions, I believe. The first is toward full acceptance of the important truth that during the era of industrialization, the normative concept of culture served a variety of purposes that we trivialize if we reduce them to the single agenda of "social control." More important, if historians want to reap the full benefits of a pluralist approach, we need to address an issue I consider in more detail in the four chapters that follow: the changing context within which the work of building new cultural institutions and practices actually went forward during the era of industrialization. Save for Neil Harris, the leading lights have displayed remarkably little interest in breaking down the last three decades of the nineteenth century. Thirty years ago, in a provocative essay on "Four Stages of Cultural

Fig. 1.3. Jane Addams, 1907.
Division of Photography and
Prints, Library of Congress

Growth: The American City," Harris argued that at some point in the
1870s the character and motivation of patrons of cultural institutions in
older eastern cities began to change. Their concerns shifted away from
popular distribution and participation to what he called "certification"—
of either the experiences and objects elite cultural institutions protected
or the good taste and social standing of their affluent supporters.

Harris noted that the popularizing phase lasted somewhat longer
in new western cities such as Denver and San Francisco. But it is
arguable that even in older eastern cities, the overall pattern, as well as
the pace, of change were complex and ambiguous in ways that even his
more flexible periodization does not manage to suggest. Well past the
turn of century, for example, it is clear that "participatory" and "certifying" understandings of the meaning of culture remained closely inter-
twined in the thinking and activities of the founders of the leading
American settlement houses in Boston, New York, and Chicago. A vivid
brief illustration of such thinking appears in Jane Addams's 1901 speech

to a national convention of women's clubs. In explaining how the Social Extension Committee of the Hull House Women's Club was a successful example of what settlement houses were trying to do, Addams described a winter "social evening" activity that unexpectedly brought together the women of the club and the husbands of Italian immigrant women who lived nearby. She recalled that one of the Italian men "did a number of pretty tricks, such as one sees in the streets of Naples," and another "sang rousing songs." "The evening went happily," Addams concluded, and she recalled that at its close one of the women of the club said to her, "I am ashamed of the way I used to talk about Dagoes. I used to say that we must move off the street because there were so many Dagoes coming in. But they are just like other people, only you have to take more pains to find them out."

Speaking to an audience that already understood the term "culture" to encompass a very wide variety of self-improvement projects, Addams then went on to account for the woman's change in attitudes in terms her listeners would have had little difficulty in grasping: "That was the result of cultivation, if we take the definition that it is extended experience. It is exactly the thing we send our children to Europe for, the result we hope for when we read books about all kinds of people—to get over the differences raised by barriers and traditions, that really we may be fair-minded and may know people as they really are. And if we can do that in our social life as in our intellectual life, or if we are without much intellectual life, and do it with our social life it is a great achievement."[29]

In explaining and promoting the settlement house movement, Addams often assumed the role of spokesperson for a new class of already "cultivated," college-educated American men and women. When she did so, however, it typically was to show how settlement houses had broken down conventional understanding of what cultivated men and women could or could not do and what cultivation actually entailed. Her 1901 speech is a case in point. At a time when many native-born Americans scoffed and some earlier immigrants distanced themselves from "new immigrants" from eastern and southern Europe, Addams and the founders of other settlement houses embraced an inclusive understanding of culture that counseled tolerance, reciprocity, and a benign recognition of cultural multiplicity. And the specific episode Addams recalled in her 1901 speech was one of countless similar "social evenings" at settlement houses in Boston and New York, all of which came to life with pictures, songs, and dances from the new immigrants' native lands.[30]

In Addams's mind Hull House and other American settlement houses had created a world where the distinction between "participatory" and "certifying" concepts of culture existed but had little meaning. Two years after Hull House opened its doors in a poor, ethnically mixed neighbor-hood on the near west side of Chicago, Addams and Ellen Starr were wel-coming eight hundred to a thousand people into their home every week. Men, women, and children came for a variety of reasons and joined with Addams and Starr to create a remarkably complex intercultural space. Faculty from the University of Chicago came to teach "College Exten-sion Courses" on topics that included the history of art, mathematics, and zoology. The Chicago Public Library fitted up one of its five new branch library stations at Hull House, staffed it with two librarians, and supplied it with French, Italian, and German newspapers. Hull House itself also sponsored the Working People's Social Science Club, where each week Chicago labor activists, businessman, civic leaders, university professors, and ordinary working people openly debated the merits of capitalism, socialism, progressive taxation, and anything else that sparked their inter-est. Residents and neighborhood volunteers also mounted art exhibits in the Butler Gallery, which they built next door to Hull House, and trans-formed a nearby saloon into a gymnasium. Every morning except on Sundays, they managed a day nursery and operated a kindergarten, and all the while they also ran interference between their neighbors and Chicago's court system, hospitals, landlords, and city hall.[31]

This characteristic effort to address simultaneously the needs and in-terests people who already considered themselves cultivated and people whose "faculties are untrained and disused" remains the most striking aspect of the American settlement house movement.[32] And the fact that it persisted and gained strength during the first two decades of the twen-tieth century should remind us, among other things, that the immediate results of late-nineteenth- and early-twentieth-century efforts to estab-lish new institutions grounded in a "certifying" concept of culture hardly matched the high hopes that elite urban patrons invested in that con-cept. The actual number of people who visited museums and attended operas and symphonies during that period can only be guessed at, but it certainly was never large enough to signal the successful establishment of a new cultural hierarchy in America.[33] History of course is not chronol-ogy. But if we are ever fully to understand the unprecedented importance culture assumed during the industrial era, that understanding should rest, in part, on a more refined temporal articulation of the various set-tings, and various ways, in which the pursuit of culture went forward in that era.[34]

Finally, pluralist historians can do more work of the kind I pursue in this chapter by developing or strengthening narrative interpretations that allow us to recognize and understand the richness of the American rhetoric of culture on its own terms. The notion that the attitudes and interests of Americans who championed culture during the industrial era are best understood simply as applications of British Victorian values to new circumstances ought to be put to rest. If we go looking for the actual historical origins of America's interest in culture, there seems little question that the Unitarian ideal of self-culture must be counted among its prior and primary sources. Although it was that lapsed Unitarian Ralph Waldo Emerson who gave this ideal its most memorable expression during the middle decades of the nineteenth century, calls for the full development of the individual, and an optimistic faith in the almost limitless capacity of human nature implied by those calls, had been sounded by a long list of Unitarians who preceded him or could be counted among his contemporaries.[35] The pursuit of culture during the industrial era of course was not simply Unitarianism detached from its theological foundations. Yet a remarkable number of the most prominent advocates of culture in fact did come from Unitarian families, especially during the immediate postwar years. Jane Cunningham Croly, for example, the founder of Sorosis and arguably the single most important figure in the early history of the women's club movement, was the daughter of a Unitarian preacher. And what Charles Eliot called his non-denominationalism was viewed by some of his critics as "Unitariansim raised to the nth power."[36] Various other attitudes and ideas, some considerably less confident that individuals on their own could bear the responsibility for fostering self-development, inevitably influenced public understanding of what counted as culture. Yet just how a distinctively American ideal of self-culture was maintained, updated, and reinterpreted forms a central theme in the complex story of how American men and women went about "building culture" during the industrial era.[37]

TWO

"Our national glory"

Emerson in American Culture, 1865–82

Any effort to understand American cultural and intellectual life during the industrial era must pay special attention to Ralph Waldo Emerson. It would be a mistake to say it was during this period that he secured his identity as the "founder" of his nation's culture. No one figure ever has earned that title. Emerson also never claimed it for himself. By the time of his death in 1882, however, he was as inescapable a presence in America's intellectual and cultural life as Lincoln was in its politics, and he would remain so for at least another twenty years.

But how and why? When I began work on this essay, the received account encouraged us to think of Emerson as an uncomplicated, almost predictable presence in the cultural and intellectual life of late-nineteenth-century America. Rather than a figure somehow still active in responding to or shaping historical events, the late Emerson worked mostly as a symbol—the Apostle of Culture or Transcendentalist par excellence—and to appreciate the symbol we apparently needed to know little about his activities and ideas, let alone new developments within the institutional organization of late-nineteenth-century America that allowed him to remain such an highly valued figure.

It is not easy to say exactly why Americans valued Emerson so highly during the industrial era, but that is what I try to do in this essay and the one that follows. Emerson spoke in various ways to Americans living in the industrial era. If we make a systematic effort to grasp what they were, he becomes something more than a stick figure frozen in time and we in turn have a deeper understanding of the cultural and intellectual life of the industrial era.

I

Emerson's post–Civil War career is best understood as a time when his contemporaries came to see him as both America's leading man of letters and one of its preeminent public moralists, a figure whose life and writings urged them on to more strenuous efforts to realize shared national ideals. "He is an accepted fact," one contemporary reviewer of *Letters and Social Aims* (1875) commented more bluntly, "just as we accept Shakespeare." There is still a tendency among biographers, cultural historians, and literary critics to treat Emerson's entire postbellum career as a prolonged mental twilight, a tendency encouraged by the gradual but relentless decline of his eyesight and memory and by the uncertainty surrounding his precise role in the arrangement of his final publications.[1] There is an element of truth in that familiar picture, but it needs to be complemented by study of the various reasons Emerson was such a highly visible figure during the last seventeen years of his life and of how his activities and views figured in public debate about the shape of postbellum culture.[2]

This is especially true of the years 1865–72, the period that is the main focus of this essay. The years immediately following the Civil War, one contemporary witness later observed, were a time when "none but Emerson himself noted the approach of old age." More significant, they were also a time when Emerson became "an accepted fact" in American life. He entered into a sort of Indian summer as a public speaker early in 1865 and over the course of the next five years enjoyed his most active and lucrative years on the national lecture circuit. The first collected edition of his writings, the pirated two-volume *Complete Works of Ralph Waldo Emerson,* appeared in London in 1866, and by the late 1870s three other multivolume collected editions had been published in Boston. Honors, such as election to the Harvard Board of Overseers and to a vice presidency of the New England Woman Suffrage Association, also pressed upon him, as did a new set of admirers ("Emersonidae," James Russell Lowell called them) who made Emerson himself into something of a cultural cause—figures such as Franklin Sanborn, Moncure Conway, James Elliot Cabot, and Charles William Eliot. Further evidence of his fame can be found in the steady stream of invitations to lecture, publish, sit for photographs, and travel that continued to find their way to his Concord home over the course of the 1870s. There can be little question that when Emerson reached the end of his creative life in 1872, he was among the most famous figures of his time.[3]

Most phases of Emerson's career, and almost all aspects of his writings, have been subject to intensive study and are comparatively familiar. But neither the last two collections of essays published during his lifetime nor the final, and in many ways distinct, phase of his public career have received adequate scholarly attention.[4] A step-by-step recounting of every facet of the development of the late Emerson's reputation, however, would extend well beyond the boundaries of a single chapter. So here I touch only in passing on his poetry and literary essays. What I offer primarily is a picture of Emerson as an aging but still active public moralist who presented his views to a growing variety of audiences that became available to him as one of postbellum America's best-known figures. My two main concerns are to recover an Emerson who wanted to help his contemporaries grapple with the problems of their lives and in the process to characterize a set of ideas and a particular style of presentation that defined his stance as a public moralist. I also aim to reconstruct some of the more important ways in which his activities and ideas gained national attention during the last years of his life. My commitment to restore Emerson to his historical context has made for a study that is comparatively short on theory and long on efforts to allow the late Emerson to speak for himself (something he is rarely allowed to do in modern scholarship) and to attend to the various ways in which his contemporaries viewed his career and his postwar lectures and writings. One consequence of this approach is a fairly generous supply of quotations. Another is a sensitivity to the importance of questions surrounding the history of Emerson's reception that nonetheless resists their promotion to an infallible method of identifying the immediate significance of Emerson's body of work without careful reference to the work itself. Doubtless it makes sense to think of Emerson's lectures and essays in terms of the economic and social interests of those willing to pay for or write about them. Whatever truth this familiar approach may contain, however, it is not very near the whole truth. I try to develop a broader view in this chapter and the one that follows.

II

This was part of an editorial eulogy that appeared in the *Boston Daily Advertiser* the day after Emerson died of pneumonia on April 27, 1882, in Concord, Massachusetts: "He is not the property of any class, but our common possession and our national glory whose works read like the great ledger entries of our merchants, whose acts betray the shrewdness and prudence of the typical New Englander and whose words are the outcome of our national development, our joy, our honor, and withal a part of every fine American, so that his axioms and surprises of 1840 have become our proverbs of 1882. If one wishes to have the summary and quintessence of this new continent, and its people, their thought and the very spirit of modern New England, it is all in Emerson, of whom only the mortal frame can be destroyed by the angel death."

Doubtless writing the obituary of a "national glory" is a daunting task, and this passage betrays the strain by not going on to answer the question of how "axioms and surprises" of a typical New England in the 1840s became the entire nation's proverbs in the early 1880s. Yet the *Daily Advertiser*'s characterization of Emerson as a "national glory" was amplified and echoed in countless other obituary tributes across the country during the spring and summer of 1882. The *New York Herald* proclaimed that "nobody who has watched the growth of the intellectual life in America can have a doubt about the permanence of his influence upon its development. No American writer of any time is acknowledged by a wider intellectual audience to have been the stimulus to it most liberal thinking." The *Chicago Tribune* said that at the time of his death Emerson had come to be "recognized as the representative mind of his country." The *San Francisco Chronicle* offered perhaps the most lavish praise of all, observing that Emerson "belongs like DANTE, GALILEO, MONTAIGNE, NEWTON and DARWIN, not so much to his own as to future times, and his works will be classics in all languages centuries after his contemporaries of higher-flown pretensions and reputations are forgotten." Dissenting notes, predictably, were sounded in southern newspapers, but usually they were qualified with grudging recognition of his achievements. At the time of his death, began the obituary in the *Charleston Daily News and Courier,* Emerson was widely recognized as "the most distinguished of American essayists"; he "had no prototype and will have no successful imitator."[5]

We can see this nationwide tribute as both a symptom of Emerson's extraordinarily high public standing and a cause of its further growth. In tracing the historical origins of this final remarkable apotheosis, however, we should not let it obscure the very different character of Emerson's reputation during earlier stages of his career. In the 1830s he had first gained national attention as a figure who had inspired a radical break with existing Protestant literary and philosophical traditions in New England. In the 1840s and into the 1850s, his lectures, essays, poems, and other publications won him a transatlantic reputation as the most original man of letters American culture had yet produced. In 1859 and 1860 he joined Thoreau in defending John Brown at a time when news of his Harpers Ferry raid met almost universal condemnation in northern states; and when the Civil War began, one of his most widely known contributions to public debate was his controversial description of Brown as "the Saint . . . whose martyrdom, if it shall be perfected, will make the gallows as glorious as the cross."

Against this background it is interesting to speculate how different Emerson's obituaries would have been had he died, say, early in the summer of 1863, after major Union military defeats at Fredericksburg and Chancellorsville. Not only would it have been more difficult to place him in the history of American culture—"Twenty years before his death," William Dean Howells once reminded students of Emerson's popular reputation, "he was the most misunderstood man in America"—but it seems likely he would have been remembered by many, North and South, as something of a sectional ideologist whose antislavery speeches had given abolitionism an important measure of cultural legitimacy.[6] Nor would Emerson have established a close attachment to Harvard, the full story of which forms an important episode in the development his postbellum reputation. Only when Harvard's "own darling sons [started] dying on the field of battle," Sanborn observed in the year of the Emerson centenary, did its official appreciation of him begin to rise to "something like justice."[7] He could have added that, during the last decades of the nineteenth century, the increasingly close association of Emerson's name with Harvard would provide new ground for the building of his reputation.

It is difficult to say what Emerson himself made of his postwar fame. While he hardly thought of himself as a sectional ideologist, he did prize his regional identity. And yet he never longed for followers. Emerson said he found satisfaction not in his possible direct influence on others but in successfully encouraging kindred spirits to pursue their own paths. ("This is my boast," he had written in his journal in 1859, "that I have no school & no follower. I should account it a measure of the impurity of insight if it did not create independence" [*JMN* 14:258]).[8] Nor did he view his own publications as sacred texts. In some moods he dismissed the commercial success of his later publications as the predictable byproduct of his longevity. Referring to *Society and Solitude*, he remarked in an 1870 journal entry, "My new book sells faster, it appears, than either of its foregoers. This is not from its merit, but only shows that old age is a good advertiser. Your name has been seen so often that your book must be worth buying" (*L* 6:55). As he grew older he also became increasingly uncomfortable with his status as cultural celebrity. "We should all be public men if we could afford it. I am wholly private," he wrote in a journal entry of July 12, 1872, "such is the poverty of my constitution" (*JMN* 16:275–76). His discomfort with popular acclaim was fed by his sense that he often came across as a "hack lecturer" (*L* 6:123).

As much as he believed in the transforming power of good lecturing, Emerson never escaped doubts about his effectiveness as a speaker, doubts that were intermittently triggered in the late 1860s by indifferent audiences and satirical newspaper accounts of his talks. Finally, several entries in his letters and journals betray a growing frustration at his inability to keep up with his many commitments; and by 1868 his sense of dwindling intellectual energy crossed with an anxiety that expressed itself in various ways, including efforts to block newspaper coverage of his lectures in Boston and New York.[9]

All that said, there is little question that Emerson recognized his services as a lecturer and a writer were more in demand between 1865 and 1872 than at any previous time in his career. "I have never had so many tasks as in the last twelve months" (*L* 6:123), he commented in a letter of July 7, 1869, looking back on a year during which he had given forty-five lectures in Massachusetts, Rhode Island, Connecticut, and New York, corrected six earlier volumes of his essays for publication in a new two-volume collection of *Prose Works* that Fields, Osgood and Company would publish in October, participated in deliberations that led Harvard's Board of Overseers to appoint Charles Eliot as president, served as curator of the Concord Lyceum, and begun work on the first chapters of *Society and Solitude*. And yet the two previous years in fact had been even busier, as 1866 and 1867 were arguably the most ambitious years of Emerson's entire career as a lecturer. He gave forty-three lectures in 1866 in fourteen different New England and midwestern states; the next season he accelerated his pace, delivering eighty lectures altogether, and for the first time he went as far west as Minnesota and Kansas. During the late 1860s his fame as a lecturer also came to be matched by his economic prosperity. In the mid-1850s Emerson had begun to command a comparatively large income from lecturing: his fees for individual public lectures typically ranged between $25 and $50, and the largest sum he received for private lectures was $1,166 for a series on "Topics of Modern Times" in Philadelphia in January 1854. The Civil War, however, brought a sudden and drastic reduction in Emerson's income. Dividends from his stocks and bonds were discontinued, and demand for his lectures and books largely dried up. As a result Emerson was forced to borrow to meet his financial needs and was in considerable debt when the war ended.

But his financial pinch was short lived. By the winter of 1865, the western lecture circuit had been reestablished, and that year the Unitarian Church in Milwaukee paid Emerson $300 for a series of six lectures on "American Life." By December 1867 his fee for individual public lectures in Ohio, Illinois, Missouri, and Iowa had risen to $100. Eight months later,

Fig. 2.1. Ralph Waldo Emerson, ca. 1860–70.
Smithsonian Archives of American Art

he netted $1,655.75 for a miscellany of six private lectures in Boston
managed by his publisher Ticknor and Fields—"which is by much the
largest sum I ever received for work of this kind" (*L* 6:54), he wrote in
gratitude to James T. Fields. Because of his declining eyesight and memory, Emerson rarely lectured outside New England after 1870, but his
fees remained high: $250 for "Nature and Art" in Chicago on November
27, 1871; $1,457 for six private "conversations" on literature in Boston's
Mechanics Hall in April 1871; and $300 for "Eloquence" at the Academy
of Music in Philadelphia, where three thousand people gathered to hear
him speak on March 18, 1875. The question of what contemporaries made
of his last public performances is addressed later in this chapter. Here
the point that deserves emphasis is simply that the satisfaction they took
from direct encounters with a celebrity were the currency of Emerson's
old age.

Emerson also knew that the power and prestige of his publishers had as much to do with his late success as an author as his longevity. Although publishing was never a labor of love for him, Emerson was by no means a novice when it came to the American book trade.[10] Phillips and Sampson, his publisher during the 1850s, was know for its relatively aggressive marketing of American writers. A more crucial chapter in the story of the cultural production of the late Emerson, however, began in 1860, when he was taken on by Fields, who by then had established his reputation as the first great publisher-patron of American authors. (By 1860, Ticknor and Fields's publishing list included Whittier, Longfellow, Holmes, Lowell, and Thoreau.) Fields was one of the great cultural entrepreneurs of the middle decades of the nineteenth century, and one way to summarize his role in enhancing Emerson's reputation during the 1860s might be to say simply that he used his extensive network of friendly ties with editors of newspapers and magazines in which he advertised his books to secure a prominent place for Emerson within America's emerging national literary culture. (Fields's power is most evident in the initial reception of *Conduct of Life*, Emerson's most immediate commercial success as well as his most widely reviewed book.) Yet in another sense Fields's chief service in Emerson's behalf may have been less that he helped market his writings to a national audience than that he used his power to limit the full play of market forces in determining the standing of Emerson's writings after 1860. For the advertising campaigns Ticknor and Fields launched on behalf of its writers typically were not designed to sell its costly and elegantly produced books—the first two volumes of Emerson's *Prose Works* (1869) were priced at five dollars—so much as to make national the fame of the writers it chose to sponsor. The niche within the mid-nineteenth-century literary marketplace Ticknor and Fields controlled was one where success was defined more in terms of status than sales. And so the mere appearance of Fields's name on the title pages of Emerson's publications sufficed to locate his books immediately within that niche.[11]

III

Can these disparate bits and pieces of Emerson's career between 1865 and 1872 be put into a single coherent narrative? Or, more precisely, what bearing do they have for understanding of Emerson's place in post-bellum culture? We can start to answer these questions by remembering that in his mid-sixties Emerson still thought of himself as the holder of unpopular views, despite his rapidly growing national reputation. In broad terms, it is correct to think of the late Emerson as a progressive liberal. He was democratic, egalitarian, and secular, openly sympathetic with the radicals in Reconstruction and the new movement for woman's suffrage, and even more openly suspicious of his countrymen's preoccupation with money and status—and such views hardly commanded immediate assent in the lecture halls and parlors of postbellum America. The reporter who recorded his January 12, 1866, reading of "Social Aims" before the Oberlin College Societies Library Association, for example, clearly thought he spoke for many when he underlined the unorthodoxy of his views: "Mr. Emerson has little sympathy, we suppose, with the faith that is dearest to us in Oberlin. . . . His philosophy fails beside the faith of thousands of illiterate believing souls." Five months before his visit to Oberlin, James Fields had refused to publish Emerson's new essay on "Character" in the *Atlantic,* saying it was "not suited to the magazine. Ordinary readers would not understand him and would consider it blasphemous."[12]

Such episodes help to explain why, in some moods, the late Emerson viewed himself as a figure who stood alone, a counselor without followers, sustained primarily by his desire to awaken his countrymen to their latent capacities for independent thought and action. And certainly the identity of an idealistic outsider is one that any champion of self-reliance and self-trust must have welcomed, since it simultaneously celebrates the inner resolve of a solitary individual, defines a sense of public purpose, and explains away perceived failure. Occasionally, then, the late Emerson still sounds like an American Jeremiah, and although he encountered other reminders of his unpopularity in the late 1860s, it is fair to say that exaggerating the strength of popular opposition to his views at times remained one of his polemical strategies.[13] The most important instances of this—not surprisingly—involved discussions of popular attitudes toward religion and education. It is particularly noticeable in "Character," where Emerson depicted mankind at large as resembling "frivolous children" who were "impatient of thought and wish to be amused. Truth is too simple for us; we do not like those who unmask our illusions" (*W* 10:109), and in "Education," where he described advocates of educational reform as confronting a society in which "the word Education has so cold, so hopeless a sound" and "a treatise on education, a convention for education, a lecture, a system, affects us with slight paralysis and a certain yawning of the jaws" (*W* 10:133). "Character," it is worth noting, first appeared in the April 1866 *North American Review,* three months before Emerson received an honorary doctor of laws degree from Harvard. "Education" was the lead lecture in a successful series on "American Life" he initially presented in Boston, Worcester, and Milwaukee, in the winter of 1864, a year that had begun with his election to the American Academy of Arts and Sciences.[14]

As the invocations of "us" and "we" in "Character" may suggest, however, even in his most polemical moods Emerson projected his differences with his contemporaries in ways he intended to be reassuring. He in fact did not see himself speaking from a position located entirely outside the circle of mankind. "The religions we call false," he acknowledged, "were once true. They also were affirmations of the conscience correcting the evil customs of their times" (*W* 10:104–5). Emerson, while pointedly questioning popular belief in the need for any particular institutional manifestation of religion—especially, of course, Protestant Christianity—remained confident of the enduring moral energy of his contemporaries. His task as public moralist, then, was to persuade them to continue to move in the right direction, and central to that task was persuading them to recognize that the route he recommended was an extension of a path that others before had already followed successfully. The following passage in "Character" is particularly revealing:

> The Church, in its ardor for beloved persons, clings to the miraculous, in the vulgar sense, which has even an immoral tendency, as one sees in Greek, Indian, and Catholic legends, which are used to gloze every crime. The soul, penetrated with the beatitude which pours into it on all sides, asks no interpositions, no new laws—the old are good enough for it,—finds in every cart-path of labor ways to heaven, and the humblest lot exalted. Men will learn to put back the emphasis peremptorily on pure morals, always the same, not subject to doubtful interpretation, with no sale of indulgences, no massacre of heretics, no female slaves, no disfranchisement of women, no stigma on race; to make morals the absolute test, and so uncover and drive out false religions. There is no vice that has not skulked behind them. It is only yesterday that our American churches, so long silent on Slavery, and notoriously hostile to the Abolitionist, wheeled into line for Emancipation. (*W* 10:114)

This doubtless was one of the passages that made "Character" "blasphemous" in Fields's view.

But Emerson's purpose was complex in ways this label does not manage to suggest. The passage is notable, as David Robinson has observed, in its equation of nineteenth-century movements for feminism and racial equality with the struggle against the most egregious historical examples of religious bigotry. But the passage at the same time served to voice Emerson's overriding concern with the new American culture he saw emerging from the success of the cooperative effort represented by the antislavery movement and the Civil War. Here Emerson wanted to drive home at least two related points. First, the specific "immoral tendency" of the American churches had been their commitment to defend an arbitrary resting place along the route of moral progress; and second, the moral impetus of American culture as a result had passed from its churches to its various reform movements.[15] Taken together the two claims reflected not so much Emerson's "heretical" views as they did his renewed confidence in his countrymen. "We see the dawn of a new era," he wrote in an 1865 journal entry, "worth to mankind all the treasure & all the lives it has cost, yes, worth to the world the lives of all this generation of American men, if they be demanded." Emerson knew what the Civil War had cost in lives, but he also wanted to believe it had "made many lives valuable that were not so before" and so had effectively "*moralized* cities & states" (*JMN* 15:64).

As careful reading of "Character" suggests, Emerson did not stand in a purely adversarial relation to postbellum American culture precisely because he was appealing to certain shared national values and experiences at the same time as he was criticizing his contemporaries for not living up to their agreed shared standards. His essays, Oliver Wendell Holmes remarked in a letter of October 30, 1869, were "peaceful battle songs"; they did not make men "set their teeth and knit their foreheads, but sent them forward smiling to think their thoughts and say them."[16] Emerson was not attempting to reverse or subvert his country's cultural and moral sensibilities, in other words, but instead to refine them and to call them more effectively into play on public issues. In these circumstances, however, he was also running at least two risks as he contrasted the far-sightedness and consistency of his own positions with the generally self-interested confusions and inconsistencies he had to impute to those who, while sharing the same premises, had failed to draw the same conclusions. The first, ironically enough, was the risk of not being understood at all ; the second was that of standing too close to those he criticized—of sounding too "peaceful" in his criticism—and thereby not being understood correctly. Both of these considerations also bring us to the final aspect of Emerson's general performance as public moralist I want to discuss here: his characteristic style and manner of argument.

Nothing seemed more apparent about Emerson to his postwar listeners and readers than the difficulty of his language. Some admirers (such as Bret Harte) praised him for doing more than any other American thinker "to voice the best philosophical conclusions of American life and experience." But others remarked that he did so in ways that made it difficult to sum up neatly the conclusions he was endorsing. It also appears that by the end of his public career contemporary audiences had come to expect Emerson's lectures and essays to sound obscure and often heard them as obscure even when Emerson's prose was comparatively straightforward. There is no need for extensive citation here except to illustrate briefly how the difficulty of Emerson's prose sometimes served to obscure his performance in the role of public moralist. An instructive example in this regard would be the laudatory review of *Letters and Social Aims* that appeared in the February 26, 1876, *Saturday Review*. At first glance the review appears to be a straightforward rebuttal of the complaint that Emerson's writing was "fanciful and rambling, and does not teach one anything in particular." As the rebuttal unfolds, however, it becomes clear that the complaint contains an important element of truth. For Emerson's achievement, according to the *Saturday Review*, lay precisely in the fact that his writings were not accessible to those who approached them looking for "rules and propositions." In his work "matter" and "form" were as inseparable as they were in "the best talk," yet also as with the best talk, this meant there was something in Emerson's writing that "would not be fixed." The *Saturday Review* was by no means divided in its praise of Emerson's achievement. What makes its defense of the difficulty of his prose instructive, however, is that it loses sight of the fact that Emerson thought of himself as a social critic who was describing what was wrong with his culture in ways that suggested practical remedies. The more difficult his language, then, the greater the distance between him and his audience and the more obscure his criticism was likely to be.[17]

It would be misleading to suggest, however, that most encounters with Emerson's language during the 1860s and 1870s produced the impression of a writer whose views resisted straightforward translation. The young Henry James, for example, had little trouble in offering a reliable precis of his ideas in an otherwise historically threadbare and somewhat condescending account of Emerson in his 1879 biography of Hawthorne.[18] What is perhaps more striking about the language of *Society and Solitude* and *Letters and Social Aims*, especially when read in conjunction with contemporary newspaper accounts of Emerson's lectures and public addresses in the mid- to late 1860s, is the extent to which his prose in fact took various forms. Throughout his career, no one ever doubted that Emerson's language presented a formidable challenge to ordinary intelligence. But his essays, lectures, and speeches also displayed mastery of prose styles that ranged from moral indictment and political censure at one extreme to satiric comment and utopian speculation at the other. This list may sound strange to some modern literary critics and theorists, but I expect it captures the experience of many of

Emerson's contemporaries who knew him mostly by way of listening to him talk or reading excerpts from his books in literary reviews and summary accounts of his lectures in newspapers. Any one interested in understanding the growth of Emerson's reputation in the 1860s and early 1870s would be wise not to lose track of a lecturer and writer who could employ this sort of rhetoric:

> I think the genius of this country has marked out her true policy. Opportunity—doors wide open—every port open; if I could have it, free trade with the world, without toll or custom-house; invitation as we now make to every nation, every race and skin—white man, red man, yellow man, and black man; hospitality, a fair field, and equal laws to all. (*UL*, 6)

> The young men in America at this moment take little thought of what men in England are thinking or doing. That is the point which decides the welfare of the people; *which way does it look?* . . . We have come to feel that "by ourselves our safety must be bought;" to know the vast resources of the continent, the good will that is in the people, their conviction of the great moral advantages of freedom, social equality, education, and religious culture, and their determination to hold these fast, and, by them, to hold fast to the country and penetrate every square mile of it with this American civilization. (*W* 8:101–2)

> Therefore I praise New England because it is the country in the world where is the freest expenditure for education. We have already taken, at the planting of the Colonies . . . the initial step, which for its importance might have been resisted as the most radical of revolutions, thus deciding at the start the destiny of this country,—this, namely, that the poor man, whom the law does not allow to take an ear of corn when starving, nor a pair of shoes for his freezing feet, is allowed to put his hand into the pocket of the rich, and say, You shall educate me, not as you will, but as I will: not alone in the elements, but, by further provision, in the languages, in sciences, in the useful and elegant arts. The child shall be taken up by the State, and taught, at the public cost, the rudiments of knowledge, and, at last, the ripest results of art and science. (*W* 10:125–26)

Here clearly was a public moralist ready to offer "rules and propositions" and confident enough of his standing that he did not need to use specialized or esoteric language to convey his message. Here too was a figure who openly identified himself as a member of his community and whose

Fig. 2.2. Ralph Waldo Emerson. This image captures Emerson's "outward characteristics" as Emma Lazarus vividly recalled them in her 1882 memorial: "The tall, spare figure, crowned by the small head carrying out, with its bird like delicacy and poise, the aquiline effect of the beaked nose and piercing eyes" ("Emerson's Personality," *Century Illustrated Monthly Magazine,* May–October 1882, 453). Smithsonian Archives of American Art

ideals come across as strong versions of the ideals his countrymen themselves claimed to live by.[19]

All that said, perhaps Emerson's most common rhetorical strategy
was (as Richard Poirier has labeled it) troping, taking hold of the everyday language of his contemporaries and raising it to a higher pitch of
moral intensity and interpretive power.[20] This fact also underlines my
earlier point about Emerson's reliance on a certain community of values
between himself and his audience, for without a shared understanding
of the current use of language, efforts to turn that language in new and
unexpected directions seem destined to fall on deaf ears. Similarly, if
Emerson's troping aimed to free the thinking of his contemporaries
from predetermined meanings of what he took to be the key words in
their culture, at least one understanding of each term being transformed
had to be widely shared; otherwise, the attempted transformation would
have little persuasive force. The whole of Emerson's essay on "Wealth"
in *Conduct of Life* — still widely circulated in various forms during the late
1860s and 1870s — can be regarded as an extended exercise in troping
or, more specifically, an exhibit of Emerson's determination to uncover
nobler purposes he felt certain were contained with the characteristi-
cally American "demand to be rich." While the essay sometimes has been
read as providing a rationale for Gilded Age entrepreneurs, ultimately it
was a selective rationale that welcomed only those ready to join Emerson in the still-undone work of giving all Americans "access to the masterpieces of art and nature" and of creating a society whose economic
abundance would be used primarily to provide every one of its members
"the means and apparatus of science and the arts." That in essence was
Emerson's vision of the unique double meaning of "wealth": an egalitarian culture where the benefits civilization, reserved for the opulent few
in Europe, would now be enjoyed by all in America.[21]

The rhetorical strategy of troping so characteristic of Emerson's essays
and lectures in the 1840s and 1850s also figured prominently in those he
composed in the second half of the 1860s. It was evident, to begin with,
in his choice of titles: "Character," "Success," "Courage," "Hospitality,"
"Greatness," and "Eloquence." All these pieces are "Emersonian," as
Poirier has defined the term, in wanting both to "prevent words from
coming to rest" and to "dissuade us from hoping that they ever might."
The "constant interest" in "manners" Emerson appeared to affirm at the
outset of "Social Aims," for example, was grounded in an understanding
of "manners" that expanded and redefined the term to include Emersonian ideals of self-command and independence. Emerson accepted the popular definition of manners, in other words, only to turn that definition on
its head. The man of true "manners and talent" does not need a fine coat,

for "it is only when mind and character slumber that the dress can be seen. If the intellect were always awake, and every noble sentiment, the man might go in huckaback, or mats, and his dress would be admired and imitated" (*W* 8:87). The late Emerson offered no praise for a life of voluntary poverty, otherwise he sometimes sounded much like Thoreau.[22]

As a rhetorical strategy for a public moralist, troping was not without its drawbacks. There is little evidence showing that Emerson's contemporaries understood the full complexity of his challenge exactly as he offered it. As we have seen, some despaired of understanding it at all; others heard Emerson's acknowledgment of their concerns and then overlooked or ignored his criticism.[23] Robinson's description of the prose in "Success" as "walking a thin line" could also be applied to several of his postbellum essays. Emerson was a figure who thought he could speak to his culture, Robinson reminds us, because he so deeply shared its values, and this familiar characterization draws attention to the fact that his effort to reclaim the notion of success by divorcing it from the search for quick and superficial achievement was of a piece with his effort to preserve the ideal of success on individualistic grounds. In recognizing that these two views of success were of piece, however, we can also see why contemporaries who put Emerson back into close company with American prophets of the gospel of material success did not entirely misconstrue his original intentions. The potential for such a half-reading was latent in the strategy of troping itself. In speaking the language of his countrymen, Emerson never managed to sustain an oppositional tone strong enough to prevent many of them from mistaking his language for a roundabout endorsement of existing social and economic practices. Emerson's protest against the culture of his day, Holmes remarked in looking back on the course of his career, was one that "outflanked the extreme left of liberalism" yet it was at the same time "so calm and serene that its radicalism has the accents of the gospel of peace." Emerson was, in short, "an iconoclast without a hammer, who took down our idols from their pedestals so tenderly that its seemed like an act of worship."[24] Not entirely true, and curious coming from Holmes since he doubtless knew that slavery and the Civil War had prompted Emerson to deliver openly partisan, and at times fiercely polemical, lectures and addresses. But Holmes also knew that Emerson was never comfortable with the role of political spokesman.

IV

In considering Emerson's identity as a public moralist during the final years of his life, as well as the whole complicated question of his status as one of the nation's leading cultural celebrities, special attention has to be paid, finally, to his role in the transformation of American higher education. Here the chronological framework employed so far in this chapter needs be broadened somewhat. Emerson's influence in this realm, especially in the case of Charles Eliot's implementation of the elective system at Harvard, has provoked conflicting interpretations in modern scholarly commentary. And these interpretations, interestingly enough, mirror divisions of opinion first displayed by late-nineteenth-century observers of Emerson's career. A general conviction that Emerson was a spokesman for fundamental educational reform was first voiced during the 1840s and 1850s, when he emerged as a favorite lecturer on college campuses and before various young men's associations. After the Civil War, Emerson also found admirers who argued that his condemnations of the "deadness" of American education had prompted his most concrete recommendations for reform: "It would be well for those who affect to regard him as a harmless mystic, to know that no other man, for years, has left such an impress upon the young collegiate mind of America; that his style and thought go far to form the philosophic pothooks of many a Freshman's thesis; that from a secular pulpit he preaches better practical sermons on the conduct of life than is heard from two-thirds of the Christian pulpits of America."[25]

In a similar though much less defensive vein, Eliot would announce in the Emerson centenary year that he had "laid down in plain terms the fundamental doctrines" on which Harvard's new elective system rested. Supporting his position with quotes drawn from essays ranging from "The American Scholar" to "Education," he identified Emerson as "a prophet and inspirer of reform" who had left the hard work of "giving practical effect to his thought" for others to do. But Eliot, perhaps the most influential academic reformer of his generation, left no doubt that it was Emerson, above all others, who had inspired the work of curricular reform that had begun when he took office as Harvard's president in 1869, with Emerson himself—then in the second year of his first term on the Board of Overseers—sitting among the front-row guests at his inaugural address.[26]

Several years before Eliot underlined Emerson's credentials as an American "prophet," another set of admirers had put forward a different and apparently contrasting image. James Elliot Cabot's *Memoir of Ralph Waldo Emerson* (1887) provided an influential early statement of this view with his observation that Emerson's doctrines in fact had never gained many converts because he "had never identified himself with his precepts, but was always ready to reverse them, however categorical they might be, with equal emphasis and as coolly as if he had never

heard of them. He was not compiling a code." Cabot's alternative suggestion here was that Emerson was important not because he had helped
reshape nineteenth-century American culture but because he had con-
templated that culture from the vantage point of an original mind. This
was an Emerson who, George Santayana later would say, admiringly,
"had no doctrine at all." Those who knew Emerson personally, he remarked, never judged him as a poet or philosopher, or identified his
"efficacy" with that of his writings. Yet his cultural efficacy, on Santayana's account, was beside the point, since the picture of Emerson he
presented was that of a detached, Olympian figure who generally held
himself above the fray of controversy and so was "in no sense a prophet
for his age or country."[27]

On closer inspection, it may not be hard to see that these two interpretations are not quite the opposites they may appear at first. They im-
plicitly agree, after all, in discounting the modest effectiveness Emerson
claimed for himself in reflecting on his career. Both "American prophet"
and "American mystic" are descriptions of a figure who wielded a pecu-
liarly powerful influence on the educated elite of his time. (By the end of
the century Emerson's better-informed admirers collectively had begun
to sense that he could be enlisted in many causes or none at all.) And
yet I suggest that if we also consider Emerson's complex and disputed
contribution to the transformation of American higher education in the
broader context of this chapter's discussion of his role as public moralist, that contribution falls into place if we approach it as an integral part
of his distinctive effort to interpret and defend the newness of American
culture. Santayana was right in saying that Emerson had no gospel to
proclaim, at least not in the usual sense. But that hardly meant he was
prepared to defend American "education" as he found it. For what he
found spoke only of mistrust and timidity, that is to say, of failure to
honor the distinctively American belief that all the nation's institutions
"existed for the individual, for the guardianship and education of every-
man."[28] The entire system was "a system of despair," Emerson complained. It omitted "the vast and the spiritual" as well as "the practical
and the moral" (*W* 10:133). The true object of education was both more
idealistic and more worldly than its current generation of providers
chose to recognize.

The content of a distinctively American education, then, had yet to
be determined, and Emerson hoped to have—and for a time clearly did
have—a voice in that determination. Several lectures he delivered frequently during the second half the 1860s—especially "Resources," "Social
Aims," "Education," and variously titled lectures on the topic of culture—
should be read in terms of his longstanding commitment to a cultural

transformation in which his central strategy was to awaken his listeners to their own deepest values. The chief objects of his criticism were skepticism and complacency: "There is much criticism, not on deep grounds, but an affirmative philosophy is wanting." Emerson called on a new generation of American scholars to join him in assuming the responsibilities of "counselor" and "upholder," "imparting pulses of light and shocks of electricity, guidance and courage" (*W* 10:325). "Guidance" here was, in part, synonymous with a renewal of faith in "the good will that is in the people," a renewal that, in Emerson's case, had been wrought by the Civil War: "The whole history of the Civil War is rich in a thousand anecdotes affecting the fertility of resource, the presence of mind, the skilled labor of our people" (*W* 8:139). During the war itself Emerson had said, "We will not again disparage America now that we have seen what men it will bear" (*W* 11:322). Another part of his guidance was focused on longstanding cultural questions: "Amidst the calamities which war has brought on our county this one benefit has accrued—that our eyes are withdrawn from England, withdrawn from France, and look homeward." Emerson himself was "looking homeward" in his postwar lectures and essays, and what he saw was a profound cultural transformation in the making and a transformation whose accomplishment he held up as the primary measure of America's worth as a reunified nation.

Despite his free-trade convictions, the late Emerson was neither a spokesman for a rising professional middle class nor an idealistic mouthpiece for a new entrepreneurial elite. (Unlike other northern celebrants of the Civil War and its heroes, he also never waved the bloody shirt.) His vision of the "progress of culture" in America took other forms. One—largely overlooked by students of the last phase of his career—was a remarkably pointed defense of immigration. Emerson's message at the outset of his second Phi Beta Kappa address at Harvard in 1867, for example, was that there had been an unprecedented "fusion of races and religion" in America, a fusion that had made the nation "the answering facility of immigration, permitting every wanderer to choose his climate and government" (*W* 8:197). The generational categories in which Emerson often expressed himself arguably fit immigrants better than the middle class or corporate entrepreneurs. The new postwar American nation was one where "men come hither by nations" (*W* 8:197) and promised, as he had put it in an 1864 lecture before the Parker Fraternity in Boston, by "perpetual intermixture to yield the most vigorous qualities and accomplishments of all."[29] Emerson was also sympathetic to new efforts to speed the political and economic assimilation of freed African Americans. He had identified himself publicly with the great revolution of the middle of the Civil War, the acceptance of black men into the Union army.[30] After the war he endorsed the Reconstruction as an end to the "false relations" of slavery and the beginning of an effort to create a just order in which "every man shall have what he honestly earns" and an "equal vote in the state, and a fair chance in society" (*JMN* 15:301–2).

What would "education" in this America become? Emerson professed not to know: "We confess that in America everything looks new and recent" (*W* 8:202). He knew only that the very purpose of America entailed embracing the"new and recent"—thereby promising an escape from "the ruts of the last generation"—and that here education would not imitate the European model, with churches and "hereditary aristocracy" imposing their values on ordinary people. With the Civil War over, Emerson also knew that his own exemplary New Englanders no longer formed a separate country but were now caught up in America's "fusion of races and people," and they would betray their own democratic values if they resisted the assimilation of those coming "from crowded, antiquated kingdoms to the easy sharing of our simple forms" (*W* 8:203). "The democratic opening of all avenues to all," Emerson proclaimed, "is the fixed advantage which our institutions give, the solver of all conceits" (*UL*, 7).The progress of democracy, then, would generate radically new concepts of culture and education whose richness could only be intimated. Repress American "hospitality," constrain the choices of ordinary men and women, and the result will be to extinguish the egalitarian spirit that is "our power." America's alternative to European education, its "one point of plain duty," was "to educate every soul. Every native and every foreign child that is cast on our coast shall be taught, at the public cost, the rudiments of knowledge, and at last the ripest results of art and science" (*UL*, 7).

A multinational America, the "answering facility of immigration" where individual identity is not static but progressive and ever-changing, and where the object of education is to teach every person "self-trust," was Emerson's vision of a postwar America. How much of this version of Emerson reappeared in Eliot's famous centenary address? Important parts of it, to be sure. Eliot recognized and shared Emerson's confidence in the uniqueness of what was transpiring in America. The same was true for Emerson's belief that there was no preestablished model for American education available in Europe. But this perhaps is the wrong question to explore at length here if we want to understand the main historical significance of the Emerson-Eliot connection. It does not require close reading of Eliot's centenary tribute to see that it was largely a picture of Emerson in his twenties and thirties. Emerson's career as a lecturer received only brief mention, and its remarkable revival in the

late 1860s—including his second Phi Beta Kappa address at Harvard—
went unmentioned. The part of Emerson's life that interested Eliot ended
in 1843, because in that year he saw the development of the central max-
ims of his thought as coming to an end. Emerson's contributions to the
abolitionist movement in the 1840s and 1850s were more important than
Eliot may have known or remembered at the time, though there were
other voices celebrating Emerson in 1903—above all, Franklin Sanborn,
then the chief eulogist and self-appointed historian of American Transcendentalism—who already had made much of this side of his career.
Moreover, it was almost entirely in antebellum New England that Eliot
put Emerson—the world of Concord, Harvard, and Boston, not the postbellum America of immigrants and entrepreneurs. Finally, and perhaps
most obviously, he saw Emerson through the spectacles of his own understanding of what counted as progressive reform at the outset of the
twentieth century, with the result that Emerson was viewed as a prophet
of various other developments ranging from "the cultivation of manners" and the ascendancy of "athletic sports" in American higher education to "the absurdity of paying all sorts of service at one rate, now a
favorite notion with some labor unions." Even Eliot's claim that Emerson had been the main source of his commitment to the elective system
turned out to be somewhat self-serving. We know that elective reforms
endorsed by both of Harvard's governing boards were already underway
at the time of Eliot's inauguration, and the new president was expected
to continue the advance. And while it was hardly surprising that Eliot
traced his intellectual pedigree back to Emerson, he in fact had displayed little concern with the elective principle before his election.[31]

Whatever its limitations, Eliot's centenary lecture on Emerson forms
an important part of the larger story of how Emerson's name and ideas
continued to receive national attention and authorityduring the late nineteenth and early twentieth centuries. Eliot was in no position to dictate a
national consensus regarding Emerson, even if he had managed a more
faithful rendering of his career and ideas. But he did hold institutional
power that he used to provide what was arguably a more important service: the publicity needed to keep Emerson visible in American culture
at large. The entire course of their relationship might be described as
something of a feedback loop. At first Eliot borrowed strength from the
reputation of a living, embodied Emerson. Here we should remind
ourselves how young Eliot was when, after he was elected president,
he began to have frequent contact with Emerson—he was thirty-five
(younger than any previous president) and Emerson was sixty-six—just
as we should remind ourselves that he had not been the overwhelmingly
popular choice of Harvard's Board of Overseers. The Emerson whom

Eliot sought out in the 1870s was not simply one of the sixteen overseers who had voted for him—eight had voted against his appointment—but a figure recently accepted as part of Harvard's great past and an eager ally in the cause of institutional reform.[32]

Near the end of his term, however, it was Eliot, now widely recognized as the most influential educational reformer of his generation, who helped to build Emerson's posthumous reputation. In fact, by the turn of the century, Eliot's public identity within American culture began to resemble the late Emerson's in some respects. The labels "oracle," "prophet," and "sage" were now used to describe his relationship with the public at large. Harvard's President Eliot had become America's President Eliot, and it was in that role that he helped to confer new luster on Emerson. Two years after the centenary address, he found what turned out to be a more permanent way of identifying Emerson as a vital agent of Harvard's past and future, dedicating the University's new Emerson Hall—the first building in American dedicated to the study of philosophy—on the occasion of both the one hundredth anniversary of his birth and Harvard's hosting the annual convention of the American Philosophical Association. Four years later, Eliot made Emerson the chief American beneficiary of his labors as editor of the new "Harvard Classics," in yet another project that served to tie his name even more closely to an institution that once had wanted nothing to do with him. In Eliot's fifty volumes, Emerson was among a remarkably small handful of American writers who earned inclusion in an otherwise all-British and European pantheon; and while he was one of two Americans whose writings earned publication as a separate volume, Eliot singled him out as "the greatest of American thinkers."[33]

V

The story of the late Emerson's career told in this essay differs in several important respects from that usually told by his modern interpreters. First of all it suggests that the best word to describe the public image of Emerson in America during the 1860s and 1870s is "manifold." "Emersons," not some monolithic "Emerson," is what we have been talking about. The familiar image of the late Emerson as a revered literary figure of the recent past, a New Englander who survived during the onset of the industrial era as a symbolic remnant of a better age, is simply too foreshortened (if not altogether misleading) to take in all the details displayed in a full history of his postwar activities and reputation. Against the familiar image of "exquisite" Emerson (the adjective comes from the young Henry James), I support a more complicated one first sketched shortly after his second Phi Beta Kappa address. Here is how that sketch appeared in the September 21, 1867, issue of *Every Saturday:*

> The enthusiasm with which Ralph Waldo Emerson is greeted in every part of the United States is a phenomenon which cannot escape the attention of those who study the affairs and tendencies of that country. During the last few years we find him at one time called to Washington to address the national representatives on the condition of the country, and afterward engaged in a consultation with President Lincoln; last year Harvard University bestowed on him the honorary degree of Doctor of Laws; during the past winter he visited the West, and addressed the populations of its most important cities which turned out crowds to welcome and listen to him; at St. Louis he held conversations with a Hegelian club, which certain educated Germans have formed there; and more recently he has been unanimously chosen to deliver the chief oration at the Cambridge Commencement, having the day before been elected by the legislature of Massachusetts an overseer of that institution, the oldest and most important in the country. Thus in his sixty-fourth year, and after a literary career of more than forty years, in which he has advocated the most sweeping heresies of the age, and been regarded as an incomprehensible visionary, the seer opens the "garden-gate," once sternly slammed in the face of the world, and steps into the arena; the prophet's mantle is thrown aside for the captain's armor.[34]

The verdict here is not precisely the one I support—and it was Harvard alumni, not the Massachusetts legislature, who elected Emerson to the Harvard Board of Overseers—but it comes close. It was in the second half of the 1860s that Emerson first achieved the stature of a national presence, although the story told here, I believe, also shows that his "heresies" were not forgotten, and that his countrymen did not suddenly stop viewing him as an "incomprehensible visionary" as they sought greater familiarity with the man and his writings and ideas. The broad opening claim of this assessment, however, seems accurate enough, if in proclaiming Emerson a national presence *Every Saturday* meant to draw attention to two relatively straightforward points. First, despite the fact that actual sales of American editions of Emerson's writings remained relatively modest, over the course of the 1860s and 1870s, some sort of confrontation with Emerson—the man, the image, his lectures, and his writings—became virtually obligatory for literate Americans of diverse backgrounds and interests. And second, during those decades, the same could not yet be said for any other nineteenth-century American writer and lecturer, either in Emerson's own generation or in its successor.

There was in fact no one else who had lived a life quite like Emerson's or represented what he had come to represent: a poet/philosopher central to the emerging high culture of America's industrial era and yet at the same time a peripatetic public moralist who, for more than three decades, had attempted to address the cultural and political concerns of everyday Americans.

These conclusions are also significant in pointing to questions I take up in the chapter that follows. As with the story of his post–Civil war career, the story of what became of Emerson's reputation during the two decades immediately following his death is a complicated. But it is easier to sort out if we keep in mind what this chapter tries to show, that during his lifetime the centrality of Emerson was not imposed on his countrymen but accepted, sometimes with amusement, confusion, and reluctance. As important as his ties to Ticknor and Fields and post-bellum Harvard may have proved to be, no one set of cultural institutions ever "constructed" Emerson's reputation while he was alive. It is of course true that he needed to be familiar to be respected—to become "an accepted fact" before he became "our national glory." But over the entire course of his lifetime the repeated performances most important to public acceptance included his lectures and newspaper accounts of those lectures as well as his publications and institutional attachments under his direct control. To carry the story beyond 1882, then, we will need to attend more carefully to the cultural identities of those who guaranteed the familiarity of an Emerson who would live on largely as the author of books. Charles Eliot was only one of a large number of players in this story, and a latecomer at that.

THREE

"More than Luther of these modern days"

The Social Construction of Emerson's Posthumous Reputation, 1882–1903

This chapter grew directly out of the one that precedes it. As its somewhat laborious subtitle may suggest, it also is the most methodologically self-conscious piece in the book. In tracing the development of Emerson's posthumous reputation, part of what I do in this study is what historians routinely do when asked to explain how certain ideas, individuals, or practices happen to gain and hold great cultural value: respond by employing the methodological concept of "social construction." More specifically, to explain how and why Emerson remained such a highly revered figure during the decades immediately after his death in 1882, I recount a story that not only took place in time but also entailed construction in the literal sense—an actual assembly of different parts in particular stages as well as a temporal process in which later stages were built upon, and out of, earlier stages.

All construction stories are guided by the concept that value is never just a matter of natural ability or talent. Yet as Ian Hacking has pointed out, this apparently simple methodological concept allows for various grades of commitment. The most controversial argues that we should abandon the notion of evaluation as a neutral account of objective qualities and accept in its place one that sees evaluation as invariably contingent on personal interests and needs. Less contentious is the historical grade of constructionism I commit to in this piece. Most workaday intellectual and cultural historians (among whom I number myself) are content to employ the concept of social construction as a heuristic device. They view enduring reputations more as empirical phenomena than as objects of suspicion. And the stories they tell about enduring reputations typically include careful reconstructions of a dynamic process made up of distinct stages as well as discussions of what over time would count as reasons for endurance.

In the workaday historian's approach, insisting that all things of enduring value have a construction history hardly represents a breathtaking insight. Reputations endure in various ways and for different reasons. Not all construction stories are the same. So it is the particulars of such stories that usually attract our interest. Not too many of the particulars of this chapter are given away by noting here that, as with Emerson's career between 1865 and 1882, what interests me most in telling the story of the construction of Emerson's posthumous reputation is the light it sheds on the much larger story of how Americans went about building new cultural institutions during the industrial era.

I

"The pathos of death," William James observed at the start of his fine address at the Concord celebration of Emerson's centenary, "is that when the days of one's life are ended, those days that were so crowded with business and felt so heavy in their passing, what remains of one in memory should usually be so slight a thing." The Emerson who remained in James's memory, however, was an obvious exception to this rule. Not "so slight a thing" but one of a select few whose "singularity gives a note so clear as to be victorious over the inevitable pity of such a diminution and abridgment." The living figure who once walked Concord's streets and country roads, awaiting "the beloved Muse's visits" in its fields and woods, had departed some twenty years earlier. But his "soul's note" and "spiritual voice," James proclaimed, still rose "strong and clear above the uproar of the times" and seemed "destined to exert an ennobling influence over future generations."[1]

Doubtless James knew that an Emerson centenary celebration held in Concord's town hall was not the occasion for systematic reflection on the question of Emerson's posthumous reputation. But optimistic forecasts about his staying power must have looked like a safe bet on May 25, 1903, since an important part of what made Emerson an active presence at the time—numerous well-placed Americans across the country who (like James) could say they had actually seen Emerson, or spoken with him, or in some fashion experienced his "ennobling influence"— had yet to pass from the scene. Even so the terms James used in characterizing what he remembered of Emerson's "singularity" deserve some scrutiny. The identification of Emerson as the pride and ornament of Concord (then already well established as America's first shrine of literary tourism), the omission of any mention of his remarkably long public career as a lecturer and writer, and the concentration on Emerson as a reclusive "artist" and "spiritual seer," according to received scholarly accounts, must be regarded as characteristic elements of a late-nine-teenth- and early-twentieth-century view of Emerson that centered on a reverent idealization of his personality and life. Composed at a moment in America's cultural history when Emerson's authority apparently had come to rest on what Charles Eliot Norton (in his Concord centenary address) called the "consistent loftiness" of his character, James's invo-cation of the "ideal wraith" of Concord reinforces a still-familiar story about the ascendancy of Emerson as America's first secular saint and an accompanying delayed recognition of the full complexity of what he had accomplished during his long lifetime.[2]

While this story has some measure of truth, I set a more complex and eventful narrative against it in this chapter. "It was in college that I read [Emerson's] books and reread them" and "came gradually to recognize him as being what he was, the most resolute reformer not excepting [William Lloyd] Garrison, whom our nation has produced." Putting Emerson at the head of the long line of nineteenth-century American re-formers is only the more conspicuous of two significant differences here. William James at least mentioned in passing that the struggle against slavery had "appealed" to Emerson. Anyone listening closely to his address, however, heard nothing of the many books Emerson had pub-lished over the course of his lifetime, let alone of the flood of inexpen-sive new editions of his work that had appeared during the two decades following his death.

The author of this text-driven and more politically charged charac-terization of Emerson was Thomas Wentworth Higginson (1823–1911), who immediately preceded James on the stage in Concord. Some nine-teen years older than James, Higginson was himself something of a longstanding "reformer." In the 1850s he had led demonstrations in Boston against the Fugitive Slave Law and was part of the "Secret Six" cabal behind John Brown; after the Civil War, during which he com-manded the first regiment of freedmen in the Union army, he had be-come a vocal feminist as coeditor of the *Woman's Journal* (1870–84). In recounting Emerson's record as a reformer, Higginson explained that he had been "not merely a technical reformer, but stood to the world as a vital influence and represented the general attitude of reform." It was "Emerson, and he only" who was "the more than Luther of these mod-ern days," and the picture of him that lingered in Higginson's mind was not that of a reclusive artist but that of a passionate fellow abolitionist whose writings, early in the Civil War, had inspired freed slaves under Higginson's own command.[3]

Higginson's Concord address repeated more widely circulated remarks he had published two days earlier on the front page of the *Boston Daily Advertiser,* where he also had complained that Emerson's identity as one of America's preeminent democratic reformers appeared to be fading from sight. Underlining what he took to be the misleadingly conservative character of the two most popular biographies of Emerson, those by Oliver Wendell Holmes and James Elliot Cabot, Higginson voiced his distress over their "constitutional reticence" in discussing Emerson's once prominent role in both the antislavery and the women's movements. He faulted Cabot's biography in particular for failing to mention the "well-known fact" that Emerson had spoken several times at woman suffrage conventions, "and this cordially and sympathetically."[4]

Higginson's pronouncements hint at the more eventful narrative I want to develop in this chapter. They do so inadvertently, however, because no elaborate historical investigation is needed to show there was little ground for the complaint he voiced in the *Boston Daily Advertiser.* Nine days before the Concord celebration, for example, in a testimonial commissioned by the editors of *Harper's Weekly,* William Dean Howells had proclaimed that Emerson stood "next after Lincoln" as chief "interpreter of the American spirit." Similar sentiments were also voiced at Emerson centennial celebrations outside of Concord. In Boston's Symphony Hall, Harvard's President Charles W. Eliot praised Emerson as an early advocate of many of the reforms that had come to define the progressive reform movement. Similarly John Dewey argued in a paper at the Emerson Memorial Meeting held at the University of Chicago that he was best remembered as "the Philosopher of Democracy." Emerson had stood for "restoring to the common man that which in the name of religion, of philosophy, of art and of morality, has been embezzled from the common store and appropriated for sectarian and class use." Finally, alongside Higginson and William James on the stage at the Concord celebration were two other figures who had not forgotten Emerson's services to the cause of reform. President Caroline Hazard of Wellesley College reminded listeners that "the dignity" Emerson "gave to the individual with his call to awake and arise—this splendid call to personality—sounded not only for men but for women." Similarly Moorefield Story, one-time secretary to the venerable abolitionist Senator Charles Sumner and now a well-known leader of various reform movements and spokesman for Negro rights, used the occasion to condemn the persistence of racism in American society, telling the Concord audience that it could be viewed as a failure to express a "living faith" in the ideas of the man they had gathered to honor.[5]

This list of prominent examples could easily be extended. What is interesting for my purposes here, however, is not merely the fact that Emerson's identity as a champion of democratic reform was not, as Higginson feared, fading from sight in 1903. Rather it is that, even among Emerson's most well-placed admirers, the broader question of what made him a figure of enduring value invited responses that do not seem compatible at first glance. How could Emerson have been essentially both an artist and a democratic reformer? An angelic presence and a committed abolitionist? An "ideal wraith" who hovered over Concord and the "more than Luther" of the entire modern era? The contrast between these characterizations, however, can serve as a point of departure for exploring neglected aspects of the development of Emerson's posthumous reputation. This chapter does not pretend to offer a full survey of various interpretations of Emerson's life and writings in the late nineteenth and early twentieth centuries, still less a story of his "ennobling influence" in this period. Instead it aims to draw attention to certain developments within the institutional organization of American culture that allowed Emerson to remain a highly visible presence during an era of decisive cultural and economic change. It also attempts to account for some of the substantially different ways in which various groups and individuals came to enlist "Emerson" to secure or negotiate their own cultural identities.

II

During the decades immediately following Emerson's death, three successive stages marked major changes in the relationship Emerson's name and writings had with various culture-bearing entrepreneurs and institutions of that period. It is important to remember that these stages closely overlap one another chronologically, and so at times they may seem indistinguishable. To preview one example, at the time of Emerson's death most obituarists celebrated the example of his life and personality yet also wondered how long his essays would continue to be read because they did not seem to fit anywhere in the existing American literary order. Only two years later, however, Emerson's essays and poetry began to appear in countless cheap cloth and paperback editions, thereby helping to assure that by the turn of the century reading Emerson would become something of a national practice. Although the three stages in the development of Emerson's reputation between 1882 and 1903 do overlap, I approach them here in succession to develop a more detailed understanding of the various ways in which his life and writings continued to find widespread public notice and acclaim.

Fig. 3.1. Ralph Waldo
Emerson in the *Illus-
trated London News,*
May 6, 1882, 437

The first stage was that in which the iconic status Emerson's name
and writings had already gained over the course of his lifetime remained
largely unquestioned, sustained and enhanced as it was by the activities
of a variety of individuals and groups, ranging from personal friends and
admirers who made Emerson into a cultural cause to newspaper and
magazine editors for whom reporting about Emerson's career and work
remained a form of popular entertainment. During the 1880s and 1890s,
Emerson remained what one of his contemporaries had labeled him late
in his life: an "accepted fact" in American life, a figure who seemed to
stand entirely on his own and whose "magic touch" had helped countless "thoughtful people" grapple with the great problems of life.[6] That
Emerson continued to have some currency in this way well past the turn
of the century—essentially, he was America's first great cultural sage—
raises some important questions about standard notions of how his
canonicity has worked over time.

During the second stage, Americans were invited to consider Emerson's significance primarily against the background of a sudden and

explosive growth in the available supply of his writings. While late-nine-teenth- and early-twentieth-century views of Emerson were less text-centered than our current understanding, there can be no question that it was in the mid-1880s that his writings first became a major publishing commodity and that hundreds of thousands of Americans who ten years earlier were unlikely to have encountered his essays and poems first-hand could now afford to own them. During his own lifetime Emerson's writings had found their way into the hands of ordinary Americans mostly by way of excerpts and partial reprintings that appeared in anthologies, gift books, literary magazines, and newspapers. But the average price of his books put them well beyond most Americans' reach. It was only dur-ing the last two decades of the nineteenth century that his essays and poems became available in anthologies, books, and pamphlets that were priced and distributed for sale on every level of the American literary marketplace.

The third and final stage was that in which widespread classroom study and academic specialization first began to attend to the develop-ment of Emerson's reputation, as he was increasingly identified as a fig-ure whose career and writings helped to give rise to the tradition of "American literature." His presentation as a founding author of distinc-tively "American" literary texts depended on a variety of new cultural institutions and practices, ranging from the steady expansion of enroll-ments in American public schools to the establishment of English de-partments at elite American colleges and universities. By the turn of the century, dozens of literary anthologies and textbooks carried Emerson directly into American classrooms, where he has of course remained a fixture ever since.

Among academics who study enduring reputations, it has become commonplace to explain them as social constructions that often proceed through distinct stages that reflect accompanying (and more or less con-scious) changes in public understanding of their subjects. What has not been fully appreciated or understood in Emerson's case, however, is that while "Emerson" has been central to American culture since the middle decades of the nineteenth century, the actual construction of his reputa-tion has been a remarkably complex and scattered phenomenon. From the very start of his career, several conflicting, overlapping, and even contradictory representations have operated simultaneously in popular perception and discussion. During the antebellum era, Emerson was vilified as an atheist and an unintelligible thinker. Edgar Allen Poe dis-missed his early essays as "twaddle."[7] Yet at the same time Emerson was celebrated as a democratic visionary and a uniquely gifted writer. Con-tradictory assessments also had regional valences: Emerson's prominent role in bringing cultural legitimacy to the abolitionist movement and his forceful defense of John Brown were widely known and rendered his name anathema to educated southerners during the second half of the nineteenth century.[8] Not surprisingly there were no Emerson centenary celebrations below the Mason-Dixon line.

Even so, because Emerson's image, name, and writings were everywhere in American culture by the turn of the century, it seems correct to say that he had become part of the public domain and hence possessed a drawing power independent of the status of any who claimed authority to interpret him. Put another way, things Emersonian had a broad, deep, and diverse market that was the historical precondition for Emerson's "magic touch" during the late nineteenth and early twentieth centuries. And to understand how his posthumous magic worked, we should return for a close look at assessments of his career that appeared in the spring and summer of 1882, when the machinery of American publicity made his passing into a major publishing event.

III

"Ralph Waldo Emerson was recognized as the representative mind of his country," announced the *Chicago Daily Tribune* on April, 30, 1882, "and he is dead—dead at the age of 79 years; dead with a purer and more enduring fame than is often the mead of mortal men." In the days immediately following Emerson's death on April 28, just about every major American and English newspaper ran an obituary or eulogistic editorial, sometimes both. After all, in the opinion of the *Boston Daily Advertiser,* if one wished to have "the summary and quintessence of this new continent and its people . . . it is all in Emerson, of whom only the mortal frame can be destroyed by the angel death." Public concern had mounted several days before, when the *New York Daily Tribune* reported in stories reprinted in newspapers across the country that Emerson had contracted pneumonia. During the days that followed, newspaper headlines and stories multiplied up through May 1, with reports of his burial in Concord, and tailed off only after May 8, with a final flurry of mostly eulogistic assessments of his career.

Interestingly enough, Emerson's obituaries in English newspapers were often as effusive in their praise as their American counterparts. Eulogistic tributes appeared in the *London Daily Telegraph,* the *London Standard,* and the *London Times* the day after Emerson died. Five days after his funeral, the widely circulated *Illustrated London News* featured a full-page portrait. Other English newspapers that ran flattering tributes included the *Spectator,* the *Literary World,* the *Pall Mall Gazette,* and the

Manchester Examiner Times. Alluding to the recent death of Henry Wadsworth Longfellow (on March 24), the May 1, 1882, *London Daily Telegraph* appeared to voice the general sentiment of the English daily press when it observed that, while America had just lost "another of the illustrious band of New England worthies who will constitute in after-days her classic authors, Emerson's loss is no more confined to the New World than the previous bereavement; all the republic of letters shares it, for he who is no more belonged to all humanity."

The immediate aftermath of Emerson's death was hardly the time to form a fair estimate of his place in American culture. But numerous journalists, scholars, ministers, and literati pursued the task as best they could. The sheer volume of their efforts can be viewed as testimony to his high standing. Emerson's death signified much more to Americans than the passing of a distinguished essayist, lecturer, poet, and reformer; it marked the demise of a national institution. Many of his obituaries were also polemical, however, and their broad range of interests and observations is worth noting as a reminder that Emerson is no exception to the rule that national recognition comes in different shapes and sizes. Three largely neglected examples will suffice. Among the most widely circulated obituaries of Emerson were those that appeared in Sunday school newspapers and magazines—for example, the *Christian Advocate,* the *Independent,* the *Sunday School Times,* and the *Christian at Work*—all of whose editors used the occasion to raise what they considered the still-controversial question of his religious views, and in the process paid him only grudging respect. After denouncing the "indiscriminate" eulogies he had received in the secular press, F. D. Huntington stressed in the *Sunday School Times* that Emerson had to be given different marks for three distinct aspects of his career: his personal life, his contribution to American thought and letters, and his relations with Christianity. Huntington gave him high marks in the first two areas but then firmly denounced him as a figure who had done more than anyone else "to unsettle the faith of educated young men of our age and country," adding that he found it incredulous that other contemporary Christian ministers would now extol his thinking.[9]

Julia Ward Howe, on the other hand, viewed Emerson's legacy in simpler and more flattering terms. Her obituary in the *Woman's Journal* was written primarily to remind its readers that chief "among all of Emerson's great merits" had been "his loyalty to woman." "He believed in woman's power," Howe explained, "to hold and adjust for herself the scales in which character is weighed against attraction" and at "more than one woman suffrage meeting" had entered his public protest against "the political inequality that still demoralizes society." Emerson was "for us," she continued, "and his golden words have done much both to fit us for the larger freedom, and to know that it belongs to us."[10]

Finally, several other obituaries praised Emerson by emphasizing aspects of his career they considered to have no analogues in past or present American experience. The *New-York Daily Tribune*, a longtime admirer, identified Emerson as a figure whose interests had encompassed so many different cultural and political issues that the close study of his activities and writings had come to represent "a liberal education to a large number of men and women for nearly two generations." Still others echoed the judgment of the *San Francisco Chronicle* in observing that a strictly American framework of reference could not adequately describe the significance of his ideas and writings. Because Emerson had earned his place in a pantheon of "great men" that included Dante, Galileo, Montaigne, Newton, and Darwin, he belonged "not so much to his own as to future times, and his works will be classics in all languages centuries after his contemporaries of higher-flown pretensions and reputations are forgotten." Even among those who did not wish to single out Emerson as a "great man" or "the representative mind of his country," there was little hesitancy in acknowledging that he could not be compared with anyone else in the existing cultural order. "Although a New Englander of the New Englanders," Lafcadio Hearn wrote in the *New Orleans Times-Democrat*, he "had no prototype and will have no successful imitator. . . . [He] stands alone in his century by the peculiarity of his methods and the range of his philosophy."[11]

Earlier studies of Emerson's obituaries have noted that admirers and critics alike agreed that, by the end of his remarkably long life, Emerson could be viewed as a figure who stood apart from and even, in some minds, above any of his publications. Yet here too there were disagreements about which aspects of his personality and career ought to be regarded as the foundation of his reputation. The *Chicago Tribune* described Emerson's life as "uneventful," commenting that he had "lived in his thoughts and lived for composition alone." Yet others recalled that Emerson had been, as Bronson Alcott put it, "before the public for forty years, and may fairly said to have made the American lecture." The *Boston Commonwealth* remembered Emerson as a "reformer and patriot" who "early opened his Church in Boston to abolitionists with whom he enrolled himself" and later "took all the leading reformers of his era to his heart, whether Theodore Parker, Charles Sumner, John Brown, or Abraham Lincoln." More generally, the fact that Emerson was widely perceived as a religious man who was "not a Christian" was regarded by critics and admirers alike as the foundation of his public identity. Some critics found this the most disturbing aspect of his career. The

Charleston Daily News and Courier, for example, observed disapprovingly that, because Emerson was blind to the reality of sin, he had wrought evil among his "weaker imitators" by giving them an excuse "to believe nothing, feel nothing, and hear nothing."[12] Others insisted that his often sharp criticism of institutional religion had served the nation well. "I think one of Emerson's chief services to his countrymen," John Albee wrote in the *New-York Daily Tribune,* "is, and will continue to be, in untangling the connection between forms of religion and morals, in once more planting prostrate man upon his feet and revealing to him the moral beauties and dignities of life."[13]

Given such contrasting assessments aroused by his death, it is hardly a surprise to find that Emerson's passing did not end his hold upon the attention of his countrymen. What is striking is the fact that he would remain more in the public eye in the years immediately following his death than at any time since the late 1860s, when he had enjoyed his most active and lucrative years on the national lecture circuit. During the mid-1880s, Emerson was the subject of four book-length biographies, numerous biographical sketches, dozens of appreciations, and scores of reminiscences.[14] His longtime publishers in Britain and the United States also cashed in on the publicity generated by his death by issuing new editions of his work. In April 1883 George Routledge and Sons, Emerson's British publisher since 1850, published a single, double-columned edition of his *Works* in its inexpensive Books for the People series. That same month Houghton and Mifflin issued the first volume of its more elegant and expensive, six-volume Riverside Edition of his works. There were also new posthumous publications—such as *The Correspondence of Thomas Carlyle and Ralph Waldo Emerson* (1883), *Miscellanies* (1884), and *Lectures and Biographical Sketches* (1884)—all of which were widely reviewed and continued to attract popular interest in his career and writings. The same was true of Matthew Arnold's controversial address on Emerson in Boston in December 1883. Local response to Arnold's attempted demotion of Emerson from the heights of Anglo-American culture was fierce and swift, and the controversy received nationwide newspaper and magazine coverage. After his death, as before, many newspaper editors considered talk about Emerson to be an item of popular interest.

Many of the new things Emersonian that appeared in the mid-1880s, including much of the counterattack on Arnold, were the work of an influential set of personal friends and admirers who made Emerson into something of a cultural cause, figures James Russell Lowell once called "Emersonidae." Among the more influential of these was James Elliot Cabot, who had been appointed Emerson's literary executor in 1876 and after his death labored to make him appear as an even more productive author than he had been in life. Between 1884 and 1893, with the assistance of Emerson's daughter Ellen, Cabot collected or re-created dozens of previously unpublished lectures, addresses, and essays in *Miscellanies, Lectures and Biographical Sketches,* and *Natural History of Intellect* (1893). The five book-length biographies that appeared in the 1880s were also the work of Emersonidae, and they have an interesting history of their own. Biographies by George Willis Cooke, Moncure Conway, and Alexander Ireland highlighted Emerson's involvement in the antislavery movement. As Len Gougeon has pointed out, it was the publication of Oliver Wendell Holmes's *Ralph Waldo Emerson* (1884), commissioned for Houghton Mifflin's influential Men of Letters series, that marked the moment when the story of Emerson's ties to the abolitionist movement first began to blur both in matters of fact and of interpretation. Holmes barely mentioned Emerson's extensive antislavery activities in the 1840s and 1850s and quickly passed over his controversial support for John Brown. The immediate impact of Holmes's biography, however, is difficult to measure. Three years later, in his two-volume *Memoir of Ralph Waldo Emerson* (1887) Cabot presented the most detailed account of Emerson's abolitionist activities in all the early biographies, and several reviewers welcomed it as a corrective to what they saw as Holmes's more one-dimensional portrait.[15]

Emerson's reputation also gained strength from the continuous attention it received from Franklin B. Sanborn, who arguably was the most active of all the late-nineteenth-century Emersonidae. Sanborn had begun to write about Emerson for the *Boston Commonwealth* in 1865 and continued to do so for various other newspapers and magazines until the year before he died in 1917. While his biographical sketch in the American supplement to the ninth edition of the *Encyclopedia Britannica* was perhaps the most widely circulated of many publications concerned with Emerson, Sanborn's chief means for keeping Emerson in the public eye was through his longstanding connection with Samuel Bowles's *Springfield Republican,* then one of the nation's most respected newspapers, with a readership scattered throughout the country. Sanborn served as resident editor there from 1868 to 1872 and for most of the rest of his life contributed two weekly columns on Boston's cultural and political affairs. Emerson was one of the threads that held these columns together, and over time Sanborn came to fashion a complex and lifelike figure by printing and discussing letters, documents, and other previously overlooked memorabilia. Emerson's poetry received frequent and lavish homage, with Sanborn often insisting that his verse compared to that of the greatest English poets. Finally Emerson also figured prominently in Sanborn's efforts to preserve an honorable place for John Brown in the patriotic mythology of the nation, and his 1885 biography of Brown included three pages of previously unpublished passages from Emerson's journals.

As a group the Emersonidae surely held institutional power that provided Emerson with an important element of the publicity needed to keep him visible in American culture. It would be a mistake to say, however, that they also were in a position to dictate a national consensus regarding Emerson or that their activities alone were sufficient to perpetuate his fame. To be sure, Emerson's high standing in the late nineteenth century certainly depended on influential personal connections. But it depended on far more than that. For Emerson continued to have what might be described as a separate "physical existence" in the form of numerous texts he had once authored, and which continued to be produced, distributed, and read in some fashion. Moreover, if we go back to the last decades of the nineteenth century with this consideration in mind, what we find is another (and largely neglected) aspect of Emerson's career—the complex history of the reprintings of his texts—which must be viewed against the background of changes that would have more far-reaching consequences for his reputation.

IV

Historians recently have come to see the last two decades of the nineteenth century as a time when a new kind of culture was forming in America. For simplicity's sake, some now speak of the outcome of this transformation as the creation of a mass-print culture—a sweeping change that saw the mass production of books, magazines, and newspapers flourish for the first time and ordinary and affluent Americans alike come to live in an environment increasingly permeated by the printed word and the printed image. Such a culture, to be sure, had begun to form during the antebellum era, when thanks to the development of the telegraph New York newspapers such as the *Herald* and the *Tribune* reprinted stories for readers around the country. By midcentury books also were available everywhere, and in growing numbers; initial press runs of ten thousand were not uncommon, and some first editions even went as high as one hundred thousand. Between 1840 and 1856, the value of books made and sold in the United States tripled, and with an accompanying drop in price, the sheer number of books in circulation increased even more substantially.

Yet the parallel growth of publishing and of a national audience habituated to reading newspapers and books was a necessary, not sufficient, cause for the successful development of new print media produced for a national marketplace. More important in extending their range were technological developments such as the development of groundwood paper for books and more rapid methods of papermaking, which did not appear until the Civil War had ended. Beginning in the mid-1870s, these innovations not only allowed for a dramatic reductions in prices of printed publications but also prompted an even more sweeping cultural orientation that initially took shape as an enormous flood of cheap books, in both paperback and hard cover, that swept through American society during the 1880s.

Precipitated by a steep decline in the price of paper after the war, production of cheap books began with a sudden proliferation of new "libraries" of paperbound, uncopyrighted British and French novels. Low prices were supported by other developments, including the physical uniformity of the books (all were in quarto, with two or three columns of very closely printed type on each page), the elimination of royalties on books that were either in the public domain or left unprotected in the absence of an international copyright law, and, perhaps most important, the fact that cheap reprint companies issued books for which regular publishers had already created a national market. By the mid-1880s, with most "cheap books" selling for as little as twenty cents at newsdealers or in dry-goods stores across the country, the number of books extant began to reach astronomical figures. "Libraries" of inexpensive books also continued to grow in size, with nearly fifteen hundred titles added to these series in 1886 alone and their widespread sale now persuading some regular publishers to issue their own new series of paperbacks. In 1886, the peak year of what had become a fiercely competitive market in paperback publications, there were some twenty-six cheap "libraries" extant, printing thousands of titles by both American and European writers. Growth in the actual numbers of books printed was even greater. One of the most successful of the first cheap "library" series—George Munro's Seaside Library, launched in 1877—delivered 5.5 million books to newsdealers during the first two years of its existence; when the company was taken over in 1890, an inventory estimated at nearly 30 million volumes had been sold.[16]

The emergence of American mass-print culture during the last decades of the nineteenth century can also be traced, and in the view of some historians traced more clearly, by examining data on the sudden growth and development of America's first national magazines. When passage of the International Copyright Law in 1891 brought an end to the large-scale production of cheap paperbacks, the nation's leading monthly magazines—the *Atlantic, Harper's, Century,* and *Scribner's*—were all produced by leading publishing houses. They sold for a quarter or thirty-five cents. *Century* was the best seller of the group, with a top figure of two hundred thousand for a single issue. Two years later, however, in the middle of the economic panic of 1893, a quick sequence of events ushered in a new era of magazine publishing.

The "magazine revolution of the nineties" began abruptly in July 1893, when S. S. McClure brought out a new, copiously illustrated monthly designed to compete with the established "quality group" and marketed at the unprecedented price of fifteen cents. *McClure's Magazine* boomed from its inception, and within two months it also prompted other existing magazines to cut prices. First came *Cosmopolitan,* which dropped its price to twelve and a half cents; two months later *Munsey's* went down to ten cents a copy. By 1895 both *McClure's* and *Cosmopolitan* followed *McClure's* down to ten cents, where, joined by several other general monthlies, magazine prices remained for the next ten years. While exact circulation figures for the many ten-cent magazines born in the mid-1890s are unreliable, it is certain they too reached unprecedented levels. In the year of Emerson's centenary, for example, *McClure's* boasted a circulation of 377,000; *Cosmopolitan,* 350,000; and *Munsey's* about 600,000. (Meanwhile, circulation for the leading elite magazine, *Century,* had declined to 150,000.) By 1905 there were some twenty mainstream monthly magazines with circulations of 100,000 or more, reaching an audience of some 5.5 million readers.

The sudden success of national magazines brought with it a diverse bill of fare. In their effort to challenge the dominant position of the respectable monthlies, editors of mass-circulation magazines attracted many thousands of new readers with stories about contemporary social and political developments, as well as with an abundant supply of illustrations and photographs. But they also continued publishing the same eclectic blend of literary genres that had been concocted by the elite monthlies. Stories about the newly rich and powerful ran side by side with articles on American and European artists and features on American and European novelists and poets of the past. The practical consequence of this mixing of genres, as Matthew Shneirov has pointed out, was an innovative blurring of the boundary between "high" and "popular" culture.[17]

All this is now well known to specialists who study changes in the institutional organization of American culture during the late nineteenth century. What precisely does it have to do with the development of Emerson's posthumous reputation? Although still largely untraced by modern bibliographers, discussions of and references to Emerson are not hard to find in the pages of America's first mass-circulation magazines.

One fairly prominent example will suffice here. During the last months of 1893, shortly after the price of *Cosmopolitan* had been cut to twelve and a half cents, the magazine published a series of glowing, abundantly illustrated articles on various aspects of the World's Columbian Exposition in Chicago, popularly known as the World's Fair in the "White City." One of the last articles in this series—"A Farewell to the White City," by Paul Bourget, then a well-known French literary and cultural critic—enlisted Emerson's authority and language to explain the particular "promise" the World's Fair had left to Americans. The extraordinary popularity of the White City's "palatial monuments of human achievement," Bourget wrote, had demonstrated the existence of a "feverish, often touching craving for culture" that was driving Americans in "bewildering haste towards the libraries, theaters, and museums of Europe." But he also stressed that the fair's imitation Beaux Arts "palaces" in fact had not realized "the absolute originality of Emerson's dream" of American culture, a dream that still beckoned his countrymen to act on their own capacity to build their own new and more "durable counterparts" to the White City's now demolished structures.[18] And yet, while other examples are easy enough to find, Emerson can hardly be described as a fixture in the new world of mass magazines. The magazine revolution of the 1890s did not undermine his reputation, but it probably did not do much to enhance it either. Emerson's centenary, it is worth noting, went unmentioned in the pages of the major national monthlies. Even so, in the absence of a systematic survey, it would be a mistake to offer broader pronouncements about what further research might reveal.

What bearing did the "cheap books" phenomenon have for the making of Emerson's reputation? Here the evidence speaks more plainly.[19] In the realm of American "cheap books," Emerson's writings seem to have appeared first in New York and Chicago in the mid-1880s, when they were reprinted by John B. Alden and Thomas D. Hurst. Following the common practice of marketing inexpensive books in library series formats—Brilliant Books, in Emerson's case—Alden published new editions of *Nature, Essays [First Series], Essays [Second Series],* and *Representative Men,* with prices of individual books ranging from twenty to fifty cents. He also used his new bookplates to produce separate pamphlet publications of several individual essays, pricing them between three and five cents. Two years after Alden launched his inexpensive reprints of Emerson's writings, Hurst and Company produced the first of several cheap editions of *Essays [First Series],* and in the late 1880s and early 1890s it went on to publish new editions of *Essays [Second Series], Poems, Representative Men, English Traits,* and *The Conduct of Life.* Hurst marketed Emerson's work in its Arlington Edition of popular twelvemos,

Fig. 3.2. Cover of Emerson's
Essays: First Series (New
York: Hurst, n.d.). Joel Myer-
son Collection of Nineteenth
Century American Literature,
Rare Books and Special Col-
lections, University of South
Carolina

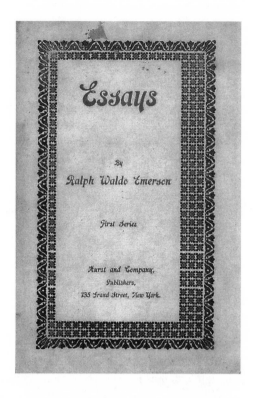

which included over three hundred bound volumes of both standard
and popular works. Listed at one dollar each, books in the series sold at
retail for much less. Hurst also leased his plates to the United States
Book Company, which printed its own cheap editions of *Essays [First
Series]* and *Essays [Second Series]*.

Alden and Hurst perhaps were the most influential popularizers of
Emerson's writings during the 1880s, but they were hardly alone. Several other New York and Chicago publishers known chiefly for issuing
cheap books—such as John B. Lovell, A. L. Burt, and Richard Worthing-
ton—also produced inexpensive new editions of his writings. We also
know that while New York and Chicago were the chief centers for production of cheap books, numerous other now largely forgotten publishers and printers across the country were in the business of publishing
inexpensive books, and its seems likely that they too helped to put
Emerson's writings into the hands of ordinary Americans. English publishing houses with offices in New York also produced their own cheap
book editions of Emerson for sale in the American market. The first of
these—George Routledge and Sons' double-columned, 643-page edition
of the *Works of Ralph Waldo Emerson*—seems to have been the most

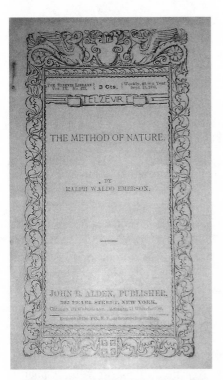

Fig. 3.3. Cover of Emerson's
Method of Nature (New York:
John B. Alden, 1890). Joel Myerson
Collection of Nineteenth Century
American Literature, Rare Books
and Special Collections, University
of South Carolina

ESSAYS.

BY

RALPH WALDO EMERSON.

FIRST AND SECOND SERIES.

COMPLETE IN ONE VOLUME

A. L. BURT COMPANY, Publishers
52-58 Duane Street, New York

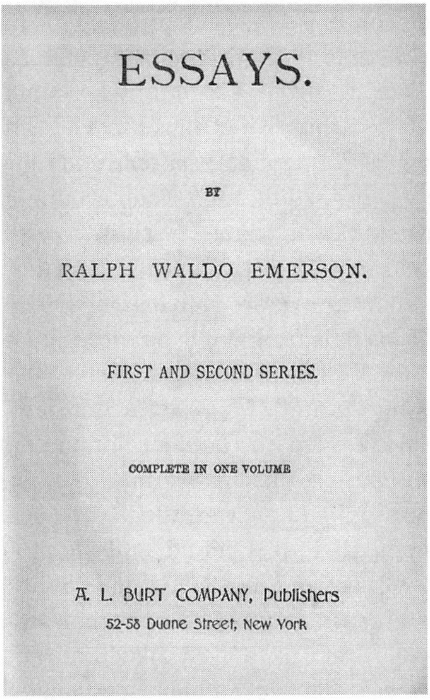

Fig. 3.4. Cover of Emerson's
Essays: First and Second Series
(New York: A. L. Burt, n.d.). Joel
Myerson Collection of Nineteenth
Century American Literature, Rare
Books and Special Collections,
University of South Carolina

successful, appearing first in 1883 and selling some forty thousand copies before going out of print in 1905. Routledge also marketed Emerson's writings in its popular Morely's Universal Library series, reprinting *Essays, Representative Men,* and *Society and Solitude* in double columns in a three-volumes-in-one format.

All this said, we should not ignore the fact that there remain certain difficulties in answering the question of how American and British "cheap book" editions of Emerson's writings may have helped to sustain or reshape his reputation. Many of these editions have no publication date, and in most cases there is scant information about numbers of individual books that were actually produced. Those who took notice of the "cheap book" editions of Emerson's writings when they first appeared marveled at the fact that his work had suddenly become available at prices that the "poorest could afford." One observer remarked that Emerson, along with other great European writers such as Thomas Carlyle, George Eliot, Victor Hugo, and Walter Scott, was now being "read in the backwoods of Arkansas and the mining camps of Colorado."[20] And yet, while it is easy enough to gather evidence showing that late-nineteenth-century Americans could find Emerson's writings in a wide variety of formats and settings, it is quite another matter to attempt to read over the shoulders of Arkansas farmers and Colorado miners who encountered Emerson reprinted in quarto with his poems and essays formatted in two or three columns of closely printed type to the page. Did the inexpensive quarto editions dilute Emerson's significance or somehow integrate him into the lives of people who could never have afforded his books and probably would never have read them had it not been for the price? Was Emerson read carefully for instruction and edification or simply skimmed through as entertaining filler? It is hard to resist the conclusion that we will never know.

Yet several things can be said with confidence about these issues. The mere fact that Emerson's writings were widely available as "cheap books" during the 1880s and early 1890s tells us that during those years he was not the exclusive property of the Emersonidae or other elite custodians of American culture. No single group of admirers controlled Emerson's image during these years. Likewise, the familiar notion that during this period Emerson was valued more "for his manner than for anything he actually wrote" ought now to be put to rest. Clearly the circulation of his writings grew exponentially in this period, and the producers and buyers of cheap editions of his work might be said to afford an illustration of a "grass roots" interest in Emerson that earlier students of this phase of his posthumous career have overlooked entirely. Finally, while it may be too much to say that "cheap book" editions of

Emerson's writings made his reputation for a new generation of readers in the 1880s and 1890s, they very likely did prompt Houghton Mifflin, the American publisher most actively concerned with promoting Emerson's reputation during this era, to develop various new formats that brought his writings to every level of America's burgeoning book market.[21]

Perhaps the best known of these remains the 1883 Riverside Edition of the Complete Works, marketed in two different formats that allowed Emerson to appear as both a staple item for new middle-class home libraries and as a collector's item in a new, deluxe edition. Yet Houghton Mifflin also published Emerson's books in several other, less expensive formats, all designed to present them as the work of a potentially popular author. Among the more successful were the Cheap Edition of *Essays [First Series]*, priced at fifteen cents and reprinted several times in 1884 and 1885; and the Popular Edition of *Essays First and Second Series*. Printed and priced in two different formats—cloth for one dollar, wrappers for fifty cents—this two-volumes-in-one edition of the essays was reprinted several times between 1889 and 1898. Houghton Mifflin also continued to publish Emerson in two formats initially developed by James R. Osgood in the late 1870s: the nine-volume Little Classics Edition, launched in 1876 and still in print as late as 1923, and the two-volume collection of miscellaneous essays first marketed in the 1882 Modern Classics Edition, which remained steady sellers to the end of the century.

Houghton Mifflin's most remarkable marketing innovation in the late nineteenth century, and perhaps its most important service in helping to secure Emerson's reputation in an era of mass publishing, would come when he was first added to the list of American writers reprinted in its new Riverside Literature Series. Driven partly by the firm's desire to capture a more substantial share of the rapidly expanding textbook market, Houghton Mifflin began to reissue its formidable list of American classics as texts for high schools in the late 1880s. And its successful promotion of Emerson's writings among those it confidently identified as having given ordinary Americans their existence as a people gave him yet another new measure of strength in American national culture. Priced mostly at fifteen cents and marketed nationwide, each of several different Riverside Literature Series editions of Emerson's poems and writings had sold in the tens of thousands by the time of his centenary.

A full survey of the publishing history of Emerson's writings during the last quarter of the nineteenth century would extend well beyond the boundaries of a single chapter. What we have considered here, however, suggests quite plainly that during America's first great boom in mass publishing, his work did not disappear into a rarified cultural space. In fact, by the turn of the century, Emerson's writings were everywhere,

Fig. 3.5. Cover of Emerson's *Ralph Waldo Emerson, Essays: First Series* (Boston: Houghton Mifflin, 1884). Joel Myerson Collection of Nineteenth Century American Literature, Rare Books and Special Collections, University of South Carolina

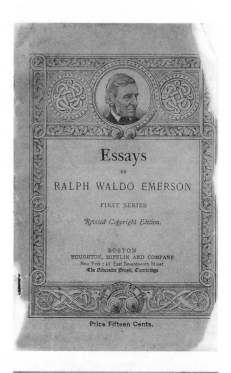

Fig. 3.6. Cover of Emerson's *Fortune of the Republic and Other American Addresses* (Boston: Houghton Mifflin, 1889). Joel Myerson Collection of Nineteenth Century American Literature, Rare Books and Special Collections, University of South Carolina

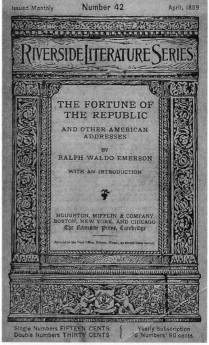

selling in the hundreds of thousands and perhaps even in the millions, in cheap pamphlet and paperback reprints as well as in deluxe, multi-volume cloth editions, in books that could be found on the shelves of public libraries as well as in the parlors of middle-class homes, in books produced for high school students as well as for rare-book collectors. Or put another way, we can say that during the decade immediately following his death, Emerson, a figure who during his life had pursued a many-sided career as lecturer, essayist, poet, and reformer, assumed another cultural identity: author of writings that were a major publishing commodity in the burgeoning Anglo-American literary marketplace.

V

In tracing Emerson's reputation after the collapse of the "cheap books" in 1891, we need to turn our attention to the third and final stage of its development, the emergence of "American literature" as a new and increasingly dominant construct for shaping popular understanding of his career and writings. In the 1880s prominent nonacademic professional writers such as Horace Scudder and E. C. Stedman were among the first figures to engage in the work of arranging and celebrating writing known as American literature. By the end of the century, however, this work had become something of a new cottage industry for college and university professors who introduced American literature courses in recently established English departments at roughly the same time as the subject was also first entering the curriculum of public schools. During the 1880s and 1890s, dozens of professors across the country made names for themselves by writing the history of American literature in a plethora of nationally marketed textbooks. Among the most influential of these were *Initial Studies in American Literature* (1887) by Henry A. Beers of Yale and *American Literature* (1897) by Katherine Lee Bates of Wellesley College (each of which was widely distributed as a Chautauqua text), as well as *A History of American Literature: With a View to the Fundamental Principles Underlying Its Development, a Textbook for Schools and Colleges* (1896) by Fred Lewis Pattee of Pennsylvania State and *An Introduction to the Study of American Literature* (1896) by Brander Matthews of Columbia (each of which sold at least a quarter million copies after publication).[22]

By the turn of the century, the commercial success of books devoted to outlining the history of American literature had served to create a new literary tradition, at the same time as it had helped to establish the cultural authority of a first generation of academic specialists in this field. The sheer volume of literary history textbooks, however, also served a

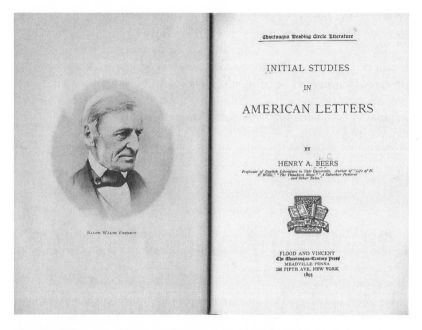

Fig. 3.7. Title page of Henry A. Beers's *Initial Studies in American Letters* (1887). Howard-Tilton Memorial Library, Tulane University

more immediate purpose: providing high-minded advertisements for the individual subjects of their academic expertise. In an age when a great boom in mass publishing had kicked the machinery of American publicity into high gear, and the abundantly illustrated pages of cheap, mass-circulation magazines such as *Munsey's, McClure's,* and *Cosmopolitan* helped to invent the cult of celebrity that has remained so integral to American culture, one could say that American literary history textbooks did something of the same for those figures who composed the canon of American literature as it first came to be known in the late nineteenth century, principally Longfellow, Hawthorne, Lowell, Whittier, and of course Emerson. Indeed, beginning with Beers's *Initial Studies,* which featured a photograph of Emerson as its frontispiece, many textbooks attempted, as Brander Matthews put it, to "arouse a student's interests in the authors as actual men" by including illustrations that provided portraits of individual writers, views of their birthplaces or residences, and facsimiles of their manuscripts. The biographical format of most textbooks, largely uncluttered by lengthy quotations or textual analysis, probably did little to encourage careful reading. On the other hand, this format reflected and reinforced the new emphasis on the personal, and on personalities, that figured so prominently in American mass-print media.

We also know that American literary history textbooks figured prominently in a broader process of national cultural self-definition that gained new momentum in the decades following Emerson's death. As Nina Baym has carefully demonstrated, in celebrating American literature, authors of late-nineteenth-century textbooks configured it to serve two of the primary aims of American public education at the time: forming character and ensuring patriotism. In essence the story they told about American literature—and about Emerson's role in bringing it to life— ran as follows. In the face of many obstacles, a bona fide literary culture had developed during the decades before the Civil War. Before 1830 there had been no such culture; after 1830, according to the story, a literary culture emerged in New England among groups of Cambridge and Concord authors joined socially by the amenities of Boston, where powerful publishing institutions also supported them and circulated their writings around the nation. The main authors in the first American literary canon—Emerson, Hawthorne, Lowell, Longfellow, Holmes, and Whittier—were descendants of Puritans whose writings expressed Puritan values in the language of the nineteenth century. The new literary histories encouraged veneration and gratitude toward figures they presented as having created American literature for the rest of the countrymen, often stressing that knowledge of their careers and writings would help to assimilate readers to the national culture they at once represented and displayed. Emerson's specific role in this story was that of founder. Typically he was presented as the New England writer most responsible for moving beyond Unitarianism into forms of literary expression that were separate from particular doctrinal programs and hence for transforming Puritanism into a distinctively American literature. Emerson was seen, as well, to have been at the center of a group of several writers who had consciously engaged in building American literature and were, in various ways, also exemplary of the New England mind.[23]

There is no need here to rehearse the limitations and inadequacies of this narrative, and its long-term bearing upon the evolution of Emerson's reputation should be fairly obvious. Beginning in the mid-1890s, as this view of American literature and its attendant interpretation of Emerson took hold, custody of his reputation in time fell primarily to academic specialists who viewed him as a legitimating national symbol and made his career and writings objects of classroom instruction and professional academic inquiry.

Even so, it is worth taking time to consider some of the peculiarities that marked this process in its initial stages. Literary historians have a tendency to speak of the creation of the first version of an American literary canon as if it were, by the turn of the century, a single, fully accomplished process.[24] But it was not. It is more accurate to speak of two parallel efforts to institutionalize the study of Emerson and other New England writers as American classics. The first played itself out within the now relatively well-mapped territory of new English departments at American colleges and universities, the other in the much larger yet almost entirely unexplored terrain of countless high school classrooms across the country. Because publishers very rarely differentiated between college and high school textbooks in this era, we know that college and university professors figured centrally in both efforts. Only in the second, however, did the publications of the professors enjoy any substantive success before the late 1920s.

What explains the discrepancy? Within the English departments of American colleges and universities, it was primarily the prominence of philology that made for the very slow and uneven progress of efforts to establish separate courses in American literature. Philology was europhilic and anglophilic, and its practitioners in English departments generally assumed that American literature had been and still remained simply a branch of English literature. The story was much the same in professional meetings and scholarly publications sponsored by the philologically top-heavy Modern Language Association (MLA), where for several decades after the association's founding in 1883 papers and articles on American literature were scant. It is true that by the turn of the century courses in American literature were offered at most American colleges and universities. Yet these were limited to a handful of general survey courses for undergraduates. At the graduate level efforts to institutionalize study of American literature were almost a complete failure. In 1900 scarcely a dozen (less than 10 percent) of the country's 150 universities had developed graduate programs in American literature, and only four doctoral degrees had emerged. The first doctoral dissertation on Emerson appeared in 1896; only eight more would be completed over the course of the next thirty years.[25]

Why, in contrast, did the first efforts to institutionalize study of American literature enjoy such remarkable success in high school classrooms? The ready commercial accessibility of the late-nineteenth-century American literary canon surely had something to do with it. So too did the substantially different requirements of the more rapidly expanding realm of American secondary education, which invited open expressions of cultural nationalism. For high school teachers, the value of American literature rested chiefly on the grounds that it could serve as a agent of acculturation. Collectively Emerson and the other great New England writers had forged the channel for disseminating the ethos that gave Americans existence as a people and, above all, the means by which a now-burgeoning population of immigrant outsiders could be brought inside it. American literature, as Richard Broadhead has put it, was taken literally to be that which "Americanizes," and it was in such terms that hundreds of thousands of new readers began to find their way to Emerson in the mid-1890s.[26]

This curious mix of condescension and reverence had several consequences for the making of Emerson's reputation. Given the broader argument in this chapter, two stand out. First of all, clearly the cultural phenomenon we are considering here remains "Emersons," not "Emerson." Far from revealing a widely shared agreement about Emerson's significance, the mixed results of early efforts to institutionalize study of American literature reflected a longstanding and continuing division of opinion. Intent on serving two related yet distinct cultural causes, professionalization and acculturation, the first generation of academic specialists in American literature were unable or (in many cases) unwilling to present themselves as something other than students of a provincial branch of British culture. Hence their failure to open up Emerson to widespread and sympathetic professional academic study. It also seems fair to say, however, that their quick and parallel commercial success in promoting American classics as school texts resulted in Emerson's continued engagement in, and overlap with, American culture at large. School texts certainly were not the first innovation to create a mass audience for Emerson's writings. As we have seen, it was "cheap books" that first put his writings within the physical and financial reach of ordinary people across the country. But there can be little question that mass-produced school texts ultimately proved a more reliable vehicle for securing Emerson's place in the public cultural domain, as reading about his career and selections from his writing now became a familiar and endlessly repeated exercise for generations of American high school students.

VI

A final point in conclusion. As with the story I told about Emerson in the previous chapter, I believe there were some late-nineteenth- and early-twentieth-century Americans who anticipated the broad outlines of the story I have told in this one. One example should suffice here, and it comes from a memorial given by George Willis Cooke, one of the lesser known Emersonidae, at the time of the Emerson centenary. In the May 1903 issue of the *New Englander,* Cooke issued a more concise assessment of Emerson's posthumous career: "The two decades that have passed away since Emerson's death have clarified our judgement of him, and have given him a more assured and a loftier place than he occupied when he departed from us. There is no indication that he is losing his hold upon us or that his fame will wane at any time in the future. What remoter generations will say of him we cannot foresee, but that he will be outgrown or suffer neglect we cannot think."[27] Cooke's verdict is not precisely the one I have tried to support in this chapter, but it comes close. While I believe Emerson's precise significance for American culture remained an unsettled issue in 1903, the emergence of a mass-print culture had resulted in his gaining an "assured" place in the public cultural domain. My story is more complex than Cooke's because it recognizes that the explosive growth in the supply of and demand for his writings has to be set against the background of other new institutions and practices that sought to define public understanding of the significance of the man and his writings and ideas, and especially important among these was a two-sided effort to enshrine Emerson as the founder of American literature.

That said, Cooke's refusal to speculate on what future generations might say about Emerson can serve as a reminder that, as with many other new cultural practices that came to life in the late nineteenth century, the immediate results of efforts to promote the study of American literature did not fully match the high hopes its earliest promoters had invested in these efforts. Just as important, it also can serve as a reminder that the continuing phenomenon that was "Emerson" was not shaped primarily by the interests and ambitions of a new class of academic professionals. The essential development in these decades was simply a dramatic and unprecedented expansion of America's public cultural domain, making it one in which Emerson's essays and poems now found their way into the hands of an increasingly broad range of men and women, who could and did enlist him to serve their particular purposes. Little wonder, then, Cooke saw no indication that Emerson was losing his hold on the American public. His hold, in 1903, was tighter than ever.

FOUR

The Academic Public Sphere

The University Movement in
American Culture, 1870–1901

This chapter proposes what I consider a new approach to the question of how the American university system—undoubtedly the most important of the many new cultural institutions that came to life during the industrial era—first secured its now central place in our national affairs. Historians have assumed several different vantage points in accounting for the early success of the American university. Many emphasize the professionalization of knowledge; others focus on class ambition and definition. More recently Thomas Bender has made a major point of the early civic purpose of the new research universities in 1870s and 1880s. The new point of concern in this chapter is what I call (borrowing but also substantially modifying Jürgen Habermas's well-known concept) the "academic public sphere."

In examining certain parts of eighteenth-century western Europe, Habermas has argued for the existence of "bourgeois public sphere," defining it as a new social space—and a set of attendant norms—that encouraged democratic public debate. In his account newspapers, pamphlets, coffeehouses, and salons were among the key instruments that made this new public sphere possible. I do not see the American university movement as fostering a coherent set of norms, but I believe it too can be said to have created and occupied a new social space in late-nineteenth-century America, the academic public sphere. Mass-marketed books, mass-circulation magazines, and local and national newspapers were among the instruments that made this possible. So too were the complex career paths followed by leading university administrators and academic intellectuals, as well as the adult education movement in its various forms. It also should be noted that, unlike Habermas's idealized model of a public sphere that lies beyond the influence of economics and politics, America's emerging academic public sphere drew life from, as well as helped sustain, many of the changes typically associated with the industrial era: population growth, rising literacy rates, growing per capita income, and the rapid spread of urbanization joined with immense improvement in the ease and speed of communication and transportation. Indeed all these changes not only gave unprecedented relevance to academic inquiry and training but also made them accessible to a larger public than ever before.

I

Late in July 1893, Daniel Coit Gilman, then in his eighteenth year as the first president of Johns Hopkins University, traveled by train to Chicago to deliver the opening address at an International Congress on Higher Education that the National Education Association (NEA) had organized in conjunction with the World's Columbian Exposition. Staged in Chicago's massive, new Memorial Art Palace seven miles north of the exposition, it was the first of nine such sessions that would assemble over the course of two weeks, all with the shared design of promoting public understanding of the strengths and weaknesses of America's various school systems. The roster of participants in the opening session included most of the figures we remember as architects of the modern American university: James Angell of the University of Michigan, William Rainey Harper of the University of Chicago, Seth Low of Columbia University, David Starr Jordan of Stanford University, Martin Kellogg of the University of California, James H. Baker of the University of Colorado, and of course Gilman himself.[1] William Torrey Harris, former president of the NEA and then the U.S. commissioner of education, chaired the committee assigned to make arrangements and helped ensure that the university presidents' speeches and commentary received for broad public notice. In return for a two-dollar registration fee, each of the several thousand NEA members who had traveled by train from across the country to attend the various congresses in the Art Palace later received an edition of the complete conference *Proceedings* (1895).[2]

It also was Harris who had asked Gilman to make the opening address, one he hoped would focus attention on the first session's organizing theme, the problematic relationship between the college's traditional ideal of "liberal education" and the university's new ideals of "specialization" and "research." But Gilman had other things in mind. He began by remarking that, while the American public showed "an amount of interest in universities and colleges unequaled, and perhaps unapproached, in England, France, and Germany," it would be a mistake to ask them to think about the current state of higher education in terms of the neat binary Harris had proposed. The sheer diversity of American higher education, Gilman explained, was the new and relevant circumstance: "No established churches exercise either legal or traditional control. No central national authority has any right of superintendence, oversight, or inspection. Each separate state has its own organization." Gilman also noted that, with all its variety, late-nineteenth-century higher education was a landscape populated by a multitude of sinners. New academic titles were plentiful, but they had no significance, he cautioned, "unless the source is known from which they are derived. Anybody who chooses may call himself "a professor," and the "only rebuke that he incurs is the gentle rebuke of his neighbors." Too often the label "university" was being "applied to institutions of the humblest character." Even so, at a time when much of American higher education seemed both confused and diffused, Gilman stressed that the nation's "highest institutions" had not lost their way, and he moved on to outline four "functions" he urged his audience to "recognize unanimously" as identifying all legitimate universities.

The first was the teaching of well-trained students. Whatever else the university might undertake, Gilman said, its primary purpose was to educate "youth who have been prepared for advanced work by previous disciplines in certain branches of knowledge." As opposed to "collegiate education," university education assumes students who have already developed "habits of attention, memory, discrimination, classification, and judgment." The university's second function was to conserve knowledge. "Libraries and museums are the dwelling-places of universities," Gilman explained, because they are "comfortable stalls" for those "whose pleasure it is to trace from their origins" our language, laws, religions, and customs, as well as for "those who are able to collect, arrange, describe, and interpret all natural objects."

The third function of the university brought Gilman directly to the issue Harris had wanted him to address at the outset, and he did not mince words here: "Call it research, call it investigation, call it scientific inquiry, call it seeking for truth—never has the obligation been so strong as it is now." Yet even while acknowledging that new ideals of specialization and research were in ascendancy, Gilman quickly moved on to emphasize that "the results of scholarly thought and acquisition" ought not to be treasured as "secrets of a craft; they are not esoteric mysteries known only to the initiated." The fourth function of the university, then, was to deliver the results of specialized research to the world at large, and there were multiple ways in which this could be done, ranging from textbooks and magazine articles to lyceum lectures and teaching in then-booming university extension programs. Thus would

American professors themselves become "sowers of seed which will bear fruit in future generations."

The details of Gilman's account of the four functions of the university also provided another explanation of why he considered it a mistake to think about the condition of American higher education in terms of an alleged opposition between "colleges" and "universities." While many university reformers found colleges wanting, the main source of their concern—the inability of colleges to reduce current variations in their entrance policies—had little to do with the question of "liberal education." That ideal in fact was holding its own, he argued, thanks in part to the new emphasis universities were giving to "the dividing line between undergraduates and postgraduates."[3]

Gilman acknowledged there were some vexing problems on the horizon: the uncertain prospect of creating a national university, unresolved questions concerning higher education for women, and the proliferation (already) of unread scholarly publications. But he also knew what was expected as a conclusion to public addresses made in Chicago in the summer of 1893. So he closed with a rousing and expansive forecast of what lay ahead. American universities and colleges, Gilman proclaimed, "are the hope of our future," for they were entering an era when

> professors of law will be taken from our universities for arbitration and counsel in questions affecting the peace of nations; when men of letters, or at least of academic culture will be sent, as the best representatives of the American people, to the most cultivated courts of Europe; when students of finance will be asked to leave chairs of instruction and assist the officers of government in disentangling financial problems . . . when men of science will be more and more relied on in the solution of the world problems pertaining to life and force . . . when the daily press will more and more readily open its columns to the mature opinions given out by learned men; and when the barriers (slight and transitory barriers, we may well believe) which have grown up between the common schools and the universities will disappear from every part of the country; and when knowledge, accurate, scientific, comprehensive knowledge, will be regarded not only for its own sake but as the parent of wisdom and virtue.

The "day of universities" in fact has dawned, Gilman concluded; our "higher institutions" have "won that position that entitles them to the confidence, the admiration, and the support of the American people."[4] Academic culture and the national culture, in short, were destined to become one.

II

I start with this extended look at Gilman's address for several reasons. When he spoke at the opening of the International Congress on Education in Chicago in 1893, the modern American university system was just beginning to secure its now central position in our national affairs, and his address allows us to glimpse with unusual clarity the keen sense of public purpose that drove architects of that system as well as the prominence of public stages from which they regularly broadcast their pronouncements. Gilman's late Victorian rhetoric, confident tone, and expansive vision harken back to the era when spokesmen for the American university promised it would become an agency of enlightened economic and political reform as well as an arena within which sustained reflection on the cultural, intellectual, and professional life of the nation would now largely take place. I want to think again about the meaning of that promise, especially about transformations in late-nineteenth-century American culture that lent it almost immediate credibility.

That a story of all-encompassing changes must be told here is hardly a breathtaking insight. Yet given Gilman's account of the multiple functions (and perhaps not entirely coherent ideals) served by American universities, it is not easy to see how the story should best be told. Twenty-five to thirty years ago, many historians believed the term "professionalization" captured the primary cultural mission of the American university movement.[5] And for certain purposes, it remains an indispensable term. Gilman did not speak of "professionalization" in his Chicago address, but the concept certainly captures part of what he had in mind in saying that the third function of a university was contributing to "the progress of observation, measurement, and experiment." Yet as often happens with terms that are assigned integrating roles in historical narratives, scholars returning to this field in recent years have come to recognize what Gilman saw quite clearly in 1893: "professionalization" captures only some of the complex variety of developments that gave rise to the university. The phrase "organize it on a more professional basis" accurately describes much of what universities ultimately accomplished in reshaping American cultural and intellectual life during the half century before 1920. But the implied assumption of a unilinear path of development during these five decades may lead us to underestimate the complexity of what was actually happening, let us say, in the summer of 1893, when professionalization of intellectual life within the university was still in an early and uncertain stage of development, and when the very figure we now remember as the person most responsible for launching the university's campaign to ensconce itself as the gate-keeper to the professions stressed that this campaign represented only one of four tests of a legitimate university.

Such thoughts suggest it would be a mistake to offer a new account of the emergence of the university that did not resist as well as endorse professionalization as an organizing theme. But the particular story I tell in this chapter, while drawing attention to the complexities of academic professionalization, is not an exercise in revisionism. That would be unnecessary in any case, since over the course of the last two decades detailed histories of the disciplines provided by other, more specialized scholars have shown that professionalization not only occurred at a ragged and uneven pace but also took different and not mutually reinforcing forms.[6] Instead I want to build on their work to launch discussion of a related but much less well-remarked development in late-nineteenth-century American culture: the emergence of what I call the "academic public sphere."[7] I use that concept to track two closely interconnected developments Gilman alluded to when he spoke of the American public's "unequaled" interest in higher education. The first concerns various ways in which steady expansion in the size and diversity of the American higher education during the late nineteenth century caused activities taking place within colleges and universities to assume unprecedented significance in American life. The second is the growing demand by those outside the emerging university system to have a continuous supply of information about, as well as alternative forms of access to, pursuits taking place on campuses across the country.

Here is a preliminary illustration of what I have in mind. During the last two decades of the nineteenth century, as steady growth in the range of subjects taught in American colleges and universities served to increase the number of "professors," it also prompted professors to make new efforts to make themselves more visible and influential in American culture at large. When Johns Hopkins opened in 1876, for example, it employed a core of professors, such as Herbert Baxter Adams and Richard T. Ely, intent on bridging the gap between academic intellectuals and the American public. We now remember Adams primarily as the driving force behind the organization of the American Historical Association (AHA) in 1884. Four years later, however, it also was Adams, inspired by the experience of lecturing at the summer Chautauqua Institute in upstate New York, who announced plans to establish Johns Hopkins as the hub of a nationwide program in adult education, with printed study programs, books written for such an audience, lecturers recruited from Hopkins graduate students, and examinations set and graded by its professors. While Adams never realized his goal of converting John

Hopkins into a "veritable school of peripatetic historians," he did join Ely and other extension-minded colleagues in undertaking local initiatives that made university extension courses widely available in Baltimore under the sponsorship of voluntary associations, Chautauqua circles, teachers' associations, and the YMCA.[8]

To explain how the university first came to occupy its central place in American culture, then, what matters is not so much the often tangled story of the emergence of its constituent disciplines as the ways in which that story forms part of the larger story of how the university itself first gained visibility in American culture at large. My thesis is that, whatever weight historians choose to assign to professionalization as the main driving force behind the university movement during its first three decades, we should recognize that the changing circumstances that eventually allowed professionalism to succeed had the more immediate effect of assigning unprecedented significance to academic life in general. Or put another way, what allowed the university to gain its central place in our national affairs was not in the first instance the sudden ascendancy of the new ideals of professionalization and research. It was, rather, the sheer growth in the size and diversity of American higher education, the steady expansion of public notice of the university itself, and the involvement of dozens of presidents and countless professors into spheres of American life previously untouched by their goings-on. In short, to understand the rise of the American university I want to shift attention away from its relatively well-mapped internal history to some of the less recognized ways in which the university succeeded in persuading the late-nineteenth- and early-twentieth-century American public at large that its various activities and concerns identified it as the new locus par excellence of the nation's cultural and intellectual life.

III

Detailed discussion can begin by looking at the consequences of rapid numerical expansion during the industrial era The bare facts perhaps are familiar. But they remain striking enough to bear some repeating. At the beginning of this period, the number of students enrolled in American colleges and universities was very small: a total of 52,000 undergraduates. By 1890 there were 157,000, and the figure rose to 230,000 in 1900, 355,000 in 1910, and 598,000 in 1920. As a percentage of eighteen to twenty-one year olds in the total American population, these figures represent 1.68 in 1870, 4.00 in 1900, 5.2 in 1910, and 8.09 in 1920. During these decades graduate training also began to feature prominently in American higher education for the first time. Yale awarded the first doctoral degree in 1861; national enrollment in graduate programs rose from 198 students in 1871 to 2,382 in 1890, 9,370 in 1910, and 16,000 in 1920.[9]

The exact number of career university and college "professors" is harder to determine. In 1893, Gilman correctly warned against applying that title to all who served on American college or university faculties because he knew the lower limit of college work was itself notoriously unclear. Degree-granting colleges abounded in the 1890s, but the distinction between them and the large number of academies, "collegiate institutions," seminaries, and high schools was very loosely defined. (Some state superintendents in fact lumped colleges, academies, and high schools together in their statistical summaries, thereby providing tacit recognition of low standards in hopefully titled tertiary institutions.) Yet compared to previous eras, figures charting national growth in the size of faculty in American higher education are remarkable: 5,553 in 1870, 23,868 in 1900, 36,480 in 1910, and 48,615 in 1920. An important related development, particularly as far as the growth of a sense of corporate professional identity was concerned, was the de-clericalization of leading institutions. Driven primarily by a new respect for "science," the process began from the top down, with the gradual disappearance of clergymen from the ranks of administrators and governing boards. To be sure, university and college presidents were not interested in emphasizing differences between science and religion. But during the last quarter of the nineteenth century, as the American university and "science" became almost identical for the broader public, it is clear that acceptance of evolutionary science and of the ideal of "scientific" research served to enlarge and reinforce claims that professional competence should serve as the primary criterion of faculty appointments. Or as Charles W. Eliot put it more succinctly, "A university cannot be founded on a sect."[10]

Expansion of the range of subjects taught in colleges and universities also prompted a slow but steady increase in the number of specialized academic departments. Before the university era, specialization was not generally recognized as the prerogative of college teachers. (As late as the 1870s, when David Starr Jordan, later Stanford University's first president, taught at the short-lived Lombard University in Illinois, his classes included natural science, political economy, evidences of Christianity, German, Spanish, and literature.) During the last quarter of the century, however, the spread of the elective principle allowed for the establishment of a large number of new courses in the natural and social sciences, as well as in English literature and modern languages. Initially state universities in the West and the Midwest, with their linked commitments to science and public service, embraced the elective principle more eagerly than any other group of institutions; they also offered more instruction in commercial and vocational subjects. By the turn of the century, however, the elective principle in various ways had come to dominate leading private institutions as well, and led eventually to a multiplicity of innovations—either further extensions of the principle or various attempts to curb its perceived excesses—that became characteristic of twentieth-century university and college curricula. (The fact that the elective principle was so closely identified with Charles W. Eliot, not simply Harvard's president for forty years but also one of the leading cultural celebrities of his time, clearly helped encourage this process.) While the elective system also helped foster organization according to more numerous and specific areas of study, the ascendancy of the research ideal made departmentalization even more desirable. At Cornell and Johns Hopkins, departments enjoyed autonomy as early as 1880. Harvard moved in this direction in 1891. The new University of Chicago appeared fully organized in this sense in 1892, and by the end of its first year had twenty-seven departments—including fields such as neurology, elocution, and physical culture—each with its own head.

Such changes were substantial. But did they signal a triumph for the "research ideal" in the intellectual life of late-nineteenth-century colleges and universities? Yes and no. The spread of departmental organization certainly represented the faculty's research specialization. But in some areas, especially in the new social sciences, terminology remained hazy for some time. Until at least 1890 the term "academic department" was regularly used to designate that part of a university where studies for bachelor of arts degrees were pursued, as opposed to, for example, the medical school. As late as 1920 sociology and political science remained subgroups within some departments of economics and history. The research ideal also was shaped and limited in various ways by a persisting emphasis on the traditional ideal of teaching. Even presidents of universities at which the research ethos most clearly dominated in this period stressed the advanced level of their undergraduate students and never suggested that scholarship be isolated from their instruction. What Gilman once described as the informing ideal of a university—"personal contact of young men and young women with scholars and investigators"—in fact was continuous with traditional college ideals of character formation and moral guidance rather than with any purely academic notion of professional training. (Even new subjects, then, had to justify their claims partly in terms of these ideals, as in the case of philologists who, in putting their subject forward as a replacement for Greek and Latin, argued it would serve as a more up-to-date form of "mental discipline.") The upshot was that the degree of specialization in teaching was never as pronounced as it was in research. Moreover, for many late-nineteenth-century university-based "scholars" and "investigators"— William James is perhaps the most striking among many possible examples—the older professional ideal of the "college professor" as public moralist and mentor of a broadly literate community remained as appealing as, or simply continued to take precedence over, new professional disciplinary labels.[11]

All that said, there can be little question that sheer growth in the size and diversity of American higher education served to channel traditional ideals and practices in a variety of new directions. By the turn of the century, the doctoral degree or some time studying in Germany had almost become a prerequisite for any one who wanted to win a permanent appointment at leading institutions.[12] And with this prerequisite came another: demonstrated competence in some new "scientific" technique. Here new choices included the chemistry laboratory, what James called "brass-instrument" psychology, the new science of language (philology), and new historical methods. New and independent professional associations also reflected divisions that were being institutionalized in academic departments during the last quarter of the century. And over time they took various steps to formalize and standardize their particular fields of inquiry, including the promotion of graduate studies and providing assistance in the production of a plethora of new academic journals.

But by no means all of the identities made possible by numerical expansion in late nineteenth century can be neatly mapped with the concepts of specialization and professionalization. The foundation of professional associations, as we shall see, served various purposes, some strictly intellectual, others more practical and pedagogical. Especially in the case of associations that spoke for history or one of the new social sciences, requirements for membership at first were not very demanding. Early professional associations in these fields recognized the claims of bona fide scholars who had private income or were employed in other occupations. They also aimed at forging alliances between a still relatively small number of college and university teachers and a broader community of nonacademic professionals whose financial support they needed and whose cultural status they longed to share. Finally, during their early decades new professional associations in the social sciences included a substantial number of university teachers intent on using their knowledge to provide solutions to economic and social problems. And as their careers played themselves out, many discovered their hunger for public influence and authority not only could be satisfied in various ways but also frequently was an object of national interest and publicity.

IV

During the last two decades of the nineteenth century, national interest and publicity that attended university-based efforts to professionalize the organization and study of academic disciplines was particularly visible in the new field of economics. And much of it focused on the complicated figure of Richard T. Ely. His purpose in launching the American Economic Association (AEA) at Saratoga Springs, New York, under the auspices of the American Social Science Association (ASSA) in 1885 remains a subject of disagreement among historians. One well-established version of the story, which begins with Ely circulating a prospectus that gave the new association the appearance of a reformist organization rather than a professional one, tells of a figure determined to establish the AEA as a rallying point for critics of laissez faire and a new institutional support for economists ready to serve the cause of progressive reform. But according to this story Ely failed on both counts. His prospectus served to recruit into the AEA fifty original members a cadre of young, German-trained economists as well as more than twenty former or practicing ministers (including leading Social Gospel figures Lyman Abbott and Washington Gladden) who were on hand for the ASSA's annual meeting. But it also threatened to split the small existing community of professional American economists, many of whom did not believe they could be both scientific investigators and progressive reformers. Damaging newspaper reports saying that the AEA was more interested in reform than in detached economic inquiry apparently made matters worse. So the charter AEA members moved quickly to water down Ely's prospectus and thereby eliminate its original creedlike character. (The most important changes were deletion of all references to laissez faire, a reduced emphasis on state intervention, and the addition of a statement to the effect that the platform was not binding on the association's membership.) Initial structural arrangements of the AEA also turned out to be more decisively oriented to the academic world than those of the American Historical Association, which had been launched in the same setting the year before. Of the first twenty-four members of the council, all but six were professors, and only members were entitled to vote for officers. Ely reluctantly agreed to the changes and remained among the charter members.

Here is another, perhaps rival version of the same story. In September 1885 Ely was a young untenured professor of political economy at

Johns Hopkins determined to make a name for himself both inside and outside the university. He knew he had to pursue a balancing act to accomplish that end. When it came to launching the AEA, then, he put his professional ambitions ahead of his politics. To begin with, Ely knew that President Gilman looked very favorably on Johns Hopkins faculty who promoted the name of the young institution before the national scholarly community. So while the AEA's initial platform retained some of Ely's reformist perspective, Ely saw no reason to impose it on other charter members. Indeed, at the time he freely admitted that his crusade against laissez faire had been designed largely to serve the practical purpose of advertisement. "It is not easy to arouse interest in association which professes nothing," he wrote in his 1886 *Report on the Organization of the AEA.* "This proposed economic association has been greeted with enthusiasm precisely because it is not colorless, precisely because it stands for something."[13] Nor did Ely see reason to abandon the AEA when, two years later, still seeking to grow its membership, the association quietly abandoned its statement of principles. In fact, after Ely's election as the AEA's first secretary in 1885, leadership of the organization rested largely in his hands for the next seven years, and he pursued his responsibilities with remarkable determination and energy during a critical period of the new association's existence.

Ely took the lead in gaining new members and raising funds by organizing branch societies in Springfield, Massachusetts; Buffalo, New York; Galesburg and Genesco, Illinois; Orange, New Jersey; Washington, D.C.; Kansas City, Kansas; Canton, Ohio; and Austin, Texas. He scheduled the AEA's annual meetings, set up programs for its conventions, and approved expenditures. He also promoted the sale of AEA-sponsored publications through book dealers and personally arranged sales to individuals and libraries. (The association published its proceedings as well as a monograph series; regular publication of the *American Economic Review* did not begin until 1911). Ely also assumed the role of chief publicist for the AEA, flooding newspapers and magazines with notices and articles about the organization's activities. And he worked tirelessly as a one-man clearinghouse for public information on economic issues. Each year Ely received at least a hundred letters from unknown, non-academic correspondents asking for information on subjects ranging from gas rates to labor unions. Ely sent thoughtful replies to even the most trivial request. When he left his post in 1892, membership in the AEA had grown impressively from fifty to seven hundred; its treasury balance showed more than two thousand dollars.[14]

During his years as AEA secretary, Ely never abandoned the cause of reform in his own writings, producing some of his controversial work during this time, including *The Labor Movement in American* (1886). Nor did he abandon his effort to bring his own message to a variety of popular audiences.[15] And for this he ultimately paid a price, despite all the work he did to ensure the early success of the organization. Indeed, in 1892 the AEA seemed to repudiate Ely's reformist zeal once and for all by forcing him out of the secretaryship of the AEA after he had proposed that the association hold its annual meeting in conjunction with that year's Chautauqua Institute summer session.[16] But the cultural identity of the AEA would remain something of an open question for at least another two decades. We know that at the turn of century, the organization remained unwilling to exclude nonspecialists from membership and positions of leadership within the organization. In fact, in 1899, intent on widening its constituency and increasing its public influence, the AEA invited a long list of public officials, businessmen, and other men of affairs to join.

Robert Church has pointed out that this effort was precipitated by a financial crisis that stemmed from an absolute decrease in the association's membership in the late 1890s. Yet it also reflected continuing indecision about an issue that Ely's dismissal would appear to have resolved. Indeed the election of Simon Nelson Patten as AEA president some nine years later suggests that many members continued to follow Ely's example in thinking that they did not have to choose between pursuing an irrevocable course of professional development and satisfying a hunger for popular influence and authority. Many of Patten's former graduate students at the University of Pennsylvania had become leaders of the Progressive movement on the city, state, and national level. And given Patten's longstanding commitment to the notion that the proper task of professional economists was advocacy of reform policies, few in the audience for his 1908 inaugural address could have been surprised when he exhorted them to take their place "on the firing line of civilization." By "education and tradition," he insisted, economists were secular preachers, "revolutionaries" whose vehicles for change "should be magazines and newspapers, not scientific journals."[17]

In the late 1880s and 1890s, the establishment of several new "scientific" journals—Columbia's *Political Science Quarterly* (1886), Harvard's *Quarterly Journal of Economics* (1886), the AEA's own *Publications* (1886), Pennsylvania's *Annals of the American Academy of Political and Social Science* (1890), and Chicago's *Journal of Political Economy* (1892)—probably did much more than the AEA to create the foundations of a self-conscious professional community of academic social scientists. At the same time it appeared to signal a growing isolation of that community from the concerns of the general public. Contributors to these journals produced

Fig. 4.1 Edward A. Ross,
1893. Stanford University
Archives

a steady flow of articles on a broad range of policy issues, including such controversial questions as currency regulation, public utilities, railroad regulation, and labor unions. But when their largely descriptive pieces suggested actual policy proposals, the moral and political premises of the proposals were left vague or unspecified. Or as Charles F. Dunbar put it more positively in launching the *Quarterly Journal of Economics*, such journals "would not be the representative of any special doctrine or school of economics, but would be devoted to the advancement of economic science and literature by free investigation, discussion, and criticism."[18] But Dunbar's casual distinction between "special" doctrines and schools of economists and economic "science" glossed over deep and continuing uncertainty about the scope and nature of the new science itself.[19] And that uncertainty became visible for all the nation to see in the late autumn 1900, when the forced dismissal of one of Ely's former graduate students at Johns Hopkins, Edward A. Ross, from his teaching position at Stanford University, forced reluctant members AEA to take a public stand in his support

Left in sole command of the new university after her husband's death in 1893, Mrs. Jane Lathrop Stanford had issued a total ban on faculty political activity at Stanford in 1899, not long after Ross had become the first academic economist to endorse openly the idea of free silver.[20] In the spring of 1900 Ross flouted the ban twice. In a lecture delivered in April at the Unitarian Church of Oakland, he predicted that in the twentieth century all natural monopolies, including railroad ownership, would pass into public ownership. Reported in some detail in local newspapers, this proved to be the first of two ill-advised public statements that caught the attention of Jane Stanford. A few weeks later, in a lecture to a group of San Francisco labor leaders on May 7, Ross condemned the continued importation of "coolie" labor (at a time when the Stanford railroad fortune had been built on "coolie" labor) and issued a plea for Anglo-Saxon purity. The following day, infuriated by the summary of Ross's lecture she read in the *San Francisco Call,* Stanford exercised her enormous power as sole trustee and instructed the university's president, David Starr Jordan, not to renew Ross's contract for the 1900–1901 academic year.[21]

Jordan reluctantly obliged, but in a fashion that helped make Ross's ultimate dismissal both an enormous public controversy and an event that shook the ten-year-old Stanford community to its roots. Early in June, Jordan gave Ross a temporary reappointment in the Sociology Department until he found a position elsewhere, and Ross reciprocated by submitting a letter of resignation with the understanding that it would be accepted only after he had secured new employment elsewhere. In the five months that followed, both Jordan and Ross sent out letters of inquiry, but their joint efforts produced no offers. In late October, her patience with the matter now at end, Mrs. Stanford again instructed Jordan to dismiss Ross. On November 12 Jordan reluctantly notified Ross in a private letter that he now had no choice but to ask for his outright resignation.[22]

The 1890s had been littered with similar academic heresy cases. Most of them had also involved Johns Hopkins–trained economists, and university trustees rarely lost. But none had prompted the AEA to come forward to address the question of who would control the teaching of economics within the university. The Ross case was different for several reasons. To begin with, controversial as Ross's views were in some circles, he was hardly an academic maverick. He had published articles in the *Political Science Quarterly,* the *American Journal of Sociology,* and the *Publications of the American Academy of Political and Social Science.* He also was one of the founding members of the AEA and had been elected to replace Richard Ely as secretary in 1892. More significant, Ross was a savvy self-publicist who saw to it that the account of his dismissal that first reached the American public was his own. In fact, the day Jordan asked for his resignation, it was Ross himself who lit the fuse for

Fig. 4.2. David Starr Jordan, 1908. Stanford University Archives

what proved to be the huge public controversy that followed by releasing Jordan's November 12 private letter to the local press, accompanied by typewritten copies of his version of the story in which he condemned Mrs. Stanford for interfering with a university professor's free pursuit of his "science." On November 14 and 15 the San Francisco papers reprinted Jordan's letter and Ross's statement in their entirety, leaving Jordan little choice but to announce immediately that Ross had been fired. And then the machinery of American publicity went into high gear. In the weeks that followed, Ross's dismissal was the subject of stories that appeared in hundreds of newspapers across the country, and at Stanford it produced a controversy that threatened to tear the university to pieces.

The widespread national publicity that attended Ross's dismissal also left the AEA little choice but to act. What the AEA actually did in defending Ross, however, can hardly be called a resounding public affirmation of professional solidarity. At the annual AEA convention in Detroit in late December 1900, a majority of the members who gathered at a special

Fig. 4.3. Article on the Ross controversy in the *San Francisco Chronicle,* November 14, 1900. Stanford University Archives

Fig. 4.4. Article reprinting Jordan's letter and Ross's statement in the *San Francisco Call*, November 15, 1900. Stanford University Archives

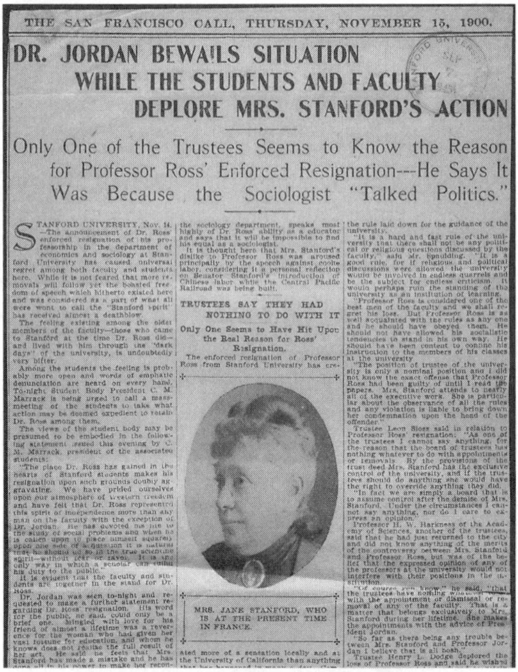

Fig. 4.5. Article on the Ross controversy in the *Denver Post*, November 24, 1900. Stanford University Archives

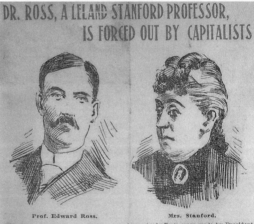

meeting to discuss the Stanford situation chose to meet ex officio rather than under the official auspices of the AEA. This assembly then established an ad hoc investigating committee whose work resulted in what Thomas Haskell has aptly described as a stage-managed, "quasi-formal vindication" of Ross.[23] After President Jordan and many members of the Stanford faculty refused to cooperate, the inquiry became bogged down in a fruitless investigation into Mrs. Stanford's motives. Lacking the imprimatur of the AEA, the committee's final report also fell flat within the American academic community. An attempt to organize a boycott of Stanford came to nothing, as did Jordan's ongoing efforts to find an appointment for Ross at Cornell or Harvard. Late in 1900 Ross left Palo Alto for the University of Nebraska, where a figure sometimes remembered as an earlier martyr to academic freedom, E. Benjamin Andrews, had recently been appointed president.[24] Five years later, as memories faded and Ross succeeded in forging a new professional identity as a sociologist, he would move on to the more tolerant atmosphere of the University of Wisconsin, where Ely had arranged a position for him and his career flourished for the next three decades.[25]

Rescuing Ross, as Haskell has put it, was no piece of cake, and things certainly could have turned out a lot worse for him than they did. But it is a mistake to say that in the absence of a self-conscious professional community such as the AEA, there would have been no one to come to his rescue. Ross in fact had other, more powerful allies at his disposal at the time he was fired, and they had rallied to his cause several weeks before AEA decided to act. Shortly after his dismissal, Mayor James D. Phelan of San Francisco, later a U.S. senator, invited Ross to a well-publicized dinner. California union officials up and down the coast also offered him their support, as did San Francisco workingmen, who held a mass meeting to protest his dismissal. The most remarkable aspect of the controversy, however, was not simply the nationwide attention Ross's case attracted in the American press. It was that only a handful of magazines and newspapers voiced support for Jane Stanford. And Ross also was quick to recognize and savor his popular triumph. In late November he hired two press clipping bureaus to send him representative articles from the national press. In less than a month the bureaus had accumulated close to five hundred clippings. By Ross's count they ran twenty-nine out of thirty in his favor.[26]

Viewed against this backdrop, it seems fair to conclude that if the Ross case drew widespread public attention to issues of academic authority and freedom in unusually stark and clear terms, those members of the AEA who came forward to save Ross on this count were latecomers to a large and diverse rescue party. Indeed, during the last months of 1900, it was mostly critics, reporters, and gossip columnists for the daily, weekly, and monthly American press who first used the Ross case to instruct a huge popular audience regarding the question of what an American university professor was—and was not—supposed to be. Typical of hundreds of similar articles from across the country was an editorial on "Science at Stanford" that appeared first in the *San Francisco Call* and later, on November 15, 1900, in the *Oakland Enquirer* shortly after Ross's dismissal, defending him because he represented "in a high degree the scientific spirit which is as ready to discard the useless as to search for the useful among the great and unchangeable facts which it is the obligation of the scientific man to discover and declare. . . . When it is known that science in a university is under bonds to prejudice or dogmatism, the usefulness of that university is at an end and its further existence is without reason." Such sentiments echoed arguments that Ross had been the first to use in defending himself. According to James Mohr, the overwhelming national support Ross received along these lines also marked a genuine shift in the attitudes of the American popular press, if not in the attitudes of the American people. Perhaps, but Mohr does not marshal enough evidence to prove the point. What can be said with confidence, however, is that by the time the official "Report of the Committee of Economists on the Dismissal of Edward Ross from Leland Stanford Junior University" finally appeared on February 20, 1901, thanks to newspaper coverage across the country, hundreds of thousands of Americans who were unlikely ever to set foot on the Stanford campus, let alone encounter Ross himself, could claim more than passing acquaintance with the controversy his dismissal had provoked. And the lesson was not lost on members of the ad hoc AEA committee investigating Ross's case. When the committee finally released its report, which supported Ross and censured Stanford, the entire text was telegraphed across the country and appeared, in whole or in part, on February 23 and 24 in major daily newspapers in Boston, New York, and San Francisco. From start to finish, the Ross case was a national media event in which newspapers and the telegraph constituted a huge and powerful sounding board for Ross and his supporters outside as well as inside the university.

V

National interest and the publicity that attended early efforts to professionalize the study of economics also were evident in another academic field whose early development was much less politically charged: literary studies.[27] During the antebellum era, gentleman amateur teachers of literature—figures such as Henry Wadsworth Longfellow, James Russell

Lowell, and George Ticknor—had understood literature as something designed for casual study, the engagement of which was designed chiefly to improve character and manners. They also had addressed a broad readership outside the colleges. At the outset of the university era, this approach to literature was challenged and temporarily displaced by that of yet another cadre of young, German-trained American scholars intent on promoting the ideal of scientific research and the philological study of modern languages. Most of the founding figures of the Modern Language Association began their careers with little or no interest in literature. They aimed instead to draw attention to the then-rising field of French and German language studies and with that end in mind created an exclusive organization that attempted to gain some measure of control over their teaching. As A. Marshall Elliot, then assistant professor of romance languages at Johns Hopkins, remarked to the forty fellow philologists who had gathered for the first meeting of the MLA at Columbia College in December 1883, "Instruction in Modern Languages . . . as in other departments of learning . . . should be such that no one, except a man of scientific training, could enter the profession, and in this way, the incompetent would naturally be shut out, and the departments would rise in the esteem and consideration of the public."[28]

American philologists were also on the rise in the 1880s because they took the lead in establishing new journals and graduate programs. The *American Journal of Philology* and *Modern Language Notes* were founded, with Gilman's enthusiastic support, at Johns Hopkins in 1880 and 1886, respectively. In new graduate schools at Cornell and Harvard, enrollments in philology also reached remarkably high levels. In the 1884–85 Harvard catalogue, almost half of the thirty-two listed doctoral candidates were in the new Department of Philology. Within ten years of the MLA's founding, its membership had grown from forty to four hundred, and so it seemed that within the steadily expanding realm of American higher education, scientific investigation of modern languages was poised to replace once more leisurely approaches to the study of literature.

Yet if we look more closely at the development of language and literature departments in the 1880s and 1890s, the oversimplifications of this account become all too apparent. From the start an opposition party of "generalist" professors determined to uphold old college ideals of liberal culture and mental discipline contested the philologists' efforts to define the terms of professionalization of literary studies. They also presented themselves as spokesmen for a missing view of literature inherited from Matthew Arnold, John Ruskin, and other British Victorian apostles of culture. Even so, most generalists also shared the philologists' commitment to the new idea of distinct departments of modern language and

English. The upshot was that institutional efforts to build late-nineteenth- and early-twentieth-century literature departments, as Gerald Graff has shown, in most cases resolved themselves in varying degrees of compromise, stalemate, and peaceful but distrustful cohabitation. At Harvard, philologists such as Francis James Child and George Lyman Kitteredge coexisted uneasily with generalists such as Barrett Wendell and Le Baron Russell Briggs. The former dominated the teaching of literature, the latter the teaching of composition courses that President Eliot himself had established in an effort to "maintain traditional culture at Harvard." Chicago's English Department—with twelve members, the university's largest at the time of its founding—offered courses that ranged from a required three-course sequence in "theme-writing" to graduate offerings that consisted of rigorous textual and linguistic study. Two members of the department also had particularly close ties to Chicago's extension division: Nathaneil Butler, who served as director of the University Extension Division in the mid-1890s, and R. G. Moulton, who in 1894 alone delivered ninety-six lectures for extension students.

Early philologists believed their efforts to make modern languages objects of scientific study would solve a problem that had thwarted the claim of literature to be an academic discipline during the first three-quarters of the nineteenth century: one could not rigorously examine it. But the move to treat literature as a professional domain in its own right must also be viewed against the background of two other developments that clearly caught philologists off guard. The first involved the growing public expectations placed on the study of English, especially as it came to include American literature, as a potential cultural force; the second was an accompanying recognition that those who approached literature as an "exact science" could not hope to meet such expectations. Nine years after the founding of the MLA, former president E. H. Magill, a French philologist from Swarthmore, gave gloomy warning to members gathered at the 1892 convention that it was "as much as you can hope for" if 5 percent of students under their tutelage "pursue courses of study which would make the investigations which you are pursuing with great interest and value to science valuable to them directly." He then asked pointedly, "Now what are we going to do with the other 95 percent?"[29]

The answer came in the form of a revival and replenishment of more literary ways of studying literature. This movement was supported by some philologists who believed literary studies could be added to the purview of their profession, but it was lead by and composed largely of "generalist" professors who charged the study of literature with a new redemptive influence that, half a century earlier, their ministerial ancestors typically had attributed to the conversion experience. Often spell-binding lecturers, generalists drew hundreds, sometimes thousands, of undergraduates to their courses, despite the scorn and derision of their more scholarly departmental colleagues. More important for my purposes here, unlike the philologists, they also reached large popular audiences outside the classroom, functioning as cultural observers for leading "family house magazines" such as *Harper's Monthly, Century, Scribner's,* and *Atlantic Monthly,* as well as for new mass-circulation magazines such as *Cosmopolitan* and *McClure's.* Generalist professors also lectured widely in the revived urban lecture circuit and produced dozens of new literary anthologies and textbooks in literary history during an era that saw the mass production of books begin to flourish for the first time.

It is true that, like that of the early philologists, the success of generalists within colleges and universities ultimately was limited in its scope. According to Graff, from the outset of the university era, generalists accepted "an unspoken partition treaty" that assigned professional authority to graduate study and left the task of "general instruction" to the undergraduate department and other college courses. A few departments violated the treaty by placing philology at the heart of their undergraduate offerings. More did so inadvertently by employing scholars whose professional training in philology simply had not prepared them to think about what general instruction in literature might mean. Within reformed colleges and universities, however, the primary constraint on generalists proved to be organizational design. As Graff has shown, nothing in the new departmental configuration of literary studies prompted professors to engage the question of how the various parts related to one another; as a result, at most colleges and universities, the conception of general instruction in literature was left to take care of itself.

By the early 1890s, then, with generalists leaving the work of professional training and accreditation to the philologists and philologists preoccupied with issues of little interest to a steadily growing population of undergraduates, it perhaps is not surprising to find that annual meetings of the philologically top-heavy MLA had become occasions when euphoric boasts of progress went side by side with sharp self-criticism. More interesting, however, is the remarkably broad scope and character of a nationwide reaction against narrow German methods that set in at roughly the same time.

Signs of that reaction were evident in the old family house magazines, as well as in more recently established literary periodicals such as the *Literary World* of Boston, the *Critic* of New York, and the *Dial* of Chicago. They also were visible in a widely distributed collection of scholarly essays on *English in American Universities* that was first published in 1895. The twenty college and university professors reporting on their departments in this volume included several of the best-known generalists of the period: Brander Matthews of Columbia, Barrett Wendell of Harvard, Katherine Lee Bates of Wellesley, Hiram Corson of Cornell, and Charles Mills Gayley of the University of California at Berkeley. Bates spoke for many of them when she commented that one happy result of their discussion was that "more than one lonely stickler for the supremacy, even in the classroom, of literature as an art has discovered, like Elijah of old, that faith has no lack of prophets." Among all the contributors to *English in American Universities*, however, none was a more severe critic of philology than its editor, William Morton Payne, who characterized it as an approach to literature "hedged about with so many thorny obstructions, that not a few young persons start bravely upon it only to fall by the way, disheartened at the sight of the forbidding barriers erected by historical, linguistic, and metrical science for the purpose of taking toll of all wayfarers."[30]

And yet new academic barriers to the study of literature in fact were not quite as forbidding as Payne believed. Only six of the twenty colleges and universities reported on in his collection of essays required narrowly philological courses of English majors; and of these, only three made linguistic philology distinctly central. To be sure, most contributors to *English in American Universities* made it clear that any "leisurely" approach to literature was now out of date. Lay "appreciation" of literature ought not to be confused with its professional "study," which at the undergraduate level now pointed toward literary history as embodied in survey courses and the new coverage model of departmental organization. With regard to particular "methods" required for such study, however, there plainly was no consensus. At Harvard the "divergence of method in detail" was in fact so wide, observed Barrett Wendell, that "no valuable generalization concerning such detail can be made." Indeed, when it came to "the matter of methods," it had "long been held by the teachers of English at Harvard that each teacher's best method is his own."[31]

How should we assess the broader cultural significance of the tangled early history of literary studies, and how does it figure in the emergence of what I call the academic public sphere? Professionalization had made its inroads during the 1880s and 1890s, but it certainly had not triumphed. Moreover, criticism of excessive specialization voiced by many of the contributors to *English in American Universities* reflected a well-entrenched effort—both inside and outside colleges and universities—to prevent specialists from freely carving up the realm of literary studies among themselves. Graff has suggested that more thorough discussions might have led to an agreement that the early professional era required an altogether different kind of literary education from either the old liberal culture of the generalists or the new scientific approach of the philologists. Perhaps, but the essays in *English in American Universities* also illustrate a different and generally unnoticed aspect of late-nineteenth-century disagreements about the proper character of literary studies—namely, that (as with similar disagreements about economics) they came to represent an academic squabble that frequently spilled over into the pages of various kinds of nonspecialist publications. All the essays in *English in American Universities*, for example, had appeared originally in the Chicago-based *Dial*, a semimonthly magazine of literary essays and reviews that had a modest but respectable circulation of five thousand. Payne's book was designed to reach a much broader readership. Apparently recognizing the strength and importance of the controversy, the Boston-based textbook publisher D.C. Heath issued *English in American Universities* as volume 26 in its popular Pedagogical Library series. While we have no circulation figures for the book, we know it was still in print as late as 1910.

Even more important and instructive is the fact that the generalists' view of English as the study of national literary history received continuous and powerful reinforcement from the great boom in mass publishing that had begun in the early 1880s. Between 1882 and 1912, D. C. Heath, Houghton Mifflin, Putnam, American Book Company, and several other publishers commissioned a plethora of textbooks on American literature for high school and college use and had them frequently revised and updated. These volumes, designed in many cases to accommodate both secondary school and college classrooms, divided into three categories—anthologies, literary history textbooks, or some combination of the two. Independent men of letters such as Horace Scudder and E. C. Stedman fashioned the most successful of the early anthologies.[32] But in time dozens of university-based generalist professors captured a major share of the expanding and increasingly lucrative textbook market.[33] As it happened, three of the most successful literary history textbooks in this period were written by generalists who earlier in their careers had contributed essays to *English in American Universities:* Brander Matthews's *Introduction to the Study of American Literature* (1896), Katherine Lee Bates's *American Literature* (1897), and Barrett Wendell's *Literary History of America* (1900).[34] Matthews's volume sold a quarter of a million copies after publication and joined Fred Lewis Pattee's *History of American Literature* (1896) to become one the two best-sellers in this new genre.

VI

The last decades of the nineteenth century saw two other related developments that perhaps point even more directly to the emergence of the academic public sphere. The first was the active and well-publicized role academic administrators and specialists played in the debates over college and university entrance requirements that developed in the early 1890s. As universities expanded and became more administratively standardized, educators set out to reduce variations in college entrance policies, and before the turn of the century the best known of their efforts in this regard was the Committee on Secondary School Studies (generally know as the Committee of Ten), which, with Harvard's Charles Eliot as its chairman and the omnipresent W. T. Harris as its chief publicist, the NEA had launched the year before its 1893 International Congress on Higher Education.[35]

It is fair to characterize the national standards recommended in the Committee of Ten's final report as something of a compromise among competing views of the goals of American secondary education. On the one hand, the proposed standards retained traditional disciplinary subjects, while including new fields of English, history, modern foreign languages, and the sciences. On the other, the four alternative curricula the committee proposed included a substantial core of academic subjects for all students—those bound for work as well as for college—with a common core substantially outweighing the different foreign language and science requirements that marked the four curricula. In some circles the report met with sharp and immediate criticism. The American Philological Association, for example, deplored the relative demotion of Greek and the idea of college admission without an ancient language and even set up its own Committee of Twelve in an effort to organize opposition to the threadbare "Classics Program" the report had recommended. Others deplored the exclusion of practical and vocational studies and saw a conspiracy upon the part of colleges and universities.

Such criticism did little damage to the committee's reputation, though it was true that the membership of the committee and its nine conferences was composed largely of college or university presidents and professors. Of the one hundred men who served on the committee and its conferences, fifty-three were in tertiary institutions, forty-five in secondary, and two in the service of the federal government. (It also is worth noting that the editors of the two leading journals in the field of education, the *Educational Review* and the *School Review*, were also university men: Nicholas Murray Butler of Columbia and Jacob Schuerman of Cornell.) In assessing the place of the committee in late-nineteenth-century American understanding of the role of academic authority, however, we also should recall that its university men included many figures who had considerable experience in the lower schools. One of the five presidents on the Committee of Ten, James H. Baker, had been principal of Denver's city high school before becoming president of the embryonic University of Colorado in January 1892. Another, Richard H. Jesse, appointed president of the University of Missouri in 1891, earlier had pursued various careers in schools and colleges after graduating from Virginia in 1875, teaching French and mathematics at academies for two years before in 1878 becoming dean of the "academic department" of the University of Louisiana, which soon thereafter was renamed Tulane. Among the people who served on the Committee of Ten's conferences, Thomas C. Chamberlain of the Geography Conference had been a high school principal before joining the faculty of the University of Chicago. Benjamin Wheeler of the Greek Conference, soon to become president of the University of California, had taught at Providence high school for several years. Harvard's A. B. Hunt of the History, Civil Government, and Political Economy Conference, was active in the Cambridge school system and had published a variety of articles on the lower schools. The list could go on.

The broader point that bears emphasizing is that while a separate sense of corporate professional identity certainly was developing among administrators and faculty in American higher education during the last decades of the nineteenth century, it did not prevent a considerable amount of movement between various levels of schools in this period. In this regard it also is worth noting that a variety of efforts assured that final report of the Committee of Ten gained widespread publicity when it was issued by the U.S. Bureau of Education in January 1894. Harris prevailed upon the secretary of interior, Hoke Smith, to print thirty thousand copies of the report and distribute them gratis to leading educators across the country. The printer's plates of the report were then transferred to the American Book Company, which published a steady-selling, inexpensive edition that would sell another twenty-four thousand copies by 1910. Additional national publicity was provided by a steady stream of laudatory magazine articles during the first several months of 1894, as well as by the "Ten" themselves, who attended numerous teachers' meeting and association gatherings in an effort to promote widespread discussion and acceptance of their proposals.

Another significant source of the external growth of academic culture was the university extension movement, which appeared in several different versions in the late 1880s and 1890s. Midwestern state universities initially saw extension as a way to establish their public usefulness and gain support from state legislators and local civic leaders. Both Wisconsin and Kansas, for example, built programs on a fairly firm base of farmer interest in agricultural education. In eastern cities, propelled by the earlier success of Chautauqua circles and the women's club movement, extension programs gained the support of independent societies, the most successful of which was the Philadelphia Society for the Extension of University Teaching, which was the brainchild of William Pepper, the provost of the University of Pennsylvania. During the first year of its operation, 1890–91, the Philadelphia Society arranged for forty courses in twenty-three local centers (most in Pennsylvania, New Jersey, and Delaware), and the 290 lectures it sponsored that year drew some fifty-five thousand people. Elsewhere, William Rainey Harper, a Hebrew and classical scholar who had left the Yale faculty and Chautauqua's short-lived College of Liberal Arts for the presidency of the University of Chicago in 1892, led the new university to establish an extension division that offered both lecture and correspondence courses. By 1898 Chicago's lecture courses alone attracted an attendance of more than thirty-two thousand in ninety-two local centers.

Interest in extension during the 1890s was also shaped by professors who wanted to bring their personal influence to bear on social and economic questions at the same time as they sought access to working-class students. The best known of these perhaps was the ubiquitous Richard Ely, who in 1892 was lured away from Johns Hopkins by Thomas Chamberlain (now president of Wisconsin) by an offer that allowed him to direct the university's extension service at the same time he organized the university's projected departments of civics, sociology, and historical science. While local centers formed the spine of Wisconsin's extension program during Ely's years, the university also supported the new People's Institute in Milwaukee, which aimed to ease labor unrest in the city by promoting the ideal of self-culture among workers.[36]

Popular interest in more strictly academic subjects such as history, literature, and economics waned by the late 1890s and thereby left the expectations of many early leaders of the extension movement unfulfilled. After 1900, however, as extension programs gave greater attention to local needs and conditions, they came to enjoy their first real flowering. The most successful and celebrated model of a predominantly service-oriented extension program in this period undoubtedly was that of the University of Wisconsin during the presidency of Charles R. Van Hise. For Van Hise the ideal of service, not scholarship, defined the preeminent goal of the American university. "I shall never be content," he declared, "until the beneficent influence of the University reaches every family in the state." Strengthening Wisconsin's research programs at the same time as he vastly expanded both technical and nontechnical extension courses, Van Hise came to preside over a steady and increasingly heavy flow of traffic between his university and agencies of state and local governments as scores of Wisconsin's professors helped to draft legislation, served on investigatory and regulatory commissions, and provided counsel to various state administrative authorities. As with the activities of the Committee of Ten, widespread publicity of "the Wisconsin Idea," in this case provided by a steady stream of laudatory newspaper and magazine articles as well as Van Hise's own relentless speaking campaigns, helped to assure that "service" joined "teaching" and "research" among the publicly recognized responsibilities of professional academic specialists.[37]

VII

The emergence of the academic public sphere can be documented from yet another angle by returning to two questions Gilman raised toward the end of his 1893 address in Chicago's new Art Palace: for whom were the results of "scholarly thought and acquisition" intended and how were they to be "given to the world"? While Gilman did more than any other university president of his era to encourage American scholars to devote more of their energy to the task of writing for a community of other competent scholars, the main stimulus for the establishment of specialized journals was competition among leading private and state universities. During the 1880s and 1890s, it was direct affiliation with a particular university that lay behind the financial viability of most academic journals, either by means of direct subsidy or (as in the case of Johns Hopkins) by providing large subscriptions that libraries would then use for exchange. New journals also figured in efforts to build and maintain faculties. Scholarly series such as the Johns Hopkins Studies in History and Political Science, the Columbia University Studies in Public Law, the University of Michigan Philosophical Papers, and the Harvard Oriental Series helped to underline the identification of scholars with the institution in which they had trained and where some of them held appointments. The formal establishment of scholarly publishing houses in the 1890s served to make the university system itself a new focal point of scientific and scholarly publications.[38] The proceedings and transactions of older academies and associations that managed to survive in this period could not compete with the specialized journals produced by universities and university presses, academic professional societies, and sometimes by commercial enterprises under academic editorship. In short, by the turn of the century universities were not only filling up much of the world of learning but also expanding that world's space.

And yet, as Gilman himself emphasized, this was not a development that proceeded without concern for the preferences of a wider reading public. Indeed, the keen sense of public mission that animated Gilman's 1893 address was grounded in his belief that the entire nation would be served by the activities of a new generation of scholars who recognized an obligation to tend to the intellectual well-being of those outside the colleges and universities. ("Publications should not merely be in the form of learned works," he emphasized, teachers in American universities, "by textbooks, by lyceum lectures, by contributions to the magazines, by letters to the daily press, also should diffuse the knowledge they possess.") Gilman was hardly alone in entertaining this belief; he expressed the outlook of other leading university presidents, all of whom sought a prominent role for professional academics in defining the central values of American society not only through research and scholarly publications but also through teaching and other forms of public intellectual activity.

A neglected example of such activity can be found in the surge in the number of what might be called "professors' books"—that is, books that began life as academic lectures of one kind or another. Most of the large supply of new American literary histories that began to appear in the 1890s, for example, grew directly from new college and university courses in American literature. Similarly William James's *Principles of Psychology* (1890), a textbook for which he had signed a contract with Henry Holt in 1878, grew out of classroom lectures in philosophy and psychology he delivered to Harvard undergraduate and graduate students in the late 1870s and early 1880s. (Because James's first book turned out to be too long, and therefore too expensive, for the college market, Holt persuaded him to prepare a *Psychology: A Briefer Course,* popularly known as "Jimmy," which was published in 1891, sold almost fifty thousand copies, and became a standard text in college physiological psychology courses during the first decades of the twentieth century.) Later *Pragmatism* (1907) illustrated another form of public speaking that enjoyed increasing prominence in the wake of the expansion of the universities: the invited or endowed lecture. The book was made up of more or less openly unrevised lectures that were published not long after James had delivered them in various settings in the summer of 1905 and the winter of 1906–1907.[39] John Dewey's early publications were of the same provenance. His first book, *Psychology* (1886), written while he was instructor in philosophy and psychology at the University of Michigan in the mid-1880s, was on his own account prepared "expressly for use in classroom instruction." After he moved to the University of Chicago in 1894 (to chair both the Department of Philosophy and Department of Pedagogy), Dewey's better-received *School and Society* (1899) collected three lectures he delivered in April 1899 to an audience of parents and others interested in the new University Elementary School, which he also headed.[40]

Ely illustrates a slightly different aspect of this trend, since he drew from both his lectures at Johns Hopkins and Chautauqua and articles he wrote for the *Baltimore Sun* in authoring five books—*The Labor Movement in America* (1886), *Problems of Today: A Discussion of Protective Tariffs, Taxation, and Monopoly* (1888), *Taxation in American States and Cities* (1888), *Social Aspects of Christianity and Other Essays* (1889), and *Socialism: An Examination of Its Nature, Its Strengths, and Its Weaknesses* (1894)—that appeared in a series of which he was the general editor, Thomas Y. Crowell's Library of Economics and Politics. Ely's best-known work, *Introduction to Political Economy* (1889), reached an even larger audience than his publications for Crowell. Written originally for the Chautauqua Literary and Scientific Society's required reading program and revised seven times over the next fifty years under the new title of *Outlines of Economics*, it became the best-selling economics textbook during the first decades of the twentieth century.[41]

In the summer of 1893, then, Gilman was right in saying that the lectures, periodical essays, and professional scholarly articles of college and university professors could serve as sources of books written for the public at large. Sometimes this even happened roughly in sequence for the same book. William James first published "Lecture I" and "Lecture II" of *Pragmatism* in *Popular Science Monthly;* and "Lecture III" and "Lecture VI" initially appeared in the first volume of the *Journal of Philosophy, Psychology, and Scientific Methods.* During Dewey's years at Michigan, his *Psychology* drew from essays he had published somewhat earlier in the *Andover Review* and *Popular Science Monthly* as well as the *Journal of Speculative Philosophy* and *Mind.* Similarly, while he was professor of political science and history at Smith College in the 1880s, John Bates Clark established his academic reputation as an economist by publishing articles in the *New Englander* (forerunner to the *Yale Review*) and in religious periodicals such as the *Christian Union* and the *Independent*, both Social Gospel publications. The bulk of Clark's first book, *Philosophy of Wealth: Economic Principles Newly Formulated* (1886), consisted of revised versions of his *New Englander* articles.

The national marketing of lectures and textbooks, to be sure, was designed to serve a variety of purposes. Most authors of American literary history textbooks, for example, attempted to configure "American literature" to serve the aims of American public education: fostering character and ensuring patriotism. James's *Principles of Psychology* was published as one of several titles in the American Science Series, which Henry Holt hoped would advance the cause of evolutionary theory in the United States. Other publishers catered openly to growing popular demand for easy access to the benefits of higher education. The publisher's note at the outset of *School and Society,* for example, commented that Dewey had made only "slight" and "unimportant" changes in his original lectures; hence the book retained "the unstudied character as well as the power of the spoken word." "The present volume is not intended primarily for specialists," Ely stressed at the outset of *Taxation in American States and Cities,* "but for American citizens generally who are intelligent enough to appreciate the vast importance" of the topic that the book addressed. The list of examples could go on. The chief interest of all this for my purposes here is simply that the steady increase in the number and variety of professors' books provides additional evidence of the growing centrality of colleges and universities in national affairs. Clearly these books also gave Americans of diverse backgrounds and interests access to a steadily expanding academic world whose inhabitants they now recognized as new and reliable sources of guidance on issues of pressing national significance.

VIII

The brings me to some final points about the story of the emergence of the American university. The first is one I stressed from the start of this chapter: during the last decades of the nineteenth century, the cultural "functions" of the American university were more numerous than modern historians typically manage to suggest. The still-familiar image of the university as a new, carefully bounded institutional space within which professional intellectual discourse found protection from the competing and superficial demands of a heterogenous American public is just too foreshortened (if not, especially in the case of the new social sciences, altogether misleading) to take in all the details that surface in a close examination of the late nineteenth and early twentieth centuries. Against the image of a safe haven for a new class of professional academics, I set a different one: a many-sided academic public sphere. This image also is one I believe matches what some well-placed observers saw in the early development of the American university system. Daniel Coit Gilman's address on "Higher Education in America" at the 1893 Chicago World's Fair has already provided one particularly telling example of this point. Here is another, which echoes Gilman's earlier remarks and comes from an article on "The Expansion of Our Great Universities" that Lafayette College president Ethelbert D. Warfield published in the August 1901 issue of *McClure's Magazine:* "No phase of social progress is more characteristic of the development of the United States in the nineteenth century than the growth of our national universities. Indeed, the whole field of education has been so fertile in ideas and undertakings that European critics, and especially English critics, have declared that America is 'education mad.' . . . One of the most marked features of our educational growth has been its spontaneousness. It has sprung from the people, from local aspirations. On this account, it has lacked unity and system; but it has gained something far better than either unity or system—vitality. It has been a part of the social life of the American people."[42]

Warfield's picture is not exactly a miniature version of the picture I paint, but it comes close, particularly in its final two sentences. American universities did lack "unity and system" in the late nineteenth and early twentieth centuries. (Or to put it in contemporary terms, they had no one essential "mission.") But they nonetheless formed a vital part of the social life of the American people. Or more precisely, despite the fact that less than 4 percent of the college-age population was attending a university or college at the turn of the century, there can be no question that engagement in some aspect of higher education—attendance at lectures of various kinds, enrollment in extension service courses or in summer sessions, study of textbooks that professors had written expressly for high schools, purchase and study of books professors had written expressly for general audiences, or simply encountering a steady stream of magazine and newspaper articles that explored various aspects of university life ranging from academic freedom and free silver to fraternities and football—had become a commonplace experience for literate Americans of diverse background and interests. And I believe the same could not yet be said of several other new late-nineteenth-century institutions—especially municipal museums, concert halls, and public libraries—whose supporters promoted them as agents of an emerging national culture. During the last decades of the nineteenth century, there was no other development that nationalized American intellectual and cultural life as quickly as the growth and spread of universities.

This last point possibly requires more evidence than I have gathered in this chapter. It is worth risking here, however, if it serves to draw attention to other developments I believe helped create and expand the academic public sphere and bear further close study. Two final examples will suffice. The first might be described as the eagerness with which American universities explained and showcased their role in national affairs when asked to participate in major public cultural events of the late nineteenth and early twentieth centuries. The occasion that gave the emerging American university system the greatest national publicity undoubtedly was the 1893 World's Columbian Exhibition in Chicago. As we saw at the outset of this chapter, the International Congress on Higher Education that the NEA staged in conjunction with the Exhibition gained widespread notice. So too did dozens of exhibits on higher education that were viewed by millions of Americans who passed through the massive Liberal Arts Building on the grounds of the exposition itself. Invited to present evidence of "the progress of education" since the Centennial Exhibition of 1876, some fifty American universities and colleges organized individual exhibits that highlighted various developments in higher education. Columbia College mounted maps and plans for a new site in Morningside Heights that would soon become Columbia University; the regents of the University of the State of New York mounted an exhibit that highlighted the state's widespread university extension programs; and Harvard showcased the growth of its endowment as well as its commitment to the elective principle and teaching and research in the natural sciences. The Chicago World's Fair has been interpreted in different ways, with some historians focusing on grandiose dreams of high culture displayed throughout the White City and others drawing attention to the rich variety of popular entertainments available in the Midway. But we have no systematic study of the various ways in which the representatives and displays of higher education figured in events at Chicago in 1893. With some digging in archives, extending the story I have told in this chapter could take place by way of a close examination of the cultural identities that universities and colleges chose to present through photographs, pamphlets, books, maps, statistics, and scientific instruments they put on display in Chicago.[43]

My story of the rise of the American academic public sphere could also be extended by exploring the various ways in which the growth of the university system coincided with the formation of a new kind of popular culture in America in 1890s. Some historians, as we saw earlier in this volume, view the outcome of the latter development as the creation of a mass-print culture, a sudden and sweeping change that saw leading monthly magazines for the first time reach millions of readers and thereby become the major form of repeated cultural experience for Americans across the country. As with the 1893 Chicago World's Fair, the question of how new mass-circulation magazines such as *McClure's, Cosmopolitan,* and *Munsey's* served to nationalize popular culture has been posed and approached in different ways. Little effort is needed, however, to discover that the ideas and activities of universities and colleges figured very prominently in the pages of these monthlies. One could say with some confidence, then, that if Americans were in fact "education mad" by the turn of the century, mass-circulation magazines were among the forces that helped make them so.[44]

A concluding point. My effort to deepen and complicate the history of the American university also suggests that historians need to bring greater specificity to the context within which its continuing expansion went forward during the first decades of the twentieth century. The story told in this chapter suggests that question is worth another look primarily because, while it may be correct to see the 1890s as marking the definitive transition to a new university-dominant model in American higher education, that decade does not, as the received account tells us, also mark the clear emergence of professional academic life as we have come to know it. Over the course of the 1890s, it is true that American higher education generally began to expand as the classical college curriculum was displaced by the elective system and new subjects had to be taught, and that growth in university and college faculties was largely in the natural sciences and social sciences. But a close examination of the evidence shows we cannot neatly track all these developments in a historical narrative that assumes the successful parallel development of professional disciplinary communities. At the turn of the century, both the AEA and the MLA, for different reasons, and in different ways, were struggling to stay afloat. The American Political Science Association, the American Sociological Association, and the American Philosophical Association had yet to be founded. The record is also muddied by several universities sponsoring new schools of social work that hired a number of nonacademic social reformers.[45] By the same token single professional academic labels simply do not adequately describe the intellectual work and complicated careers of figures such as Richard T. Ely, William James, and Woodrow Wilson—arguably the most prominent American academic intellectuals of the 1890s.[46] The story of what Thomas Bender has called "intellect's academization" certainly was well underway by the turn of the century, but it by no means marked academic intellect's retreat from public life. The rise of the American university system was a process that took place by several modes and in many settings. It served to expand the nation's public intellectual life at the same time as it transformed it.[47]

FIVE

Race and Academic Culture in 1903

The Twin Conventions, the Bassett Affair, and *The Souls of Black Folk*

This chapter began as a response to a question I agreed to address at a conference commemorating the one hundredth anniversary of the founding of the American Political Science Association (APSA): What light did the founding shed on the idea that politics is, or can be, the subject of science? As it happened, the conference took place in the same setting where the APSA was launched, Tilton Memorial Library (now Tilton Hall) at Tulane University in New Orleans, during the course of a long-forgotten joint session of the American Historical Association and the American Economic Association held December 29–31, 1903.

As I began to work through material that appeared to offer an answer—mostly contemporary newspaper and journal accounts of what was done and said in New Orleans—it quickly became apparent what my response to the question would have to be: Not much. The primary aim of the figures who spearheaded the founding of the APSA—some fifty members of the AHA and AEA who gathered at Tulane late in the afternoon of December 30, 1903—was to promote more systematic collection and exchange of information on legislation at the municipal, state, and national levels. The new association they established for this purpose, however, did not introduce any new ideas about the study of politics. Nor for that matter did it immediately inspire the significant growth of political science as an independent academic profession. Less than half of the AHA and AEA members present at the founding signed up as charter members. Ten years later, it is true, the APSA's membership had grown impressively to about fifteen hundred men and women, but of these only 20 percent identified themselves as "professors" or "teachers." As with history and economics, it turns out that modern academic inquiry into politics was supported by institutional structures built well in advance of any substantial new base of scientific knowledge and methodology.[1]

When told I had reached something of a dead end, the conference organizer was kind enough to let me address what I persuaded him was a more salient question. Why had the APSA's two parent organizations chosen to meet in New Orleans in the first place? Not much digging was needed to see that they had come to the city to proclaim and enhance the national reach of their relatively new organizations (the AHA was founded in 1884, the AEA in 1885). Equally clear, and ultimately more troubling, was that they had come at the behest of the city's cultural and economic elite to celebrate the cause of sectional reconciliation and promote the interests of the New South. Put another way, the "Twin Conventions" (as one New Orleans newspaper labeled them) were Jim Crow reunions at which most AHA and AEA conferees who chose to travel to New Orleans from other regions of the country not only had their first sighting of the South's newly segregated social order but also had advocates of white supremacy among their visible and vocal hosts.

How could this have happened? Or, more precisely, how could hundreds of well-educated and reform-minded men and women who helped to build the foundations of modern American academic culture have gathered in New Orleans freely and without protest at the very moment when racial segregation and disenfranchisement had become the new rule of life in the city and throughout the South?

The short answer to this question—which of course carries a special charge today—is that these issues were of little or no concern to any member of the AHA and AEA one hundred years ago. Admirable in so many other ways, America's first generation of academic intellectuals was almost uniformly racist and simply had no quarrel with the new Jim Crow South. The longer answer is that a careful examination of the Twin Conventions—one that focuses on both the conventions themselves and the year in which they took place—provides us with an opportunity to probe an issue I believe has not received adequate attention in discussion of historical developments that first won legitimacy for professional disciplinary intellect: the role that public and institutional expressions of belief in Negro inferiority played in facilitating the national growth and consolidation of the institutions of modern American academic culture.

This essay's guiding premise is that the real substance of academic racism at the turn of the century—its most important public manifestation, one might say—lay in certain objective actions, not simply attitudes or ideas about race. While the Twin Conventions represent an important historical event in their own right, they were at the same time the last in a series of intersecting events that made the year of the APSA's founding an extraordinarily significant one in determining how the nation's "Negro problem" would be treated in academic culture for at least another twenty years.

I

In late December 1903 several hundred men and women from across
the country traveled by train to New Orleans to participate in the annual
conventions of the American Historical Association and the American
Economic Association.[2] During their early years the AHA and the AEA
routinely convened in joint sessions. But this was the first time either
association had met anywhere in the South. Attendance was widely representative of all sections and states, with many participants descending
on New Orleans on the evening of December 28 in specially chartered
trains from New York and Chicago. The "Twin Conventions," as they
were immediately labeled in the front-page headline of the *New Orleans
Daily Picayune,* lasted three days and included a crowded social sched-
ule of luncheons, receptions, banquets, and tours of local historic sites
as well as the usual round of formal presentations of academic papers
and panel discussions, all of which were staged in a variety of prominent
settings around the city. Total attendance was not quite as a large as
at recent joint sessions. But if one counts the spouses of conferees, as
well as hundreds of other "ladies and gentlemen of New Orleans" who
attended numerous social events connected to the conventions, it easily
exceeded a thousand people. A modest number by current standards
perhaps, but certainly enough to make for an event like none other that
had occurred in the South.

The Twin Conventions have been remembered, if at all, only as the
occasion for the founding of the American Political Science Association.
This took place late in the afternoon of December 30, when some fifty
members of the AHA and AEA met briefly in Tilton Memorial Library
(now Tilton Hall) at Tulane University to review and adopt a constitution
and elect the first officers of the association. But those who actually participated in various other proceedings undoubtedly felt they had par-
taken in an occasion of much broader cultural significance. To begin
with, the list of those who attended the Twin Conventions reads like a
"who's who" of American academic social science at the turn of the century. It included some of the era's most influential economists (Henry
Carter Adams of the University of Michigan, John Bates Clark and
E. R. A. Seligman of Columbia University, and John R. Commons and
Richard T. Ely of the University Wisconsin) and historians (Charles H.
Cooley of the University of Michigan, William A. Dunning of Johns Hopkins University, Charles E. Merriam of Columbia University, and Frederick Jackson Turner of the University of Wisconsin), as well as holders
of the nation's first two university chairs in sociology (Albion Small and

Fig. 5.1. Tilton Memorial Library (*left*) and Gibson Hall, Tulane University, ca. 1903. Tulane University Archives

Franklin H. Giddings, both of the University of Chicago). Presidents of the University of Arizona (Kendrick C. Babcock), University of California (W. C. Mitchell), University of Texas (W. L. Prather), and Texas A&M University (David F. Houston) participated, as did numerous businessmen, civil servants, and lawyers who at the time formed a substantial part of the membership of both the AHA and the AEA. Newspapers reported that some fifty "lady delegates" were also on hand, including the journalist Ida Tarbell, who was president of the Ladies Committee of the AHA, and the professional historian Lucy Maynard Solomon, the first woman to have an significant influence on the development of the AHA.

While a much smaller community of southern professional academics was also represented at the Twin Conventions, their contemporary prominence added to the historical significance of the occasion. Certainly the most important of these was Tulane's ambitious and talented young president, Edwin A. Alderman.[5] In serving as official host of the Twin Conventions, Alderman not only stood at the center of activity but also appeared to have secured a prominent place for both himself and his university in the nation's emerging academic culture. At William A. Dunning's suggestion, the AHA's opening session on the second day was devoted to a discussion of the "Study and Teaching of History in the South, Past, Present, and Future." Here discussants included William E. Dodd, a North Carolinian who had received his Ph.D. from the University of Leipzig and taught at Randolph-Macon College for several years before transferring to the University of Chicago in 1908; Frederick W. Moore, a Yale-trained historian who as a professor and later as dean helped build Vanderbilt's fledgling graduate program; and Lillian W. Johnson of the University of Tennessee, a champion of higher education for southern women and of freer public access to the broadening programs of southern colleges and universities. Also noteworthy in this regard was the participation of James Ford Rhodes, who presided as president of the AHA in the absence of Henry C. Lea. Although neither a southerner nor a professional academic historian, Rhodes was a widely respected writer whose books had established him as a leading figure in the new generation of American historians who had come of age after the Civil War. This group, whose most influential representative within the university was William A. Dunning, were no longer bothered by questions of southern war guilt and had come to view the Reconstruction as a colossal mistake.[4]

The luminaries who traveled to New Orleans to participate in the Twin Conventions also arrived at a propitious time for the city's economic and cultural elite. In 1903, with a population of almost three hundred thousand, New Orleans was the only major urban center in what was still an overwhelmingly rural South. It also was home to what promised to be the South's leading university and medical school. Finding a suitable theme for the occasion proved little problem. The city had staged its own celebration of the centennial of the Louisiana Purchase earlier in the year. But it was ready to celebrate it again, although this time the celebration took place as a national event that not only commemorated and explored what one local paper called "the great historical fact" that had created New Orleans but also celebrated the South's recovery from the Civil War and the disruptive decades that followed, showing that the spirit of a New South was consolidating around its commitment to national reconciliation, industrial development, and education, with New Orleans and Tulane University as two of its focal points. So while the subjects of AHA morning and afternoon sessions of the first day bore on various aspects of the Louisiana Purchase, the subjects of AEA sessions on the first day consisted entirely of the South's agricultural and industrial problems. For local New South boosters, the high point of the Twin Conventions probably was Edwin Alderman's welcoming address of December 29—"The Value of Southern Idealism"—which confidently informed conferees that the New Orleans they honored with their presence was

"a community of boundless hope, of almost joyous self-reliance, of exhil-
arating realization of independence and self-consciousness." "The spirit
of this metropolis," he added, was also "the spirit of the whole region,"
of a South intent on recovering "industrialism in commerce and education" as well as achieving "nationalization in politics and liberalism in
opinion." Many details remained to be worked out, but there could be no
question that "twenty years from now the old patriarchal South will be
a fierce industrial region."[5]

Finally, the Twin Conventions also provided America's first generation
of professional social scientists with new evidence of its increasingly significant national identity. By 1903 sober respect for presidents and faculty
of American universities was very much in fashion across the country.
Journalists were among those who regularly engaged in the work of presenting academic intellectuals in highly flattering terms. But the Twin
Conventions provided the first opportunity for newspapers in the South's
largest city to speak at length, and the result was what today would
be called a "media event" that celebrated a meeting of academic intellectuals and their allies at the same time as it served the interests of
the New South. Indeed, for four days New Orleans' white-owned newspapers—the *Daily Picayune*, the *Daily States*, the *Item*, and the *Times-
Democrat*—proclaimed the South's infatuation with academic intellectuals,
embellishing their front pages with photographs of leading participants,
relaying detailed summaries of each day's events, and, in the case of the
Daily Picayune, even providing verbatim reprintings of scholarly papers
presented at the several AHA and AEA sessions. The Twin Conventions
were the "TALK OF THE SOUTH," ran the headline of the December 30
Daily Picayune, and little that AHA and AEA conferees said or did during
their visit failed to capture the local white press's admiration or attention. Newspapers traced their movements throughout the city, telling of
smokers at the Roundtable Club, the Athletic Club, and the Boston Club;
banquets with the local elite at the St. Charles Hotel and (on New Year's
Eve) in Tulane University's Gibson Hall; and guided tours of the Colonial
Museum, French Quarter, Kenilworth Plantation, Old Absinthe House,
and Chalmette Battlefield. At the time the extraordinarily detailed daily
reports also must have seemed a remarkable triumph for the local committee of organizers. For they both signaled that particular individuals
and institutions in New Orleans were poised to make their own contributions to the national university movement and declared that respect
for existing structures of modern higher learning was now well established across the South.

If history is what we choose to remember, how did we ever come to lose
sight of the Twin Conventions? They marked the first national gathering

The Daily Picayune.

L. LXVII. NEW ORLEANS, TUESDAY, DECEMBER 29, 1903. NO. 339.

REASON HESITATION

TWIN CONVENTIONS OF LEADERS OF THOUGHT.

American Historical and Economic Associations Meet Here To-Day.

Southern Agricultural Problems to Be Discussed by One Body, Louisiana Purchase by the Other, at Opening Sessions.

REVOLUTIONS IN SAN DOMINGO.

MINISTER BEAUPRE ARRIVES AT COLON.

Cruiser Olympia Treated With Sullen Courtesy by Colombians at Cartagena.

WAR TREMBLES IN BALANCE.

EDWIN R. A. SELIGMAN,

RICHARD T. ELY,

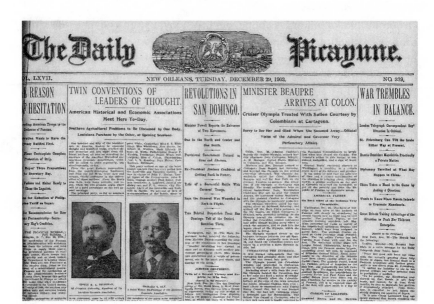

Fig. 5.2. Front page of the *New Orleans Daily Picayune*, December 29, 1903. Tulane University Archives

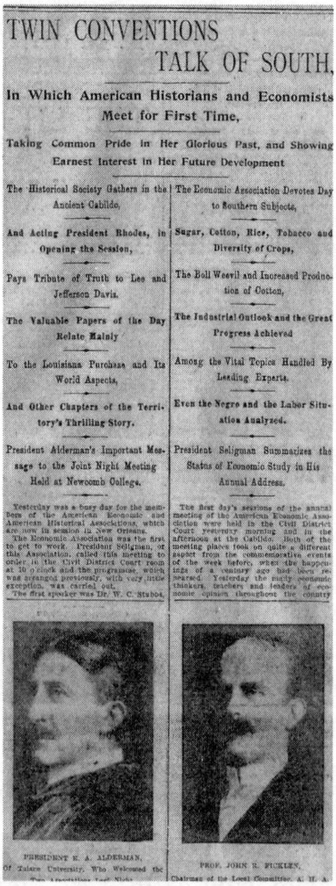

TWIN CONVENTIONS TALK OF SOUTH,

In Which American Historians and Economists Meet for First Time,

Taking Common Pride in Her Glorious Past, and Showing Earnest Interest in Her Future Development

The Historical Society Gathers in the Ancient Cabildo,

And Acting President Rhodes, in Opening the Session,

Pays Tribute of Truth to Lee and Jefferson Davis.

The Valuable Papers of the Day Relate Mainly

To the Louisiana Purchase and Its World Aspects,

And Other Chapters of the Territory's Thrilling Story.

President Alderman's Important Message to the Joint Night Meeting Held at Newcomb College.

The Economic Association Devotes Day to Southern Subjects,

Sugar, Cotton, Rice, Tobacco and Diversity of Crops,

The Boll Weevil and Increased Production of Cotton,

The Industrial Outlook and the Great Progress Achieved

Among the Vital Topics Handled By Leading Experts,

Even the Negro and the Labor Situation Analyzed.

President Seligman Summarizes the Status of Economic Study in His Annual Address.

PRESIDENT E. A. ALDERMAN,

PROF. JOHN R. FICKLEN,

Fig. 5.3. Article on the Twin Conventions in the *New Orleans Daily Picayune*, December 30, 1903. Tulane University Archives

of professional academics to take place in the South. The conventions showed that cultural leadership across the nation now increasingly resided in the universities rather than in churches and governments. Perhaps most remarkable of all, it was an event that reminds us that at the outset of the twentieth century the mere appearance in public of the nation's new class of academic intellectuals carried irresistible public appeal.[6] The Twin Conventions, on a first close look, seem a welcome exception to the rule that most academic conferences are forgettable.

But what exactly did the conventions manage to accomplish? Hindsight certainly invites us to view the contemporary praise for their achievements as so much wishful thinking. For starters the gatherings appear to have been the high point of Edwin Alderman's years at Tulane. Departing to become president of the University of Virginia in 1904, he would not stay long enough to make a sustained effort at realizing his ambition to make Tulane the South's leading university. Of more significance, the success the university movement enjoyed in the South hardly compared to that which it experienced in other regions of the country. Southern universities as a group expanded very slowly during the first four decades of the twentieth century. They also demanded, as we shall, a level of religious and racial orthodoxy that blocked even the mildest individual expressions of independent thinking. As late as 1927 the University of North Carolina Press was the only major nonreligious publishing house in the South. By 1930 only the state universities of Texas, North Carolina, and Virginia had graduate programs or libraries of national stature. In 1934 a report of the American Council of Education found that only seven southern universities had even one department adequately staffed and equipped to produce doctoral candidates. As late as 1938 the selective Association of American Universities had only four southern members: Virginia, North Carolina, Texas, and Duke.[7]

All that said, the gathering of the conventions remains, in at least four respects, a remarkably important episode for anyone interested in understanding how accommodation with racism served to promote national growth and consolidation of academic culture. To begin with the conventions proved to be the precedent for many academic Jim Crow events to come. By 1930 the AHA had met again four times in segregated southern cities: Richmond in 1908 (in joint session with the APSA), Charleston in 1913, Richmond again in 1924, and Durham and Chapel Hill in 1929. All these gatherings, the editor of the 1930 *American Historical Review* later recalled, had "left pleasant memories, and to be able to say, 'I was in New Orleans in 1903,' or 'I attended the Charleston meeting in 1913' still wins interested attention."[8] The APSA returned to New Orleans in 1929 to mark the twenty-fifth anniversary of its first annual meeting. It also began to make meetings in Washington, D.C., a regular practice in 1913, the same year Woodrow Wilson, former president of Princeton, brought Jim Crow to the nation's capital.[9]

But the Twin Conventions also had more immediate historical significance. Although the cause of sectional reunion was certainly well advanced in 1903, the conventions were the first such reunions in which academic intellectuals took center stage and where the appearance of figures the *Times-Democrat* called the "brainiest men in America" carried something of the same reconciling and uplifting appeal as then more-familiar nationwide gatherings that featured larger numbers of aging former Confederate and Union soldiers. Like other sectional reunions, the Twin Conventions were also good for business and staged in part to enhance commercial ties between North and South. In fact the business activities of the AHA and AEA turned out to be somewhat more than New Orleans could handle. On the first day of the conventions, local newspapers reported that because the city's hotels were packed to capacity, some delegates had been forced to sleep on the trains that had brought them to New Orleans and would continue to do so through the rest of their stay. Local train service was better prepared to meet demand, with both the Northeastern and Southern Pacific adding coaches to all their incoming trains on December 28 and 29.

More important, the presence of so many of the nation's leading academics in New Orleans also served as an occasion for southerners to verify if their northern visitors accepted that the terms of sectional healing were understood largely as the South had chosen to define them.[10] A considerable variety of evidence shows they did, although three brief examples will suffice here. The first was Edwin Alderman's welcoming address, given at Newcomb College at the first of two joint sessions of the AHA and AEA. Tulane's president laid out the South's terms of sectional healing for all to hear, explaining forcefully that the spirit of the New South was defined not simply by its new commitment to national reconciliation, "industrialism," and education but also by its willingness to "die" with "an amazing oneness of mind for the doctrine of racial integrity or the separateness of the two races." Alderman went on to underline that the "doctrine of separateness" did not mean "race hatred." A certain amount of race hatred did exist in the South, he conceded, but the "best Southern people not only do not hate the Negro." They believed instead that as "the forward race" they were obliged to help find "the right sort of training and education for these backward folk." But Alderman also made it clear that "the solemn duty of the white man to see that the negro gets his chance" had two a priori constraints: the Negro's "chance" could not lead either to "social equality" or to "political control."[11] Part of the New South's price for sectional healing, in other words, was rejection of a racially egalitarian society.

The second and perhaps more significant example consists of statements made by visiting northern conferees in response to New Orleans newspaper reporters who inquired about their own views of the "Negro problem." What the reporters discovered was almost entirely reassuring. E. R. A. Seligman observed in an interview with the *Times-Democrat* that the conference was a welcome occasion for leaders of northern opinion to learn to "sympathize with the best men of the South in their efforts to solve the Negro problem." He also had no doubt that "the best men of the South" were "pursuing the right path in trying to make the Negro a better working force, a more efficient industrial unit, so he may become a more capable adjunct in the development of this sector." Similar sentiments were expressed by Albion Small, who commented that "there was a growing feeling in the North, especially among university men, that the South should be allowed to solve her own problems in her own way." Perhaps the only sour note sounded by northern "university men" during the Twin Conventions was Franklin Giddings's warning that "increased immigration" might force southern blacks out of the skilled labor market, thereby "rendering it a criminal class." Yet these comments can also be read as further proof of an academic consensus about black inferiority.[12]

And then there was the "Colonial Reception," held at exactly the same time as the APSA was being founded, in the late in the afternoon of December 30, in the Garden District mansion of Mrs. T. G. Richardson, then vice president of the Louisiana Historical Society (LHS). Here "lady delegates" of the AHA mingled with "lady members" of the LHS while being served refreshments by African American women costumed either as old "mammies" in blue calico dresses with turbans and bandannas or as young "quadroon girls" dressed, as the *Times-Democrat* described them, "in fantastic garb which was worn by them in the olden days in New Orleans." Not surprisingly, the unnamed servants at the Colonial Reception were the only black people recorded in attendance at the Twin Conventions. They were not actual embodiments of the South's "olden days," however, so much as symbols of a fictitious continuity between those days and the region's new culture of segregation.[13]

III

All this tells us something about the immediate historical significance of the Twin Conventions. To take a full measure of the conventions' importance, however, they must be set against the background of more well-known events that had occurred earlier in the year 1903. While the nation's "Negro problem" was not one of the subjects AHA and AEA conferees gathered to examine in New Orleans, the conventions nonetheless had convened at the end of a year some historians now see as marking a turning point in the history of American race relations. James M. McPherson in particular has argued that, for northern liberal reformers of both races, a steady stream of horrific events made 1903 a watershed year. Not only had investigations by the Justice Department led to arrests in shocking peonage cases in Alabama, Florida, and Georgia, but the entire summer of 1903 had been marred by incidents of mob violence, including the burning at the stake of a black man in Wilmington, Delaware, cheered on by a crowd of five thousand, and an attempted lynching in Evansville, Indiana, that was prevented only when local militia and sheriff's deputies opened fire on the mob, killing and wounding thirty. The principal of an American Missionary Association industrial school in Louisiana was murdered in August 1903 and his successor driven away a few months later. In Mississippi the election of James K. Vardaman gave new evidence of the growing appeal of on unrestrained racism, even in a state where blacks were already disfranchised and thoroughly isolated. The whole of 1903, McPherson concludes, was marked by nationwide racial violence and public expressions of racial hatred that created a sense of crisis among northern liberal reformers and ultimately prompted a shift from accommodation to a new cycle of protest that led to the founding of the Niagra movement in 1905 and the establishment of the NAACP in 1910. Both organizations stood for universal political and civil equality.[14]

Any historian who uses the word "watershed" to describe a moment in time runs the risk of oversimplifying the complexity of historical events. The racial horrors of 1903 McPherson recounts certainly took place, and we will revisit them briefly later in this chapter, but there was no sense of crisis on display among the AHA and AEA conferees who gathered in New Orleans in late December of that year. Indeed, on the question of race, as we have seen, all the evidence tells us optimism was the order of the day at the Twin Conventions. And that optimism, almost certainly, was informed by knowledge of a different series of events that had occurred earlier in 1903, events that in fact seemed to hold out the promise that at least one of the barriers to racial equality—education—would be rolled back in the near future. As things turned out, this promise proved false. And explaining why makes for a rather different understanding of what the year 1903 meant in the history American race relations.

Doubtless the most consequential of this other series of events was the incorporation of the General Education Board (GEB) under the leadership of Robert Curtis Ogden at the outset of 1903. At a time when private northern philanthropy largely determined how the nation addressed the question of black education at all levels, the incorporation of the GEB marked the arrival of a new era in foundation philanthropy. Its creators were northern businessmen committed to a new ideal of efficiently organized and "scientific" philanthropy they considered fundamentally different from that which guided longstanding white northern missionary societies and black religious organizations that had established the beginnings of a private system of secondary and higher education for southern blacks during the decades immediately following the end of the Civil War. The "new philanthropy" promoted by the GEB also commanded head-spinning resources. Persuaded by his son that the cause of southern education—both black and white—deserved generous financial support, John D. Rockefeller gave an initial endowment of $1 million, supplemented it by others totaling $53 million by 1909, and by 1921 he personally had donated over $129 million.[15]

The GEB's announced mission was to promote "education across the country without distinction of race, sex, and creed." From the start, however, it was clear the GEB would not operate as an impartial force in the South. To accomplish its sectional ends, the GEB established its own offices in Richmond and Baton Rouge, but it also immediately grafted its work on to that of the Southern Educational Board (SEB), which Robert Ogden had organized two years earlier. Flagship organization of a regionwide public school crusade, the SEB was an intersectional partnership of eleven wealthy New York businessmen and fifteen progressive southern educators. And Ogden was the symbolic leader of the crusade. Entrepreneurial manager of John Wanamaker's New York department store and a philanthropist in his own right, he was a friend and admirer of both Samuel Armstrong, the white founder of Hampton Institute, and Booker T. Washington, Armstrong's protégée and the first principal of the Tuskegee Institute. Ogden also served as trustee of both Hampton and Tuskegee and was a consistent champion of the ideal of "character-building" industrial education for southern blacks. Two other influential New York businessmen who were among the SEB's original trustees— George Foster Peabody, a native of Georgia and a millionaire Wall Street lawyer, and William H. Baldwin Jr., the young vice president of J. P. Morgan's Southern Railway Company—had been associated with Ogden since 1894 as trustees of Tuskegee. And it was the three of them, with help from Andrew Carnegie, the Russell Sage Foundation, and the GEB, who financed the SEB's operations.

The southern members of the SEB's first executive board included several university and college presidents. Edwin Alderman, president of the University of North Carolina in 1901, was an original member, as were Charles W. Dabney, president of the University of Tennessee; Charles McIver, president of the North Carolina Normal and Industrial School for Women; and Hollis Frissell, principal of the Hampton Institute. Walter Hill, chancellor of the University of Georgia, became a member in 1904. Other southerners on the SEB executive board included its executive secretary, Edgar Gardner Murphy of Alabama, the leading southern opponent of child labor, champion of black education, and organizer of the 1900 Montgomery Conference on the "race question"; and Jabez L. M. Curry, a southerner transplanted to New York, where he was the main organizer of the activities of the Peabody Education Fund (established in 1867) and the Slater Fund (created in 1881), philanthropic foundations that had provided most of the money and leadership for earlier efforts at southern educational reform.

As has often been noted, when the General Education Board incorporated in 1903, its trustees formed a powerful interlocking directorate with members of the executive board of the SEB. Ogden, Peabody, Curry, Baldwin, and Wallace Buttrick (John D. Rockefeller's personal advisor on financial affairs) were founding members of both organizations, with Baldwin and Ogden serving successively as presidents of the GEB and Peabody serving as treasurer of both organizations. The SEB also met each winter in Ogden's New York office and rested each summer at Peabody's estate on Lake George, New York. Three other foundations — the Jeanes Fund (founded in 1901), the Phelps-Stokes Fund (created in 1911), and the Julius Rosenwald Fund (established in 1917) — also worked closely with the GEB, imitating its organization, responding to its initiatives, and sharing trustees. Although historians differ in offering comprehensive judgments of the ultimate impact of the "new philanthropy" across the South, there is little disagreement that, thanks to its focused goals, immense resources, and energetic and well-connected officers, the GEB quickly became considerably more visible and influential than any other northern philanthropy supporting black education.[16]

Until Ogden's death in 1913, the GEB's association with the SEB was particularly intimate, and it proved fateful on several counts. Within the GEB it resulted in a division of labor that assigned authority for determining the goals of reform to southern educators who had spearheaded the southern educational crusade since the late 1890s. As a result the GEB backed a crusade that was both openly biased toward whites and strongly opposed to any initiatives for southern black education the SEB deemed likely to undermine its primary concern to improve white education. Southern blacks played little part in the regional campaign for public elementary and high schools and failed to receive even a modest share of the educational benefits it brought. During the first sixteen years of its existence, the GEB also spent relatively little of its own money to support black education in the South. Of $27,155,446 million in GEB general appropriations during those years, only $2,462,078 went to support black education at all levels.[17]

As Eric Anderson and Alfred Moss have shown, while the GEB downplayed black education in an attempt to placate and forestall criticism in the South, northern philanthropic interest in, and support for, Negro education did not simply disappear with the arrival of the new GEB-style philanthropy. In fact, by 1903 northern philanthropists and progressive white southern educators had long since arrived at a consensus regarding "Negro education": the Hampton-Tuskegee program of training southern blacks to perform agricultural and mechanical labor was the only kind of schooling appropriate for southern blacks and should be duplicated in every southern state. Indeed, during the late 1890s it had been northern philanthropists who virtually developed the Tuskegee Institute and played a central role in projecting Booker T. Washington onto the national scene as the new leader of black Americans and Tuskegee Institute as the most famous black school in the nation. Thanks to their financial support, both the Hampton-Tuskegee idea and Washington himself were heavily advertised in national magazines and newspapers. In 1899 William Baldwin also was instrumental in obtaining for Tuskegee twenty-five thousand acres of land through special acts of the U.S. Congress and the Alabama state legislature. Baldwin then established the Tuskegee Committee on Investment of Endowment, with himself as chairman and the omnipresent Ogden, Peabody, and J. G. Phelps Stokes as board members. In 1903 he helped obtain Tuskegee's first significant endowment gift (of six hundred thousand dollars) from Andrew Carnegie. Baldwin also became chairman of the GEB that year and used his position to provide additional funds for the operating expenses of Tuskegee and other industrial schools.[18] In addition, Booker T. Washington served as one SEB's paid field agents. But neither he nor any other black leader of the time was invited attend any SEB meetings in New York or participate in its annual educational conference.

Three aspects of the new GEB/SEB alliance deserve some detailed notice, because each intersected directly with the national growth and consolidation of modern American academic culture. The first might be called the public face of the "new philanthropy" in the South. Although the SEB evolved into something of a bureaucratic organization by the end of the decade, its initial purpose was to arouse public interest and

Fig. 5.4. Booker T. Washington (*front row, seated, third from the right*), Tuskegee Institute faculty, and distinguished guests, including Robert C. Ogden (*second to the left of Washington*) and Andrew Carnegie (*to the right*), 1906. Division of Photography and Prints, Library of Congress

to fund and organize educational campaigns in every southern state. As a means of encouraging these campaigns, the SEB continued to sponsor an annual spring conference Ogden had first staged in Capon Springs, West Virginia, in 1898. After 1901 the "Conference for Education in the South" met for another six years in different cities across the South, with the intention of stimulating incipient education crusades across the region. As a rule the SEB worked through local leaders and attempted to enlist the cooperation of responsible educational officials in the various states. Individual campaign committees were organized under the direction of either a prominent southern educator or the state superintendent of education. While each campaign was conducted independently, the SEB in 1902 established and funded the Bureau of Investigation and Information on Legislation and Organization in Knoxville, Tennessee, to lend regionwide assistance. The bureau pursued surveys and investigations whose results it communicated in frequent bulletins and circulars and a weekly publication called *Southern Education.* Within a year of its organization, the bureau was regularly mailing materials to seventeen hundred newspapers across the South.

From the start, then, the GEB-funded activities of the SEB gave its educational crusade a regional orientation. From the start, too, many of these same activities served to identify all-white southern colleges and universities as important allies of the GEB and the SEB. The 1901 conference that spurred the North Carolina campaign was held at Wake Forest University in Winston-Salem, North Carolina; the 1902 conference that contributed to the organization of the Georgia campaign was held at the University of Georgia in Athens; and the final day of the three-day 1903 Richmond conference that contributed to the organization of the state campaign of Virginia was held at the University of Virginia in Charlottesville. By the end of 1903 all three of the GEB-funded state campaigns then underway were directed by southern college or university presidents: Charles McIver in North Carolina; Edwin Alderman in Louisiana; and Hollis Frissell in Virginia. The SEB's new Bureau of Information and Advice was directed by Charles B. Dabney, the president of the University of Tennessee. Beginning in 1901 Ogden also made it a practice of inviting northern professors to participate in the SEB's annual spring conferences, bringing them as his guests on the "Ogden special," a Pullman caravan that steamed out of New York in April, also stopping along the way to allow its passengers to visit select white colleges and universities and black industrial schools.[19]

From its inception, the GEB also was aware of the dangers of a northern institution working for in the South. So here, too, its officers were quick to enlist the help of southern universities and colleges in their efforts to reassure white southerners that the GEB was not seeking to impose an alien program of educational reform. Early in February 1903, for example, Edwin Alderman wrote to Ogden to tell him that Tulane University wished to award him an honorary degree on Founder's Day in March. Ogden's initial response was that he could not accept the degree in person, but criticism in the South caused him to change his mind. "I went to New Orleans for one special and only reason," Ogden explained in a letter to Hollis Frissell after he returned in April. "Some of the Southern attacks on myself and our cause are very violent. I thought under the circumstances, it might be evidence to the effect that we are not Northern inter-meddlers when an important institution of learning recognizes and compliments our movement." Seven months later GEB executive secretary Wallace Buttrick also traveled to New Orleans to deliver a similar "no northern inter-meddling" message regarding GEB policy on black education in the South. With Alderman (then also the SEB's district director for Louisiana) again in the audience, Buttrick addressed a conference of county school superintendents. "The negro, if he is to be educated at all," he informed his listeners, "is to be educated by people of the South and in the way they may be prescribe. We, as a General Education Board, have no suggestions to offer." Going a step further, Buttrick stressed, "We come to you with no notions of our own upon the subject at all."[20]

Alderman doubtless knew there was something not quite right in Buttrick's last remark. As we have seen, the GEB certainly did have its own "notions" of how the southern blacks ought to be educated. In the South, however, its officers chose to leave the work of "prescribing" black industrial education mostly to figures like Alderman and other southern university presidents and professors with close affiliations with the SEB. Shortly after taking the reins as Tulane's new president, for example, Alderman had made his opinions on this matter known in a widely noticed speech on "Education for White and Black" delivered in Baltimore at ceremonies marking the twenty-fifth anniversary of the founding of Johns Hopkins University. In Alderman's view the existing southern system of black private liberal arts colleges and universities founded by northern missionary societies and black religious organizations had failed by emphasizing "culture" rather than skills. "The dignity and necessity of labor," he told his audience, had not been "pressed upon the consideration of the race as vividly as they should have been." Rejecting the traditional liberal arts curriculum, Alderman argued that the guiding principle on the race question in the South was now the Hampton-Tuskegee program of industrial education, a program that would encourage thrift, self-reliance, and moral improvement. All "thoughtful" southerners, he concluded, denied neither the humanity of blacks nor their "economic value."[21]

At the 1903 Richmond conference, University of Georgia chancellor Walter Hill echoed Alderman's remarks when proclaimed there now was "almost a consensus of opinion, North and South, in favor of elementary education and in favor of industrial education." Hill also attributed this welcome state of affairs directly to the SEB and the Conference for Education in the South. In his view the two undertakings not only had channeled enlightened opinion toward the development of a system of biracial education in the South but also had brought that system to "into national consciousness in rational form." Sounding what by then had become a standard theme at the annual intersectional conference, Hill also proclaimed that the guiding "wisdom" of the southern education movement lay in its participants' recognition that the "national" problem of "Negro education" could only be solved by southerners.

Michael Dennis has observed that in his address to the 1903 Richmond Conference, Hill stood alone among southern university presidents when he went on to endorse a traditional college education for a limited number of southern blacks. Yet Hill also made it clear that like Booker T. Washington, he believed that the purpose of higher education for blacks was simply to train exponents of practical education, not critical thinkers who might entertain ideas of social and political equality. Hill made it clear, too, that for the vast majority of southern blacks education now "must be specialized to meet actual conditions" and that it "must be adapted to meet agricultural and industrial needs." He briefly lamented the "pathetic significance" of a large black labor force in the South that had yet to receive an education related to its "life-work." But Hill ultimately was encouraged by what he saw as the South's embrace of industrial education, a development he heralded as a new era in the history of Negro education. Under the leadership of Booker T. Washington, he concluded, "the negro" was destined to become "a home-maker, bound to the soil, a good citizen." Or put another way, for the immediate future the nation's solution to the Negro problem was plain: "Uncle Tom in His Own Cabin, or as I should prefer to say, in his own Home."[22]

Southern university presidents and professors did not invent the idea of industrial education. Nor did they control the purse strings of northern philanthropists who embraced the idea. But as Dennis has shown, it was southern university presidents and professors who provided "the intellectual medium" between northern philanthropic money and southern public opinion. Frequently addressing and writing for northern audiences during the first decade of the twentieth century, they presented their ideas about industrial education as representative of "thoughtful" southerners. In the process they also accomplished something more than simply lending the prestige of their institutions and emerging academic professions to the development of the educational program of the Jim Crow South. For northern philanthropists such as Baldwin, Carnegie, and Ogden did not merely applaud and befriend figures like Alderman, Dabney, and Hill. They made the all-white institutions they headed the primary beneficiaries of northern philanthropic support for the reform of higher education in the South. And Edwin Alderman is again a case in point here. Shortly after he left Tulane to become president of University of Virginia in 1903, Alderman set out to increase its endowment. His close ties to northern were quickly rewarded by a $500,00 gift from Andrew Carnegie, and his GEB solicitation netted an additional gift of $100,000 for a School of Education to be named after Jabez L. M Curry. All told, during the first twelve years of its existence, the GEB disbursed $3,748,406 to support institutions of higher education in the South, and $3,052,625 of that sum went to support building the endowments of thirty-two all-white colleges and universities.[23]

One historian has commented that for the cause of black education in the South, the main consequences of the new philanthropy's primary interest in industrial education were generous support for recognized industrial institutions and "fiscal disinterest" in an existing system of black colleges and universities in the South.[24] But there was more to GEB's "fiscal disinterest" than its preference for the Hampton-Tuskegee model. Until the early 1920s its fiscal disinterest was paired with a belief shared by Alderman and a vast majority of white southern educators that almost all existing programs for black higher education in the South were the futile and perhaps even dangerous work of misguided idealists. At the second Conference for Education in the South in 1899, William Baldwin proclaimed, "Except in the rarest of instances, I am bitterly opposed to the so-called higher education of Negroes." Ogden's feelings about existing African American liberal arts schools, especially Atlanta University, verged on contempt, and when the "Ogden special" rolled through Georgia it did not stop to allow its northern passengers to visit to the Atlanta campus. Ogden's animus found more significant expression in the workings of the Tuskegee machine. By the turn of the century, Ogden and other northern philanthropists had joined forces with Booker T. Washington and a supporting network of black educators and journalists in a variety of efforts designed to discredit W. E. B. DuBois and other black opponents of the Hampton-Tuskegee program. The Tuskegee machine was powerful because it consisted of large amounts of capital provided by northern philanthropists such as Baldwin and Ogden, white and black educators at industrial schools, large sections of the national black press, and powerful white politicians. Day in and day out the power of the machine was exercised by leaders of the industrial schools and editors of sometimes heavily subsidized black newspapers and periodicals, both of whom projected a positive image of Washington to propagate the Hampton-Tuskegee program.

IV

All this is a schematic recounting of events well known to specialists who study changes in the role of northern philanthropy that followed from the incorporation of the General Education Board at the outset of 1903. But what did particular events that marked the arrival of the new philanthropy have to do with the Twin Conventions? It seems likely, as I have noted, that many AHA and AEA conferees who gathered in New Orleans in late December 1903 knew the GEB had been incorporated at the outset of the year. Some doubtless also knew that in the South the GEB was pursuing its mission under the direction of the executive

board of the SEB, one of whose members—Tulane's President Edwin
Alderman—was their official host. At the end of 1903 no one of course
was in a position to predict correctly all the consequences of the new
GEB/SEB alliance. What I propose, however, is that particular events that
signaled the alliance had been formed and the decision to hold a joint
session of the AHA and AEA in New Orleans represent links in a chain
of interrelated developments that, by the time the year 1903 was over,
had substantially strengthened the nation's strategies for accommodat-
ing the workings of the Jim Crow South. If we view the rise of GEB-style
philanthropy and the Twin Conventions as intersecting events that had
important bearings on the national growth and consolidation of American academic culture, what we see in looking back on the year 1903 is
this: a significant tightening of a process of social closure whereby the
modernizing structures of American higher education—both its new universities and its new professional academic associations—would remain
the almost exclusive preserve of whites and parallel efforts to develop a
separate but equivalent system of black academic institutions would be
viewed with a mix of indifference and disdain.

A close examination of all the events that would need to be reviewed
to support this alternative reading of the significance of the year 1903
would carry us well beyond the boundaries of a this chapter. There is
space and reason here, however, to explore two of the most important,
each of which also happened to have direct ties to what occurred in
New Orleans in late December of that year. The first was publication of
DuBois's *The Souls of Black Folk* in April 1903. (McPherson comments
that DuBois's book, which included a sustained criticism of Booker T.
Washington, helped revive black militancy in 1903. But a close look at
the immediate reception of the book, as we shall see, requires a more
complicated judgment.) The second was the near-dismissal of John Spencer Bassett from the faculty of Trinity College (now Duke University) in
November and early December. Both events are relatively well known.
But their connections to the Twin Conventions have been largely overlooked. The sections that follow should make it clear that the significance of all three events is clarified and enhanced if we view them as
strands in a single, year-long story of actions and decisions that made for
social closure. Because the Bassett case had more numerous and direct
ties to the Twin Conventions, I address it first.

In October 1903, after a summer of extraordinary racial violence had
come to a close, progressive young historian John Spencer Bassett published an anonymous nine-page article titled "Stirring Up the Fires of
Racial Antipathy" in the *South Atlantic Quarterly,* a journal he had established the previous year in an effort to promote "the liberty to think" in

southern states. At a time when several northern observers had already warned that the entire nation seemed to face the prospect of a race war, Basset bravely echoed their views and urged his southern readers to heed their warning: "There is today more hatred of whites for blacks and of blacks for whites than ever before. Each race seems to be caught in a torrent of passion, which, I fear, is leading the country to an end which I dare not name." Bassett went on to say that even in the face of the nation's growing "racial antipathy," he expected American blacks "will win equality at some time." But he also stressed that he had no solution for the so-called Negro problem and certainly did not believe it could be solved by "writing anonymous articles or making speeches." The best that could be done to stoke the fires of "race antipathy," he concluded, was for "brave and wise men" across the country to step forward and "infuse the spirit of conciliation" into the "white leaders of white men."[25]

Bassett had been teaching at Trinity College since 1894 when his article appeared. He was a native of North Carolina who had attended public high school in Goldsboro, where his teachers had included Edwin Alderman, then a recent graduate of the University of North Carolina who there launched his career as a crusader for public education in the South. Later Bassett went on to train at Trinity and Johns Hopkins, where he studied with Herbert B. Adams. Although only thirty-six years old in 1903, Basset had already had made an impressive mark in his field, both as an innovative and popular undergraduate teacher and as a publishing scholar. At Trinity he had founded the *Papers of the Trinity College Historical Society* (one of a bare handful of regular scholarly publications in the South at the time), established a historical museum designed to promote undergraduate research, and launched an honor society based on academic distinction and service. During the late 1890s he also published two pioneering books on slavery and the antislavery movement in North Carolina. In a series of lectures at Johns Hopkins, he was perhaps the only southern white historian to raise the possibility that the Reconstruction had not been a colossal mistake. In 1902 he had been a member of the program committee for the AHA's annual convention.

Bassett plainly was no intellectual lightweight, nor one to shy away from controversial topics. But he was altogether unprepared for the storm his *South Atlantic Quarterly* article would trigger. On November 1, 1903, Josephus Daniels, a leading propagandist of white supremacy in North Carolina politics and editor of the highly influential *Raleigh News and Observer,* reprinted Bassett's article in its entirety and identified him as its author. In an editorial Daniels also seized on what proved to be Bassett's most controversial passage—his description of Booker T.

Washington as "the greatest man, save General Lee, born in the South in a hundred years" and his assertion that blacks "will win equality at some time"—as evidence that Bassett was unfit to teach or write about race "from the standpoint of a Southern man" and should resign his position immediately. With only a few exceptions, daily and weekly newspapers in North Carolina and other southern states followed Daniels lead, labeling Bassett a "nigger lover" whose words gave blacks a dangerously exalted opinion of their rights. He was referred to in headlines as "bASSett." North Carolina's Democratic leaders, some of whom were members of the Trinity College Board of Trustees, also joined the state's newspaper editors in demanding Bassett's resignation. When criticism grew to include hate mail and calls for parents to withdraw their children and for ministers not to recommend prospective students to apply to Trinity, Bassett privately tendered his resignation to President John C. Kilgo, who had little choice but to convene the Trinity College Board of Trustees to decide Basset's fate.

Although Bassett was professionally well connected and had friends in high places, he had good reason to wonder how much support he could count on. Only a year before Andrew Sledd, a young classics professor at Emory University who spoke out for the rights of American Negroes, was forced to resign his position. It is true that Trinity's administration, faculty, and students stood firmly behind Bassett and the principle of academic freedom, as did several alumni and local businessmen who wrote letters of support to the board, but none of them risked stepping forward with even a measured public defense of what Basset had said. More significant, the limited support for Bassett at Trinity was in sharp contrast to the complete silence of administrators, faculty, and students at all other southern colleges and universities. After an unsuccessful effort to clarify his views in a newspaper interview, the beleaguered Bassett recognized he was in no position to orchestrate his own defense and adopted a public stance of silence. In a private interview with Kilgo, he also insisted that the press had greatly exaggerated the extent of his challenge to the South's current racial attitudes and practices, explaining that the "equality" he believed American blacks eventually would win would not include any "social mingling of the races." He also conceded that it would have been more accurate to label Washington's achievement "most memorable" rather than "great."

In 1903 there was no such thing as tenure at Trinity or any other American college or university. No one could predict, then, what the Trinity Board of Trustees would decide when it gathered in a closed session in Durham on December 1. In advance of the meeting one board member proclaimed ominously it would be the "last fight for white supremacy." But Trinity's president had prepared a brilliant strategy for rescuing Bassett. Obviously convinced that Josephus Daniels's editorials in the *Raleigh News and Observer* had influenced the board's understanding of the case, Kilgo began by turning the tables on Daniels in his opening remarks, reading some of his editorials of a year before in which he had defended Andrew Sledd's right to speak freely, asserting that "a college professor ought to have the liberty to think, speak, and write as he chose without fear of prosecution." Kilgo then let Bassett's critics on the board have their say, before he played his second hand. Recounting Bassett's statements from his private interview, Kilgo explained that the views Kilgo had expressed his *South Atlantic Quarterly* article had been misrepresented in the newspapers and that any careful reader of the article would see that Bassett had posed no challenge to belief in white supremacy. Asked his own views of the "Negro question," Kilgo made it clear that while he believed blacks ultimately would make "a sure and worthy place in American life," he also believed, like Bassett, that a vast amount of work remained to be done and that the ultimate goal, in any case, was by no means equality with white Americans. Eleven trustees would speak over the course of a long and tiring meeting. When the final vote was taken at 3:00 a.m. on December 2, eighteen chose to retain Bassett, seven to accept his resignation.

Kilgo's rescue of Bassett was a remarkably skillful piece of work and is today rightly remembered as one of the proudest moments in the history of Duke University. (Had Trinity's board accepted Bassett's offer to resign, Kilgo and several other faculty were prepared to submit their resignations.) But it is by no means obvious that the board's decision should be remembered as a clear-cut triumph for the principle of academic freedom. A close examination of the immediate aftermath of the board's decision invites a more complicated and less cheerful verdict, and, as it happens, another look at the Twin Conventions.

We know that at the time of the Trinity Board of Trustee's decision, Bassett had made plans to travel to New Orleans to join his friend William E. Dodd on the AHA panel on the "Study and Teaching of History in the South, Past, Present, and Future." The ordeal of the previous weeks, however, had taken its toll. Clearly exhausted by the storm that had swirled around him, Bassett canceled his appearance at the last moment, pleading a severe attack of rheumatism. In the January 1904 issue of the *South Atlantic Quarterly,* Basset published a brief review in which he again aligned himself with the cause of approaching the Negro question in "a calm and passionate manner." But the piece almost certainly was written prior to the board's decision, and by the time it appeared in print the main lessons of the controversy were all too plain:

for the foreseeable future, the cause of moderation and reason in discussing race in the South was dead. Any effort to revive it was certain to be greeted with public harassment.[26]

Bassett apparently had little choice but to accept his exoneration in silence. It also seems clear that he had lost his appetite for promoting the "liberty to think" about race in the South. A year after the board's decision, he announced his resignation as editor of the *South Atlantic Quarterly*, explaining that his scholarly work now required more of his time. Two years later, he accepted an appointment to the faculty of Smith College, where his career would flourish for the next thirty years. Until his death, Bassett continued to correspond with his friends and former colleagues in the South. He also worked to get topics of concern to southerners included in annual AHA national conventions but apparently never found cause to include the "Negro problem" among them.

Had Bassett not cancelled his trip to the Twin Conventions, or had his case somehow found its way onto its formal agenda, it is possible that the controversy sparked by the reprinting of his *South Atlantic Quarterly* article might have been rekindled and proceedings in New Orleans perhaps would not have faded from memory as soon as they did. It is hard to believe that Bassett was not the subject of informal conversation among some members of the AHA and AEA. We have no evidence as to what they might have said. It seems safe to say, however, that given the geographical setting of the Twin Conventions, no one in attendance gave serious thought to proposing a toast to Bassett's rescue.

There is evidence that suggests, however, that Bassett ultimately did manage to make an appearance in New Orleans, if only as the thinly veiled object of comments made by President Edwin Alderman of Tulane near the end of his welcoming address. As he drew to the conclusion of his explanation of why white southerners were ready to die for "the doctrine of racial integrity," Alderman acknowledged that his address was perhaps not the proper occasion for a full discussion of the South's new "doctrine of separateness." He continued: "Discussion of it has become a national disease, and should quarantined against, for it is getting hysterical and dangerous. . . . My prescription is 'silence and slow time,' faith in the South and wise training of both white and black. I do not mean by this to echo the old sensitive cry, 'Let the South Alone'; but to emphasize . . . [the] idea that if the best people of the South cannot handle this question, it is impossible to handle it at all."[27] The veiled reference to Bassett in the first sentence, I suspect, would have been unmistakable for many in Alderman's audience at the time, although the tone of Alderman remarks may have been puzzled some of the "best people" in his audience. Was he identifying himself with Bassett's critics or with his supporters? Alderman surely knew that Bassett agreed that the problem of American race relations in the South was, for the foreseeable future, primarily a problem of how superior white southerners would understand their limited obligations to inferior blacks. Yet Bassett plainly had violated the rule of "silence," and the upshot was a controversy that, although recently settled, obviously still troubled his former teacher.

But Alderman in fact had no cause to worry. Indeed, looking back at the Bassett case through the window of his welcoming address, perhaps the most striking aspect of the case is that the storm surrounding Bassett dissipated almost as quickly it gathered. In the South it certainly was not the case that the Trinity board's decision to retain Bassett inspired other colleges and universities to undertake or defend new challenges to southern racism. Not only would there be no such challenges for several decades to come, but they were openly discouraged at the time by Basset's supporters at Trinity, all of whom made it clear that they thought he had gone too far and that there was no cause to expect that his mistake might be repeated.[28] In the eyes of his southern supporters, Basset had been silenced at the same time he was exonerated.

Perhaps more important, the Bassett case, dramatic as it was, turned out to be mostly a regional affair. As with several earlier academic freedom cases elsewhere in the country—all of which also had involved Johns Hopkins-trained professors—it was the attention of the newspapers that created an angry public controversy. But national coverage of Bassett's case in November and December 1903 hardly approached that which had surrounded Edward Ross three years earlier (explored in some detail in the previous chapter). Moreover, and again unlike Ross, Bassett was in no position to help orchestrate public understanding of his views, and his rescue took place without assistance from any of the powerful individuals within the American university system who had come to the aid of Ross and of other professors with controversial views in the late 1890s.[29] After the Trinity board's decision was announced, a few northern newspapers and the Social Gospel press praised Kilgo's victory for academic freedom. But at the time not a single university president publicly echoed their praise, nor did any leading northern academic historians, some of whom Bassett counted among his close friends. In short, the "national disease" the Bassett case represented in Alderman's mind already been effectively "quarantined" when the Twin Conventions began on the morning of December 29, and it was Alderman himself, on the evening of December 30, who slammed shut the window of opportunity for drawing nationwide attention to the controversy that had engulfed his former student.

IV

What can, or must, a historian say about this course of events? The answer is depressing but complicated. The fact of academic racism evades simple summary, and I suspect historians will never reach a consensus on exactly what share of the burden of American racism the university must bear.[30] Virtually all white Americans, for one reason or another, were openly racist at the start of the twentieth century, and their racism undoubtedly would have flourished in the absence of academic supports. It should be said too that some of the most prominent academic figures of that time maintained admirably higher standards than those of the public large. And this was true of those who pursued their careers in the South as well as those in the North. During his years at Tulane, for example, Edwin Alderman's belief in "racial integrity" did not prevent him from openly expressing support for Booker T. Washington before a mixed audience in New Orleans or from making sure that news of his support was widely disseminated. At a time when most white southerners scorned even rudimentary vocational education for blacks and viewed attendance at integrated meetings as a menacing step toward "social equality," Alderman's public endorsement of Washington was hardly an empty gesture.[31]

But to call attention to the complexities of academic racism does not entail apologizing for them. One has to look very hard to find a handful of late-nineteenth- and early-twentieth-century academic intellectuals who directly challenged conventional academic wisdom on the Negro problem, and what one finds here can only be described as passing statements that had little or no public impact.[32] Asked to summarize broadly how the Negro problem was perceived by American academic intellectuals during the first half of the twentieth century, one clear answer might be that it was viewed as much by indifference as by any deeply held views about the perceived moral and intellectual inferiority of blacks.[33] Asked his opinion about the Negro problem as he prepared to return to Wisconsin from the Twin Conventions on January 2, 1904, Richard T. Ely, once known as the boldest of American's first generation of reform-minded academic intellectuals, replied, "I have nothing to say."[34] But over time having nothing to say would have devastating results for blacks. In the South it would be powerfully reinforced by commitments of the sort that the Trinity College Board of Trustees reaffirmed when it chose to retain Bassett: commitments to both a conscious policy of exclusion and to a policy of uniform silence about the cost and consequences of exclusion. Elsewhere in the country indifference led to the creation of a system of higher education in which whites and blacks had almost no contact and progressive white academics abandoned belief in scientific racism long before they began to cast a cold eye on the workings of the Jim Crow South.[35] In short, a segregated society, for at least the first half of the twentieth century, was defined in part by what the AEA and AHA put on display in New Orleans in 1903: not simply the institutions of a segregated academic culture but institutions within which the costs and consequences of segregation were not open to systematic discussion or dispute.

These conclusions raise another troubling question that finally brings us back to the publication of DuBois's *The Souls of Black Folk* in April 1903. If that year, as I argue, marked something of a turning point in determining how the Negro problem would be viewed in modern academic culture for at least two decades to come, was there perhaps anything that happened during that year that could have made things develop in another way? Could the newly modernized structures of higher learning somehow have become even a limited force for emancipation rather than for racism and conciliation? It would be easier (and perhaps somewhat comforting) to conclude this chapter with a sweeping indictment of the consensual racism of the architects of the modern American university system. But we in fact have no evidence showing that in 1903 there were well-defined and workable alternatives to the prevailing "silence-and-slow time" approach to the Negro problem, either in direct conflict with the mainstream positions of white racism or simply working occasionally below the surface. And what little evidence there is certainly did not hold out promise of a radical departure from the status quo.

But what of the publication of the first edition of *The Souls of Black Folk*? Surely this book, which began with the now famous proclamation that "the problem of the Twentieth Century is the problem of the color line," must have asked its first readers in 1903 to imagine things might be substantially different? Well, yes and no. No one believed more deeply than DuBois that America's new universities should be deeply involved in the work solving "the problem of the color line." There also can be no question that the architects of America's university system, as well as America's first generation of academic intellectuals, were familiar with his name and his views. By 1903 DuBois, then thirty-five years old, had established his reputation as the leading figure among a small but closely connected group of black academic intellectuals who began their careers in the 1880s and 1890s. The only black member of both the AHA and the AEA, he had been professor of history and economics at Atlanta University since 1897, and there he had begun publication of Atlanta

University Studies, his own ongoing series of sociological studies of black life in America.[36] During the late 1890s and early 1900s, DuBois also had published nine of the fourteen chapters in *The Souls of Black Folk* as magazine articles. These included the crucial sixth chapter, "Of the Training of Black Men," in which he outlined the "function of the Negro College" in the New South.[37]

In this regard it also is worth noting that in late December 1903, DuBois, like Bassett, was something of off-stage actor at the Twin Conventions, and Bassett himself earlier in the year wrote an admiring review of the first edition of *The Souls of Black Folks*. Because the New Orleans meeting was a Jim Crow event, DuBois of course could not attend. But on its way to the city the New York train carrying AHA and AEA members did what no "Ogden special" allowed its passengers to do: stop for a few hours in Atlanta so that some of its passengers—E. R. A. Seligman and several other conferees—could pay their respects to DuBois. There apparently is no record of what was said at the meeting, but it seems likely that topics of conversation included the university's role in addressing in the Negro problem. It also is worth noting that Bassett's interest in this issue was the central thread of a review that appeared in the June 1903 *South Atlantic Quarterly*. Here Bassett judiciously and respectfully contrasted DuBois's goals with those of Booker T. Washington, concluding that, "while most negroes do not comprehend the very terminology of higher education," the "exceptional negro does exist; for him the door of opportunity should be left open."[38]

Yet *The Souls of Black Folk* must also be viewed as the exception that proves the rule here. In 1903 DuBois quite clearly understood that if a "door of opportunity" for university education was to be left open for black Americans, for the foreseeable future it would be an altogether separate door. Reluctantly but explicitly, chapters 5 and 6 of the book articulated DuBois's acceptance of the South's new regime of segregated education at all levels. More important, these chapters also spoke to his immediate practical purpose in publishing *The Souls of Black Folk* , that is, to gain substantial new northern philanthropic support for building the South's impoverished Negro colleges and universities. In 1903 DuBois accepted a separate system of education for southern blacks, partly because he recognized that for the foreseeable future southern whites simply would not teach them. Not only was the Jim Crow South composed of "two separate worlds," he wrote, but "the separation is so thorough and deep that it absolutely precludes for the present between the races anything like that sympathetic and effective group-training and leadership of the one by the other, such as the American Negro and all backward peoples must have for effectual progress."[39] But he had two additional reasons for accepting segregation in higher education. The first was his belief that the Negro colleges and universities in the South, if adequately funded, could grow and train a much-needed new class of black teachers and professionals, and the second was his related conviction that only Negro colleges and universities were prepared to systematically address the South's Negro problem. Manual training and trade schools were helping to accomplish "the closer knitting of the Negro to the great industrial possibilities" of the New South, but much more was needed: "The foundations of knowledge in this race, as in others, must be sunk deep in the college and university, if we would build a solid, permanent structure. Internal problems of social advance must inevitably come,—problems of work and wages, of families and homes, of morals and true valuing of the things of life; and all of these and other inevitable problems the Negro must meet and solve largely for himself, by reason of his isolation; and can there be any possible solution other than by study and thought and an appeal to the rich experience of the past?" The primary purposes of the Negro college in the Jim Crow South, DuBois concluded, were all too clear: "it must maintain the standards of popular education, it must seek the social regeneration of the Negro, and it must help in the solution of problems of race contact and cooperation."[40]

There can be little question, however, that DuBois's carefully crafted arguments for strengthening Negro colleges and universities in the South failed to change any of the existing terms of the nation's now firmly established accommodation with racism. Booker T. Washington and his allies surely recognized the first edition of *The Souls of Black Folk* for what it was, a text whose arguments were aimed at a small but closely connected community of educated blacks of which Washington now considered himself the exclusive spokesman and Washington's affluent and influential white supporters in the North, including the leadership of the recently formed General Education Board.[41] But DuBois's book was no match for Washington's power as a machine boss. In April 1903 Washington had a near personal monopoly over northern philanthropic monies assigned to provide vocational training for southern blacks and the Tuskegee machine had established itself as the largest employer of black college graduates in the nation and had spread its web tightly over hundreds of weekly African American newspapers. So while some reviewers for independent black journals and a few individuals—in private correspondence—offered high praise for the first edition of *The Souls of Black Folks,* there is little evidence to support the familiar view that *The Souls of Black Folk* inspired almost unanimous acclaim among educated black Americans at the time, let alone an immediately successful challenge to Washington's leadership.[42]

As for the recently incorporated General Education Board, we know that until the mid-1920s its recognized rule of philanthropy would remain that no arrangements for Negro education in the South could survive unless they pleased the white South. And apart from John Spencer Bassett, apparently no educated white southerner found cause to take DuBois seriously. The upshot was that between 1903 and 1914, of the paltry $695,782 the GEB disbursed to support black higher education in the South, only $140,000 went to private black colleges and universities. The largest GEB disbursement, $70,000, went to Fisk University; Atlanta University received only $8,000.[43]

Although the first edition of *The Souls of Black Folks* fell mostly on deaf ears in 1903, DuBois would cling to his high hopes for Negro colleges universities and continue to pursue his own scholarly studies of the Negro problem at Atlanta University for another seven years, before resigning—in defeat and disgust—in July 1910 to become director of publicity and research at the recently formed NAACP. Signs of defeat gathered in the years that followed the publication of *The Souls of Black Folks.* In May 1906 DuBois sent Andrew Carnegie a letter requesting financial support for his annual Atlanta Conference on black life in America and attached a report on Negro crime, the subject of the conference's ninth annual report. The object of the conference, DuBois explained, was "the systematic and exhaustive study of the American negro, in order that future philanthropists and others who seek to solve this serious problem may have before them a carefully gathered body of scientifically arranged facts to guide them." There is no record of any reply from Carnegie.[44]

By the time of his resignation, DuBois's annual conferences and careful academic studies were even further away from winning significant northern philanthropic support than they had been in 1906, and Atlanta University's trustees now doubted they would continue to sponsor DuBois's scholarly activities. A final insult came in the month just prior to his resignation, when in returning proofs of his article on "Reconstruction and Its Benefits" to the *American Historical Review* DuBois requested "as matter of professional courtesy" that he be allowed to capitalize the word "Negro." An exchange of increasingly agitated letters followed, beginning with the *AHR*'s editor J. Franklin Jameson's refusal of DuBois's initial request. DuBois then insisted on the change, curtly dismissing the argument that uniformity in editorial practice was "sufficient cause for inflicting upon a contributor . . . that which he regards as a personal insult." In a final, long reply that followed, Jameson professed both his personal innocence in all matters of racial prejudice and his astonishment that he, as the "grandson of an old Abolitionist, brought up to know

Fig. 5.5. W. E. B. DuBois, Atlanta University, 1909. Special Collection of University Archives, W. E. B. DuBois Library, University of Massachusetts

no difference between black and white," had been charged with insulting a professional colleague. "The question was simply one of typography," Jameson explained curtly, about which nothing could be done in the pages of the *American Historical Review*.[45]

DuBois engaged in later disputes about the capitalization of "Negro" in which he proved even more combative. But the message brought home by Carnegie's silence and his skirmish with Jameson—who as it happens had been among those who had attended the whites-only Twin Conventions in New Orleans some seven years earlier—must have been all too obvious as DuBois packed his bags to move to New York. Ten years into the twentieth century, the creators and first supporters of the institutions of modern American academic culture had showed quite plainly they could not be counted on to provide even modest help in solving "the problem of the Twentieth Century."[46]

Afterword

A friend and colleague with whom I discussed these studies while I was expanding and revising them reminded me that students of American intellectual history have known for some time that during the last decades of the nineteenth century, as industrialization gained momentum and our cities filled with farm-bred citizens and immigrants, a great wave of interest in culture swept across the country. After hearing my summary account of the essays, he commented that it appeared I had organized them around two questions that went to the heart of what many other intellectual historians have recently been saying about efforts Americans made to build new cultural institutions during the industrial era. First, was there a unifying conception of culture behind all its many variations? And second, did the results of late-nineteenth- and early-twentieth-century efforts to institutionalize culture turn out to be something more than pretty facades, disguising the machinations of various elites intent on imposing their own values on American society at large? Answering these questions persuasively, he concluded offhandedly, might earn me a commanding position among my peers.

Looking back on what I have done since that conversation, I think my friend was right about this volume's two organizing questions, although as things turned out the second has attracted more of my attention than the first. It also strikes me that the short version of the answers I have given is more or less the same in each case: Yes, for the most part. Of course, it remains to be seen if my peers find the longer version developed in the studies compelling or evasive.

I argued in chapter 1 that while not alone in the field, the antebellum American ideal of self-culture powerfully shaped the general course of the American debate about culture well into the first decade of the twentieth century. I argued, too, that the core features of that ideal were evident in the thinking of such figures as Ralph Waldo Emerson, Walt Whitman, Charles W. Eliot, Daniel Coit Gilman, E. L. Youmans, Richard T. Ely, W. E. B DuBois, and Jane Addams. Each understood, I think, that the American understanding of culture was authentically individualistic and thus resistant to closure around any single fixed definition of what being cultivated was to mean. Their shared insistence on space for personal choice and self-construction also provided a powerful counterforce to more authoritarian and elitist conceptions of culture.

Yet here this point probably should be restated in a way that acknowledges the slipperiness the American understanding of culture. For at its core, self-culture was a concept that incorporated a significant element of incommensurability, thereby allowing it to be appropriated to the disparate uses of very different sorts of individuals and groups. With few exceptions native-born American proponents of self-culture, beginning with Emerson, were not rigid absolutists who claimed timeless knowledge of the good, the true, and the beautiful. They did not know, a priori, what American culture would look like. But they did know it would not look European and that somehow it ought to correspond to the peculiarities of American life. Or more precisely, in America culture had to connect with the choices of ordinary men and women and therefore be fashioned to serve the uses of a democratic rather than aristocratic society. Yet if this was the case, it suggests native-born American proponents of self-culture also can be understood as people who took the first fateful steps down the road that ultimately led to a nonjudgmental conception of culture as something we humans—all of us being, in DuBois's memorable phrase, "co-workers in the kingdom of culture"—construct for own purposes, making it largely a matter of choice but at the same time sheltering it from evaluation on any single scale of values.[1]

On the question of how to interpret efforts to institutionalize culture, *Building Culture* should leave little doubt that I believe something like an indigenous "culture industry" was put into place during the last decades of the nineteenth century, and that it included elites who sought to occupy the "high" cultural ground of the era. But *Building Culture* also should leave little doubt that the culture industry of the industrial era was shaped by the aspirations of a remarkably heterogenous society. So a complete description of its workings must recognize, as I have attempted to do, contributions made by comparatively marginalized interests and groups—women, spokesmen for the new urban working class, educated African Americans, and new European immigrants. Put more simply, the culture industry of the industrial era was contested terrain. The latter phrase may be a bit overworked these days, but it provides the best and shortest explanation of why I have joined other historians before me in resisting the conclusion that any American elite was poweful enough to dictate the terms of cultural negotiation. My fourth chapter, in particular, stresses that we should not view the American university system in the late nineteenth and early twentieth centuries simply a service organization of corporate capitalism, nor as a safe haven for a new professional-managerial class of experts. It was instead a complex new and independent cultural space where, in various ways, specialists and ordinary people met and debated the issues of the day.

I acknowledge that I have avoided making many forward glances in this book. But the work of reconstructing the past inevitably comes to be a dialogue with the present, and I think several themes in this book could be profitably pursued by intellectual historians interested in telling the story of the development of American intellectual and cultural life since the industrial era. Three stand out in my mind. The first surfaced briefly toward the end of chapter 5: the lamentably slow demise of academic racism. No one doubts that American academic culture remained almost uniformly racist through the first half of the twentieth century and that at least until mid-1960s almost all of our academic institutions not only continued to practice some form of discrimination but also made remarkably little effort explore the costs and consequences of segregation. It is very hard to reflect on these facts without feelings of anger and depression. But the particular challenge historians face in considering them is this: if we believe our purpose in contextualizing past actions and attitudes is to render them coherent and dynamic, ultimately we are obliged to provide a complete and rational understanding of them.

Restricting attention to the Jim Crow South in the first half of the twentieth century, historians therefore have to ask: exactly what ought we to say about the many administrators and faculty at all-white southern colleges and universities who, following the example of Edwin Alderman, found no cause to take a more liberal public stance on the question of legal segregation? One certainly could say that, after a series of federal court decisions in the late 1940s compelled law schools at previously white universities in Oklahoma, Texas, and Virginia, and Louisiana to admit black students for the first time, Jim Crow's days now were numbered. Before the end of World War II, however, how could a historian avoid saying that, in the South, open advocacy of even a gradual policy of desegregation would have been a naïve and self-defeating gesture?

A similar sort of question arises in considering the gradual decline of the South's segregated university system in the 1950s and 1960s. What should historians make of the fact that when the decline finally set in, it occurred at different speeds and in responses to different pressures—both internal and external—from one academic institution to another? I stress immediately that to encourage closer study of such questions is not to invite an apology. Nor is it to suggest that racism is no longer an issue in American academic culture. My point is simply that if the story of the rise of academic racism is best understood, as I argue in chapter

5, as matter of objective acts and decisions, so too must be the story of its gradual decline.[2]

There also is a perhaps obvious question raised by my discussion of the rise of the American academic public sphere in chapter 4. Has the American university system yielded all that Daniel Coit Gilman and its other late-nineteenth-century architects confidently promised it would? At a time when many American professional academics berate themselves for having lost contact with the general public, it is worth noting that the academic public sphere that first came to life during the industrial era is still in plain sight.[3] In fact, it is vastly bigger and more diverse than it was a hundred years ago. Today almost two-thirds of the eligible American population goes on to some form of higher education, and the huge expansion of the American university now provides professional academics with several overlapping audiences, ranging from fellow specialists at one end to a diverse range of students at the other. There also is a downside to this, however, because one could say that today the prime brute index of the American academic public sphere is simply that there are now so many different kinds of students with so many different kinds of interests and needs. And I think we do not have a ready answer for what may be the key question of the moment: what ought we to do with this now huge audience of students that is both useful and true?

Looking backward to history of the American university during the industrial era provides no neglected easy answers. With a better understanding of that history, however, one can conclude that if the American university's past was considerably more complicated than some would have us believe, its present challenges are easier to identify than we sometimes think. On my reading the new multipurpose world that Gilman and the other architects of the American university system dreamed of during the last decades of the nineteenth century is the world that countless administrators and academics inhabit at the outset of the twenty-first. More important, it is the world we have inherited an obligation to evaluate and improve. To say that much work needs to be done, then, is no cause for disappointment or despair. The bar was set ambitiously high during the industrial era.

Finally, intellectual historians may want to take up an expanded version of the question that served as the starting point of this book: why during the era of America's industrialization did a normative understanding of "culture" gain a widespread prominence in American society it had never known before and has never experienced again? I answer the first part of this question in chapter 1 by showing that most native-born

American proponents of culture in the late nineteenth and early twentieth centuries understood culture first and foremost as a matter of individual self-construction and self-development. Culture spoke to the challenge of drawing and developing ethical, intellectual, physical, social, and spiritual faculties that all individuals were thought to possess. Or put another way, in industrializing America, culture was continuous with self-culture, an always ongoing process, not a simple possession. And conceived as such, culture therefore was open to all Americans, regardless of class, gender, or race. Little wonder, then, that it once served as a rallying cry for so many.

But what, then, should we make of the fact that we now live in a time that is no longer essentially concerned with culture understood in these highly idealistic terms? In most spheres culture today either has negative connotations that imply simply the interests of posturing and biased elites or has given way to a nonjudgmental anthropological conception of culture as an established lifestyle. Talk about self-culture has long since passed out of fashion, replaced by such expressions as "mass culture," "popular culture," "working-class culture," and "African American culture," with "culture" here pointing only to the already well-established institutions, practices, and rituals of a particular group.

One of course can only speculate about what such figures as Ely, DuBois, and Jane Addams would make of these changes. But I am fairly confident they would say that at least one aspect of culture in the normative sense—the self that was embedded in their understanding of the term—still has an important role to play in our affairs. For as we have seen, the selves envisioned by these native-born American champions of culture came from all walks of American life, and they were in turn understood as selves with a rich array of faculties and powers that could be drawn out and developed in various ways and in multiple settings. In America, cultured selves could be found in working-class brass bands, libraries and schools for adult education, women's clubs, settlement houses, and African American colleges and universities. Recovering the robustness of this once common way of thinking about culture, I suggest in conclusion, perhaps can do more than move us a considerable distance from a caricatured view of the nation's intellectual and cultural life during the industrial era. It might also help us to enrich our own.[4]

NOTES

Preface and Acknowledgments

1. Alan Trachtenberg, *The Incorporation of America: Culture and Society in the Gilded Age* (New York: Hill & Wang, 1982) and Lawrence E. Levine, *Highbrow/Lowbrow: The Emergence of Cultural Hierarchy in America* (Cambridge: Harvard University Press, 1988) provide the most influential arguments for the hierarchal view that links the rise of "culture" with the class stratification and social transformation of industrial capitalism.

2. Although for different reasons, during the 1970s and early 1980s, there was a sea change in the way in which both labor and economic historians viewed the industrial era. See James Livingston, "The Social Analysis of Economic History and Theory: Conjectures on Late Nineteenth-Century Economic Development," *American Historical Review* 92 (1987): 69–95. The literature is extensive; see references cited by Livingston (70n2–4 and 71n5).

3. Accepted on its own terms, the hierarchical view also left important questions unanswered. In *Highbrow/Lowbrow*, for example, Levine documented ways in which members of the American upper class made opera and classical music over into "high" culture. What he left unexplored is the question of why such musical forms should have been seen as indispensable new signifiers and media of class identity. Also unexplained is why elites would bestow such energy and resources on creating new institutional settings for cultural activity. Levine's restrictive view of high culture and elite rule, it appears, forces him to sidestep such fundamental questions.

4. See especially Lewis Perry's account of "The Ideology of Culture," in *Intellectual Life in America: A History* (Chicago: University of Chicago Press, 1989), 263–76; and Joseph Kett, *The Pursuit of Knowledge under Difficulties: From Self-Improvement to Adult Education in America, 1750–1900* (Stanford, Calif.: Stanford University Press, 1994), chaps. 5–7. Other important recent studies that pursue (to varying degrees) a pluralist approach include Jonathan Freedman, *Professions of Taste: Henry James, British Aestheticism, and Commodity Culture* (Stanford, Calif: Stanford University Press, 1994); Joseph Horowitz, *Wagner Nights: An American History* (Berkeley and Los Angeles: University of California Press, 1994); Abigail A. Van Slyck, *Free to All: Carnegie Libraries and American Culture, 1890–1920* (Chicago: University of Chicago Press, 1995); Ann Ruggles Gere, *Intimate Practices: Literacy and Cultural Work in U.S. Women's Clubs, 1880–1920* (Urbana: University of Illinois Press, 1997); Mary W. Blanchard, *Oscar Wilde's America: Counterculture in the Gilded Age* (New Haven: Yale University Press, 1998); Daniel G. Williams, *Ethnicity and Cultural Authority: From Arnold to DuBois* (Edinburgh: Edinburgh University

Press, 2006); and Leslie Butler, *Critical Americans: Victorian Intellectuals and Transatlantic Reform* (Chapel Hill: University of North Carolina Press, 2008).

5. It is worth noting that the study of Emerson also has undergone a remarkable renewal in recent decades. Most of our inherited commonplaces about Emerson—the anti-institutionalist with no taste for popular culture, the lover of nature, the prince of Transcendentalism, the genteel Sage of Concord, "Uncle Emerson," and so on—have been called into question. In replacement, we have been offered new accounts of his career that tell of a writer with close ties to antebellum culture and of a public moralist who inspired American abolitionists and helped give their movement cultural legitimacy. We also have been asked to look beyond a figure conditioned by his times and to recognize that his writings display a profound appreciation of certain democratic convictions and habits of mind that remain our own. And we have been invited to find in Emerson an anticipation of ideas and modes of speculation that have become fashionable under the provenance of contemporary continental theorists. In a large and still growing body of literature, especially provocative studies include Stanley Cavell, *The Senses of Walden* (San Francisco: North Point Press, 1981); Stanley Cavell, *In Quest of the Ordinary: Lines of Skepticism and Romanticism* (Chicago: University of Chicago Press, 1988); Richard Poirier, *The Renewal of Literature: Emersonian Reflections* (New York: Random House, 1987); Len Gougeon, *Virtue's Hero: Emerson, Antislavery, and Reform* (Athens: University of Georgia Press, 1990); and George Kateb, *Emerson and Self-Reliance* (Lanham, Md.: Rowman and Littlefield, 2002). No single or consistent image of Emerson has emerged from this ongoing revival. What has largely disappeared, however, is anything resembling the begrudging and qualified defense of Emerson offered by a previous generation of scholars generally considered to be his friendly interpreters.

6. Wolf Lepenies, *The Seduction of Culture in German History* (Princeton: Princeton University Press, 2006), 8.

Chapter One: "The word of the modern"

A shorter version of this essay first appeared in *Intellectual History Newsletter* 21 (1999): 11–23. This longer revised version has been strengthened by the suggestions of Casey Blake, Howard Brick, Robert Gross, Thomas Haskell, and Wilfred McClay.

1. "Democratic Vistas," in Walt Whitman, *Complete Poetry and Selected Prose*, ed. James E. Miller Jr. (Boston: Houghton Mifflin, 1959), 479.

2. "Democracy," *Galaxy*, December 1867, 919–33; "Personalism," *Galaxy*, May 1868, 540–47.

3. The entry for "culture" in the 1824 edition of Samuel Johnson's eighteenth-century *Dictionary of the English Language* lists the following items: "1. The art of cultivation; the act of tilling the ground; tillage. 2. The art of improvement and melioration." The entry in the 1893 edition of James A. H. Murray's *New English Dictionary* offers six definitions of the word, ranging from "the training, development, and refinement of the mind, tastes, and manners"

to "the training of the human body." The first entry reads: "Worship; reverential homage."

4. Matthew Arnold, *Culture and Anarchy* (1869) in *The Complete Prose Works of Matthew Arnold*, ed. R. H. Super (Ann Arbor: University of Michigan Press, 1960–77), 5:94; John H. Raleigh, *Matthew Arnold in American Culture* (Berkeley and Los Angeles: University of California Press, 1957), chap. 2.

5. Robert V. Bruce, *The Launching of Modern American Science, 1846–76* (New York: Alfred A. Knopf, 1987), chaps. 23–24; Ann Ruggles Gere, *Intimate Practices: Literacy and Cultural Work in U.S. Women's Clubs, 1880–1920* (Urbana: University of Illinois Press, 1997), chap. 5. A boom in magazines also set in during the immediate postwar years. American periodicals grew from a scant seven hundred in 1865 to somewhat over twelve thousand in 1870, and twice again that number by 1880. See Frank Luther Mott, *A History of American Magazines, 1865–85* (Cambridge: Harvard University Press, 1938), 3–24.

6. The most recent generation of historians has been prone to ignore or downplay the pervasiveness of the rhetoric of culture in the ranks of American university builders. But an older generation of post–World War II historians stressed at least one very important part of the linkage between that rhetoric and the pursuit of concrete institutional reform. The starting point in this version of the intellectual trajectory of the university movement is recognizing that a group of farsighted educators enlisted the ideal of "liberal culture" to brake the grip of religious sectarianism in American higher education. See the still-invaluable Richard Hofstadter and Walter P. Metzger, *The Development of Academic Freedom in the United States* (New York: Columbia University Press, 1955).

7. Charles William Eliot, *Educational Reform: Essays and Addresses* (New York: Century, 1898), 1–38.

8. Daniel Coit Gilman, *University Problems in the United States* (New York: Century, 1898), 1–45.

9. *Fourth Semi-Annual Report on Schools for Freedmen* (Washington, D.C., 1867), 4. Also see Alvord as quoted in Robert C. Morris, *Reading, Riting, and Reconstruction: Freedmen's Education in the South* (Chicago: University of Chicago Press, 1976), 166; and James D. Anderson, *The Education of Blacks in the South, 1860–1935* (Chapel Hill: University of North Carolina Press, 1988), chap. 7.

10. For more detailed accounts of the *Galaxy*, see Robert J. Scholnick, "*The Galaxy* and American Democratic Culture, 1866–78," *Journal of American Studies* 16 (April 1982): 69–80; and Mott, *History of American Magazines*, 361–81.

11. E. L. Youmans, ed., *The Culture Demanded by Modern Life: A Series of Addresses and Arguments on the Claims of Scientific Education*, with an introduction by E. L. Youmans (New York: D. Appleton, 1867), v–viii; E. L. Youmans, "Purpose and Plan of Our Enterprise," *Popular Science Monthly* 1 (1872): 113–25; "Mental Progress and Culture," *Popular Science Monthly* 28 (1885): 122–23. Also see William E. Leverette Jr., "E. L. Youmans's Crusade for Scientific Authority and Respectability," *American Quarterly* 17 (Spring 1965): 12–32.

12. James Freeman Clarke, *Self-Culture: Physical, Intellectual, Moral, and Spiritual* (Boston: Houghton Mifflin, 1880). Also see the discussion of Clarke in Daniel Walker Howe, *Making the American Self: Jonathan Edwards to Abraham Lincoln* (Cambridge: Harvard University Press, 1997), 256–60.

13. Edward Howland, as quoted in Arthur P. Young, "Reception of the 1876 Report on Public Libraries," *Journal of Library History* 12 (Winter 1977): 53.

14. See Sidney Ditzion, *Arsenals of Democratic Culture: A Social History of the American Public Library Movement* (Chicago: American Library Association, 1947); Dee Garrison, *Apostles of Culture: The Public Library in American Society, 1876–1920* (New York: Macmillan Information, 1979); Theodore Morrison, *Chautauqua: A Center for Education, Religion, and the Arts in America* (Chicago: University of Chicago Press, 1974); and Joseph Kett, *The Pursuit of Knowledge under Difficulties: From Self-Improvement to Adult Education in America, 1750–1900* (Stanford, Calif.: Stanford University Press, 1994), chaps. 5 and 6.

15. E. L. Youmans, "The Relation of Science to Culture," *Popular Science Monthly* 28 (1885): 557–59.

16. Charles William Eliot, "The New Definition of the Cultivated Man," in *Charles W. Eliot: The Man and His Beliefs*, ed. William Allan Neilson (New York: Harper and Brothers, 1926), 190, 204.

17. Bureau of the Census, *Historical Statistics of the United States: Colonial Times to 1957*, compiled from Series H 327–38 (Washington, D.C.: Bureau of the Census, 1961), 211–12; Mary Lee Talbot, "A School at Home: The Contribution of the Chautauqua Literary and Scientific Club to Women's Education Opportunities in the Gilded Age, 1874–1900" (Ph.D. diss., Columbia University, 1997).

18. Richard T. Ely, *The Labor Movement in America* (New York: T. Y. Crowell, 1886). Page numbers included in text refer to this edition.

19. Thomas Sewall Adams and Helen L. Summer, *Labor Problems in America: A Textbook* (New York: Macmillan, 1911), 226–27. Adams and Summer were among the first students of the labor movement to view the Knights of Labor as an example of "uplift unionism." On this account the Knights were destined for failure because their high hopes for reform were coupled with vague short-term objectives.

20. What later became the first chapter of Andrew Carnegie's *Gospel of Wealth and Other Timely Essays* (1900), his essay on "Wealth" in the *North American Review* first appeared in December 1889. For rich men, Carnegie proclaimed, the best means of benefiting the community was to place within its reach "the ladders upon which the aspiring can rise." These "ladders" included free libraries, parks, universities, art galleries and museums, and scientific observatories. In funding them, Carnegie wrote, "the man of wealth" serves as the "trustee and agent for his poorer brethren, bringing to their service his superior wisdom, experiences, and ability to administer, doing for them better than they would do for themselves." Andrew Carnegie, "The Gospel of Wealth," in *The Responsibilities of Wealth*, ed. Dwight F. Burlingame (Bloomington: University of Indiana Press, 1992), 10–18.

21. It is worth noting that *Labor Movement in America* appeared at a time when many liberal social critics and reformers viewed active labor organizations

as a threat to the ideal of "self-culture" as well as to social stability. So it is not particularly surprising that early reviewers of the book greeted it with a mix of disbelief and outrage. While Ely's understanding of culture as an inclusive ideal was in harmony with theirs, he had extended it to justify developments they considered dangerous.

22. When the Knights of Labor emerged during the mid-1870s, its initial "Declaration of Principles" (1874) proclaimed that better wages and more equitable sharing of wealth would give American workers "more time for employment of their faculties for the greater gain of their mental and moral growth." George E. McNeil, ed., *The Labor Movement: The Problem of Today* (Boston, 1887), 485. On "worker-intellectuals," see Leon Fink, *In Search of the Working Class: Essays in American Labor History and Political Culture* (Urbana: University of Illinois Press, 1994).

23. Francis G. Couvares, *The Remaking of Pittsburgh: Class and Culture in an Industrializing City, 1877–1919* (Albany: State University of New York Press, 1989), 59–60. Also see David Montgomery, "Labor in the Industrial Era," in *A History of the American Worker,* ed. Richard B Morris (Princeton: Princeton University Press, 1983), 79–113. Montgomery argues that workers' sense of social class was forged as much by their awareness of the contempt in which they were held by their "betters" as by economic deprivation. Workers in textile towns responded by creating reading rooms, gymnasiums, and debating clubs, where drinking, gambling, and profanity were strictly forbidden.

24. W. E. B. DuBois, *The Souls of Black Folk,* ed. with an introduction by Henry Louis Gates Jr. (New York: Bantam Books, 1989). Page numbers in text refer to this edition.

25. W. E. B. DuBois, "The Conservation of Races" (1897) in W. E. B. DuBois, *The Souls of Black Folk,* ed. David W. Blight and Robert Gooding-Williams (Boston: Bedford Books, 1997), 233–35.

26. Ibid.

27. As David Levering Lewis has pointed out in *W. E. B. DuBois: Biography of a Race, 1869–1919* (New York: Henry Holt, 1993), 289–90, DuBois's famous phrase, taken literally, suggests roughly a million well-educated African Americans who had reached the full measure of the best type of high European culture. A more realistic estimation, Lewis observes, at best would have been the "Talented Hundredth." The 1900 U.S. census counted 8,833,944 Negroes, of whom approximately 90 percent lived in the South. Just over 2,000 black Americans held college degrees, while 21,000 were schoolteachers. Illiteracy among blacks was 44.5 percent. Among those troubled by DuBois's elitism are Cornel West, "Black Striving in a Twilight Civilization," in *The Future of the Race,* by Cornel West and Henry Louis Gates (New York: Random House, 1997), 93–112, and Lewis, *W. E. B. DuBois,* 285.

28. Robert B. Stepto, "The Quest of the Weary Traveler: W. E. B. DuBois's *The Soul of Black Folk,*" in *From Behind the Veil: Study of Afro-American Narrative,* by Robert B. Stepto (Urbana: University of Illinois Press, 1979), 93–112; Eric Sundquist, *To Wake Nations: Race in the Making of American Literature* (Cambridge: Harvard University Press, 1993), 457–67. Also see Paul Gilroy, *The Black*

Atlantic: Modernity and Double Consciousness (Cambridge: Harvard University Press, 1993), 111–45.

29. *Club Worker,* November 1, 1901, pp. 1–2. On the role of "culture" in the American women's clubs, see Gere, *Intimate Practices,* chap. 5. Faced with the need to choose a single word to describe the terms in which a majority of women's clubs described their various activities, writes Gere, "one could do much worse that *culture*" (178).

30. I borrow here from the rich account of American settlers' attitudes toward and involvement with immigrants in Mina Carson, *Settlement Folk: Social Thought and the American Settlement Movement, 1885–1930* (Chicago: University of Chicago Press, 1990), chaps. 2–6. Carson points out that, while the settlers' attitudes fell across a wide spectrum, in a period of rising nativism, perhaps their major contribution "to national dialogue on immigration was their insistence on viewing the immigrant as the *victim* as much as the *cause*" of America's social and economic troubles (102).

31. For a vivid account of daily life in Hull House during the 1890s, see Victoria Bissell Brown, *The Education of Jane Addams* (Philadelphia: University of Pennsylvania Press, 2004), chaps. 12 and 13.

32. The words in quotations are from Jane Addams, "The Subjective Necessity of Social Settlements" (1892), in *The Jane Addams Reader,* ed. Jean Bethke Elshtain (New York: Basic Books, 2002), 16–18. In this classic essay, Addams also commented that with a thousand people coming and going in an average week, Hull House from the outside appeared to be, in her apt description, "a cumbersome plant of manifold industries" (26).

33. Neil Harris, *Cultural Excursions: Marketing Appetites and Cultural Tastes in Modern America* (Chicago: University of Chicago Press, 1990), 12–28. More recently Joseph Kett has argued that most American champions of culture continued to emphasize popular distribution and participation to the end of the 1880s. See Kett, *Pursuit of Knowledge under Difficulty,* 178.

34. More work can be done along these lines in accounting for the dramatic growth of new cultural professions in American life. For example, many of the institutions and practices that remain characteristic of American musical life were established during the last decades of the nineteenth century. These certainly included the symphony orchestras and opera houses that Levine discusses in *Highbrow/Lowbrow.* But they also included secondary-school bands and choruses, teacher-training programs for those who led them, and private vocal and instrumental studios. As a result music and music training formed a rapidly expanding job sector in the American economy. By 1900 they had grown to include 8 percent of all professional workers in the country. See Ralph P. Locke and Cryilla Barr, "Patronage—and Women—in America's Musical Life," in *Cultivating Music in America: Women Patrons and Activists Since 1860* (Berkeley and Los Angeles: University of California Press, 1997), chap. 1. It also is worth noting that several settlement houses, including Hull House, started their own music schools in the 1890s. And after the turn of the century, Addams's strong advocacy of the performing arts reflected a settlement trend. See Carson, *Settlement Folk,* 115–17.

35. David Robinson, *Apostle of Culture: Emerson as Preacher and Lecturer* (Philadelphia: University of Pennsylvania Press, 1987), provides a careful account of how central the Unitarian ideal of self-culture was to Emerson's early career as a public speaker. Also see Howe, *Making the American Self,* for a wide-ranging account of how the language of self-culture figured centrally in ideas Americans had concerning the proper construction of the self in the eighteenth and first half of the nineteenth centuries.

36. Hugh Hawkins, *Between Harvard and America: The Educational Leadership of Charles W. Eliot* (Oxford: Oxford University Press 1972).

37. Andrew Reiser, *The Chautauqua Movement: Protestants, Progressives, and the Culture of Modern Liberalism* (New York: Columbia University Press, 2003) takes a step in the direction I recommend here. Reiser argues that, by the 1880s, Chautauqua had evolved into the foremost institutional expression of the American self-culture impulse. Not surprisingly, his close inspection of its history also reveals "self-culture to be a hotly contested practice with political implications, a seemingly stable concept given new meanings as it buffeted the winds of industrialization, urbanization and state formation" (4).

Chapter Two: "Our national glory"

A somewhat longer version of this chapter appeared in Charles Capper and Conrad E. Wright, eds., *Transient and Permanent: The Transcendentalist Movement and Its Context* (Boston: Massachusetts Historians Society Publications, 1999), 459–526. Charles Capper, Geoffrey Harpham, and Teresa Toulouse provided helpful critical readings of that earlier piece.

1. The last seventeen years of Emerson's life occupy little more than twenty-one pages in the most recent, 671-page biography by Robert D. Richardson, *Emerson: The Mind on Fire* (Berkeley and Los Angeles: University of California, 1995).

2. J. A. Bellows, "Mr. Emerson's New Book," *Liberal Christian* 31 (January 22, 1876): 3–4. (The *Liberal Christian* [1845–77] was a Unitarian weekly published in New York.) As with Shakespeare in nineteenth-century America, the late Emerson was so familiar he sometimes became an object of parody, perhaps most famously in a speech Mark Twain delivered at a December 17, 1877, dinner in Boston given by the publishers of the *Atlantic Monthly* to commemorate John Greenleaf Whittier's seventieth birthday. Twain's speech—a literary burlesque in which Emerson, Holmes, and Longfellow were portrayed as seedy confidence men preying on a naïve California miner—attracted national attention. That most Boston newspapers who reported the speech presented it sympathetically as an amusing satire suggests the aging Emerson was not held in unthinking reverence in his home state. More important, the newspaper controversy surrounding the speech shows that talk about Emerson at times was popular entertainment during the 1870s. See Henry Nash Smith, *Mark Twain: The Development of a Writer* (Cambridge: Harvard University Press, 1962).

3. Franklin Sanborn, "The Portraits of Emerson," in *Transcendental and Literary New England,* ed. Kenneth Walter Cameron (Hartford, Conn.:

Transcendental Books, 1975), 184; Lowell, as quoted in Clarence Gohdes, ed., *Uncollected Lectures of Ralph Waldo Emerson* (New York: W. E. Ridge, 1932), vi. Emerson also had a substantial transatlantic reputation that reinforced his standing at home. See William J. Sowder, *Emerson's Impact on the British Isles and Canada* (Charlottesville: University of Virginia Press, 1966).

4. A more definitive assessment of Emerson's late essays and lectures awaits not only the completion of the new edition of Emerson's *Collected Works* but also a comprehensive secondary bibliography that includes all newspaper and magazine accounts of Emerson's lectures. Although missing important items, Robert E. Burkholder and Joel Myerson, *Emerson: An Annotated Secondary Bibliography* (Pittsburgh: University of Pittsburgh Press, 1982) provides the most up-to-date general inventory. My account of Emerson's career between 1865 and 1882 draws from the still invaluable Ralph Rusk, *The Life of Ralph Waldo Emerson* (New York: Columbia University Press, 1949) and John McAleer, *Ralph Waldo Emerson: Days of Encounter* (Boston: Little, Brown, 1984).

5. Anon., "Ralph Waldo Emerson," *Boston Daily Advertiser,* April 22, 1882, cols. 2–3; anon., "Ralph Waldo Emerson," *Chicago Tribune,* April 30, 1882, p. 4, cols. 6–7; anon., "Death of Emerson," *San Francisco Daily Chronicle,* April 28, 1882, 20; anon., "Ralph Waldo Emerson," *Charleston Daily News and Courier,* April 29, 1882, 22. For an extended review of Emerson's obituaries, see H. L. Kleinfield, "The Structure of Emerson's Death," *Bulletin of the New York Public Library* 65 (1961): 47–64.

6. William Dean Howells, *Literary Friends and Acquaintances* (1900), ed. D. F. Hiatt and E. H. Candy (Bloomington: Indiana University Press, 1968), 57. More recent studies of Emerson's antebellum reputation include my *Sublime Thoughts/Penny Wisdom: Situating Emerson and Thoreau in the American Market* (Baltimore: Johns Hopkins University Press, 1995), chaps. 7–8; Mary Kupiec Cayton, "The Making of an American Prophet: Emerson, His Audiences, and the Rise of the Culture Industry in Nineteenth-Century America," *American Historical Review* 92 (June 1987): 597–620; and Len Gougeon, *Virtue's Hero: Emerson, Antislavery, and Reform* (Athens: University of Georgia Press, 1990).

7. Franklin Sanborn, "Harvard's Treatment of Emerson," in *Transcendental and Literary New England,* ed Kenneth Walter Cameron (Hartford, Conn.: Transcendental Books, 1975), 351–52.

8. The following abbreviations are cited parenthetically in the text to refer to various editions of Emerson's writings: *JMN: The Journals and Miscellaneous Notebooks of Ralph Waldo Emerson,* ed. William H. Gilman and J. E. Parsons, 16 vols. (Cambridge: Belknap Press of Harvard University Press, 1960–82); *L: The Letters of Ralph Waldo Emerson,* ed. Ralph L. Rusk (vols. 1–6) and Eleanor Tilton (vols. 7–8) (New York: Columbia University Press, 1939–); *UL: Uncollected Lectures of Ralph Waldo Emerson,* ed. Clarence Gohdes (New York: W. E. Rudge, 1932); and *W: The Complete Works of Ralph Waldo Emerson* (Centenary Edition), ed. Edward Waldo Emerson, 12 vols. (Boston: Houghton Mifflin, 1903–4).

9. In a letter of November 25, 1868, for example, Emerson remarked that he had asked the leading Boston newspapers in advance of a new round of lectures not to report on him and that, for the most part, they obliged (*L* 6:45). Emerson's efforts to keep himself "safe from reporters" also reflected his desire to provide fresh material for his lecture audiences. In November 1865, looking forward to a new lecture tour in several midwestern states, Emerson told a correspondent that he was reluctant to lecture in Brooklyn and New York for fear that future audiences in the Midwest might see accounts of early versions of his lectures in the national edition of the *New York Tribune* (*L* 5:436).

10. It is worth noting that while a growing number of his contemporaries were attempting to become self-supporting writers, Emerson was well protected by money and social position from the full force of the nineteenth-century literary marketplace to shape his life and determine how would represent himself in his writings. By the late 1860s he was a wealthy man by contemporary standards. His income from investments and lectures not only provided him with financial freedom but also allowed him to pay printing and composition costs and retain copyright of all his authorized publications.

11. It is of course no less true that Emerson's growing national reputation as America's leading poet/philosopher helped confer new luster on Field's publishing house and magazines, especially the *Atlantic Monthly*. On Fields, see W. S. Tryon, *Parnassus Corner: A Life of James T. Fields* (Boston: Houghton Mifflin 1963); Richard H. Broadhead, *The School of Hawthorne* (New York: Oxford University Press, 1986); and Ellery Sedgwick, *The Atlantic Monthly, 1857–1909: Yankee Humanism at High Tide and Ebb* (Amherst: University of Massachusetts Press, 1994), chap. 3. Fields's efforts on Emerson's behalf would be continued by the several firms that succeeded Ticknor and Fields as Emerson's publisher during the last three decades of the nineteenth century: Fields, Osgood, and Company; James R. Osgood; and, after Henry Houghton bought out the failing Osgood, Houghton Mifflin Company.

12. *Lorain County News* (Oberlin, Ohio), January 17, 1866, as quoted in *L* 5:449n22; Fields, as quoted in Carlos Baker, *Emerson among the Eccentrics: A Group Portrait* (New York: Viking, 1996), 457.

13. Emerson continued to be stigmatized with the label "infidel" in the postwar years. A few weeks after he read "Social Aims" on the evening before commencement exercises at Ripley Female College (later Green Mountain Junior College), an anonymous letter in the July 27, 1865, *Christian Advocate and Journal* (New York) protested Emerson's presence by asking rhetorically, "Will not our children learn infidelity fast enough without being taught it at school by the high priest of infidelity?"

14. "Character" appeared anonymously in the *North American Review*, then under the editorship of Charles Eliot Norton and James Russell Lowell and owned by James Fields.

15. David M. Robinson, *Emerson and the Conduct of Life: Pragmatism and Ethical Purpose in the Later Work* (New York: Cambridge University Press, 1993). While my understanding of the late Emerson is much indebted to Robinson's

important study, I think (for reasons discussed later in this paper) he tends to overdraw the "oppositional" attitudes of the late Emerson.

16. Holmes, as quoted in *L* 6:78n112, wrote to Emerson after receiving gift copies of the first two volumes of his *Prose Works,* published by Fields, Osgood and Company in Boston on October 27, 1869.

17. Bret Harte, review of *Society and Solitude,* in *Overland Monthly* (October 1870): 386–87. (The *Overland Monthly* [1868–1923], published in San Francisco, was California's leading literary magazine during the last decades of the nineteenth century; its circulation was ten thousand at the time of Harte's review.) Anon., "Emerson's Letters and Social Aims," *Saturday Review* 41, February, 26, 1876, 275–76.

18. Henry James, *Hawthorne* (New York: Harper & Brothers, 1880), 80–84. Of Emerson's central ideas, James wrote, "Emerson expressed, before all things . . . the value and importance of the individual, the duty of making the most of one's self, and living by one's personal light, and carrying out one's own disposition."

19. For more extended discussions of Emerson's better-known antebellum essays along these lines, see my *Sublime Thoughts/Penny Wisdom,* chaps. 1 and 4; and Robinson, *Emerson and the Conduct of Life.*

20. Richard Poirier, *The Renewal of Literature: Emersonian Reflections* (New York: Random House, 1987), 13–19, 131–32.

21. Ralph Waldo Emerson, "Wealth," in *Conduct of Life* (1860), in *Selected Writings of Ralph Waldo Emerson,* ed. Brooks Atkinson (New York: Modern Library, 1940), 705, 700–701, 699. In 1875 James R. Osgood arranged for separate republication of "Wealth" in its new and relatively less expensive Vest Pocket series. In 1876 *Conduct of Life* was reprinted as volume 6 of the Little Classics Edition of Emerson's extant works.

22. Poirier, *Renewal of Literature,* 16.

23. Focusing mostly on midwestern newspaper accounts of early lecture versions of "Success," Cayton, "Making of an American Prophet," has argued persuasively that during the 1850s Emerson's stature grew because he was misread as a proponent rather than as a critic of the American success myth. It would be interesting to know if the same process repeated itself during Emerson's last great lecture tours of the Midwest.

24. Robinson, *Emerson and the Conduct of Life,* 162; Holmes, as quoted in Baker, *Emerson among the Eccentrics,* 472. Howells would later remark that Emerson simply was not taken seriously before the Civil War. "It would be hard to persuade people now," he wrote in 1900, "that Emerson once represented to the popular mind all that was most hopelessly impossible, and that in a certain sort, he was a national joke, the type of the incomprehensible, the byword of a poor paragraph." See Howells, *Literary Friends,* 56.

25. Hart, review of *Society and Solitude, Overland Monthly* 5 (October 1870): 387.

26. Charles W. Eliot, "Emerson," in *Charles W. Eliot: The Man and His Beliefs,* ed. William Allan Neilson (New York: Harper & Brothers, 1924). This essay was first presented as a lecture in Boston's Symphony Hall; it first appeared in print

as "Emerson as Seer" in the *Atlantic Monthly,* June 1903, 844–55, and was later reprinted in Eliot's *American Leaders* (1906).

27. James Elliot Cabot, *A Memoir of Ralph Waldo Emerson* (Boston: Houghton Mifflin, 1887), 625–26; George Santayana, "Emerson," in *Interpretations of Poetry and Religion* (1900), in *Selected Critical Writings of George Santayana,* ed. Norman Henfrey (London: Cambridge University Press, 1968), 117–27. In standard modern accounts of the emergence of the American university during the last decades of the nineteenth century, Emerson has been assigned the role of active and influential reformer; see, for example, Burton Bledstein, *The Culture of Professionalism: The Middle Class in the Development of Higher Education in America* (New York: W. W. Norton, 1976), 259–68.

28. Ralph Waldo Emerson, "Historic Notes of Life and Letters in New England," in *The American Transcendentalists: Their Prose and Poetry,* ed. Perry Miller (Garden City, N.J.: Doubleday Anchor, 1957), 5.

29. Emerson, as quoted in Cabot, *Memoir of Ralph Waldo Emerson* 2:789. Also see the better-known 1845 journal entry in which Emerson hailed the American continent as an "asylum of all nations," which drew "the energy of Irish, Germans, Swedes, Poles, and Cossacks, and all the European tribes—of the Africans and the Polynesians," creating in the process a "new race" as "vigorous as the new Europe which came out of the smelting pot of the Dark Ages" (*JMN* 9:299–300). In commenting on this passage, David Hollinger has grouped Emerson with Crevecoeur and Melville as American thinkers whose national ideal is not quite pluralist because they did not explicitly envision a series of enduring groups—nor were they unambiguously cosmopolitan—but instead emphasized "the diversity not of the final product, but only of the materials going into it." After the Civil War, the Emerson we encounter at the outset of the "Progress of Culture" might be seen as anticipating the more full-blown cosmopolitanism of figures such as Randolph Bourne. See David Hollinger, *Postethnic America: Beyond Multiculturalism* (New York: Basic Books, 1995), 86–87; and Lawrence W. Levine, *The Opening of the American Mind: Canons, Culture, and History* (Boston: Beacon Press, 1996), 105, 107, 110.

30. Emerson was also one of the *Atlantic*'s principal spokesman for the cause of rapid emancipation, after abandoning his disunionist position when the war began. On Emerson's career during the Civil War, see Gougeon, *Virtue's Hero,* chap. 8. Abolitionists saw the formation of black regiments and the regular use of black soldiers as important elements of the struggle to establish the equality of free blacks. On March, 20, 1862, Emerson spoke to a Boston fund-raising gathering for the soon-to-be-famous Massachusetts Fifty-fourth, a black regiment commanded by Robert Gould Shaw. After its ill-fated assault on Fort Wagner in South Carolina, Emerson also published the poem "Voluntaries" in the October 1863 *Atlantic* as a memorial to the regiment.

31. Eliot, "Emerson," 521–22, 526. My account of Eliot borrows from Hugh Hawkins, *Between Harvard and America: The Educational Leadership of Charles W. Eliot* (New York: Oxford University Press, 1972) and Kim Townsend, *Manhood at Harvard: William James and Others* (New York: W. W. Norton, 1996), chap. 2.

32. Hugh Hawkins has told us that during the first dozen years of his presidency Eliot attended chiefly to Harvard's internal organization and finances, and it was precisely in these areas that he enlisted Emerson's support. As a member of the Overseers Visiting Committee, for example, Emerson inspected classes in various departments. He also reviewed and voted on faculty appointments and solicited funds from his classmates. It might also be said that what makes the first phase of the Emerson-Eliot connection an important episode in postbellum cultural history—rather than simply another instance of the slippery ways in which an intellectual relationship based on "influence" usually works—is the fact that Eliot briefly seized on Emerson (along with Charles Eliot Norton and Henry Adams) as a figure of new cultural possibility: the academic intellectual. In the summer of 1870, he appointed him to the Harvard faculty as lecturer in philosophy and repeated it during the winter of 1870–71 as lecturer on natural history. Emerson's performance in Eliot's short-lived experiment in "University Lectures" was, in the view of both men, something of a failure. But it also signaled the beginning of Eliot's successful effort to transform Harvard into a graduate research university.

33. Eliot's selections from Emerson's work for volume 5 of the Harvard Classics included eighteen essays, all but one of which were published before 1844, and the entirety of *English Traits*. Selections from Benjamin Franklin, John Woolman, and William Penn appeared in volume 1; the entirety of Richard Henry Dana's *Twelve Years Before the Mast* was in volume 23; and single essays by Channing, Poe, Thoreau, and Lowell appeared in volume 28, *Essays English and American*.

34. James, *Hawthorne*, 82. "Mr. Emerson at Harvard," *Every Saturday*, September 21, 1867, 38. *Every Saturday* (1867–74) was an eclectic weekly published in Boston by Ticknor and Fields, Emerson's publisher at the time.

Chapter Three: "More than Luther of these modern days"

An earlier and shorter version of this chapter was prepared at the invitation of David Throsby and Michael Hutter for presentation at a Team Residency on "Value and Valuation in the Arts and Culture" held at the Rockefeller Study and Conference Center, Villa Serbelloni, Bellagio, Italy, February 11–19, 2004. That shorter version is available in David Throsby and Michael Hutter, eds., *Beyond Price: Value in Culture, Economics, and the Arts* (Cambridge: Cambridge University Press, 2007). Frederick Bradley, Benjamin Reiss, and Teresa Toulouse offered helpful criticism of subsequent expanded drafts of this piece.

1. "Address of William James," in *The Centenary of the Birth of Ralph Waldo Emerson: as Observed in Concord May 25 1903, under the Direction of the Social Circle in Concord* (Cambridge: Riverside Press, 1903), 67.

2. See Charles Mitchell, *Individualism and Its Discontents: Appropriations of Emerson, 1880–1950* (Amherst: University of Massachusetts Press, 1997), chap. 1, for a recent restatement of this story.

3. "Address of T. W. Higginson," in *The Centenary of the Birth of Ralph Waldo Emerson*, 58–66.

4. *Boston Daily Advertiser,* May 23, 1903, p. 1. On Higginson's career, see Tilden G. Eldstein, *Strange Enthusiasm: A Life of Thomas Wentworth Higginson* (New Haven: Yale University Press, 1968).

5. W. D. Howells, "Impressions of Emerson," *Harper's Weekly,* May 16, 1903; Charles W. Eliot, "Emerson," in *Charles W. Eliot: The Man and His Beliefs,* ed. William Allan Neilson (New York: Harper and Brothers, 1926); John Dewey, "Ralph Waldo Emerson," in *Characters and Events: Popular Essays in Social and Political Theory* (New York: H. Holt, 1929), 74–75.

6. J. A. Bellows, "Mr. Emerson's New Book," *Liberal Christian,* January, 22, 1876, 3–4 .

7. E. A. Poe, "An Appendix on Autographs," *Graham's Magazine* 20 (January 1842): 44–49.

8. On the construction of Emerson's reputation during the antebellum period, see my *Sublime Thoughts/Penny Wisdom: Situating Emerson and Thoreau in the American Market* (Baltimore: Johns Hopkins University Press, 1995), chaps. 4–5.

9. F. D. Huntington, "Ralph Waldo Emerson," *Sunday School Times* 24 (May 20, 1882): 307–8. The *Sunday School Times* was the pivotal American Sunday school paper. In the 1870s Philadelphia merchant John Wanamaker purchased and printed the paper on his own presses until the subscription rate exceeded five hundred thousand. See William Leach, *Land of Desire: Merchants, Power, and the Rise of a New American Culture* (New York: Vintage Books, 1994), 201.

10. Julia Ward Howe, "Ralph Waldo Emerson," *Woman's Journal,* May 6, 1882, 140.

11. Anon., "Emerson," *New-York Daily Tribune,* April 28, 1882, p. 4, col. 2; anon., "Death of Emerson," *San Francisco Daily Chronicle,* April 28, 1882; Lafcadio Hearn, Emerson's obituary, *New Orleans Times Democrat,* April 28, 1882.

12. Anon., "Ralph Waldo Emerson," *Chicago Tribune,* April 29, 1882, p. 4; anon., "Emerson," *Boston Commonwealth,* May 6, 1882, p. 2, col. 4; anon., "Ralph Waldo Emerson," *Charleston Daily News and Courier,* April 29, 1882, p. 22.

13. John Albee, "Reminiscences of an Emersonian," *New-York Daily Tribune,* April 28, 1882, p.1, col. 6; p. 2, col. 3. It is worth noting that the death of Emerson any time after 1870 almost certainly would have prompted a similar nationwide notice. But because it came so soon after the death of two other Anglo-American cultural legends, Longfellow (on March 24) and Darwin (on April 19), his death carried added weight in the eyes of many observers. "This will be known as the age of Darwin and Emerson," proclaimed Cyrus Bartol, "the new prophet of the animal kingdom and the unfrocked priest of the human mind." Bartol, "Emerson as an Observer," *New-York Daily Tribune,* April 28, 1882, p. 2, col. 5. The editor of the *Unitarian Review* observed that the deaths of Longfellow and Emerson had called upon Americans to give up two of their "greatest and best." Whereas Longfellow had "clothed the bareness of our commonplace lives" with "poetic vision," Emerson's chief service to "an unbelieving and materialistic age" had been to assume the role of "foremost representative of what is highest and best in our American civilization." Anon., "Longfellow and Emerson," *Unitarian Review* 17 (May 7, 1882): 458–60.

14. See Robert E. Burkholder and Joel Myerson, *Ralph Waldo Emerson: An Annotated Secondary Bibliography* (Pittsburgh: University of Pittsburgh Press, 1982) for an invaluable detailed inventory of writings about Emerson during this period.

15. See Len Gougeon, *Virtue's Hero: Emerson, Antislavery, and Reform* (Athens: University of Georgia Press), chap. 1.

16. On the "cheap books" phenomenon, see Raymond Shove, *Cheap Book Production in the United States, 1870– 1891* (Urbana: University of Illinois Library, 1937); and John Tebbel, *A History of Book Production in the United States,* vol. 2, *The Expansion of the Industry, 1865–1919* (New York: R. R. Bowker, 1972), 486–507.

17. Matthew Schneirov, *The Dream of a New Social Order: Popular Magazines in America, 1893–1914* (New York: Columbia University Press, 1994). Also see Richard Ohmann, *Selling Culture: Magazines, Markets, and Class at the Turn of the Century* (New York: Verso, 1996).

18. Paul Bourget, "A Farewell to the White City," *Cosmopolitan*, November 1893, 135–38.

19. See Joel Myerson's invaluable *Ralph Waldo Emerson: A Descriptive Bibliography* (Pittsburgh: University of Pittsburgh Press, 1982) for a detailed inventory.

20. As quoted in Shove, *Cheap Book Production in the United States*, 41.

21. On the central role played by Houghton Mifflin in establishing the first version of the American literary canon, see Richard H. Broadhead, *The School of Hawthorne* (New York: Oxford University Press, 1986).

22. My account of the early history of American literature follows Kermit Vanderbilt, *American Literature and the Academy: The Roots, Growth, and Maturity of a Profession* (Philadelphia: University of Pennsylvania Press, 1986), chaps. 7–9; Gerald Graff, *Professing Literature: An Institutional History* (Chicago: University of Chicago Press, 1987), chaps. 4–7; and Nina Baym, "Early Histories of American Literature: A Chapter in the Institution of New England," *American Literary History* 1 (Fall 1989): 459–88.

23. See Baym, "Early Histories of American Literature."

24. On the slow progress of "American literature" within the new American university system, see Lawrence W. Levine, *The Opening of the American Mind: Canons, Culture, and History* (Boston: Beacon Press,1996), chap. 4.

25. See James Woodress, ed., *Dissertations in American Literature, 1891– 1955, with Supplement, 1956–61* (Durham, N.C.: Duke University Press, 1962).

26. Broadhead, *School of Hawthorne*, 60.

27. George Willis Cooke, "The Emerson Centennial," *New England Magazine* 28 (May 1903): 255.

Chapter Four: The Academic Public Sphere

I undertook this effort at the invitation of Helmbrecht Brening, then director of the Bavarian American Academy, for presentation at a BAA conference on "Cultures of Economy— Economies of Culture," Munich, June 20–22, 2002.

A shorter version of the piece can be found in Jackson Lears and Jens Van Scherpenberg, eds., *Cultures of Economy—Economies of Culture*, Publications of the Bavarian American Academy vol. 4 (Heidelberg, 2004), 147–60. Stefan Collini, Thomas Bender, Geoffrey Harpham, Thomas Haskell, Jackson Lears, and Dorothy Ross provided invaluable comments on earlier drafts of this piece.

1. Founded in 1857, the National Education Association had suffered lean years until the 1880s, when improved transportation made it easier for its members to attend national meetings. Presidents of several American universities, including Gilman and Charles W. Eliot of Harvard, spoke at NEA meetings in that decade, and their interest in the organization lent it added prestige. The association's membership fluctuated according to the site of its annual meeting. With an average membership of 6,169 from 1884 to 1900, it seems likely that at least 6,000 members were on hand in Chicago in 1893. See Theodore Sizer, *Secondary Schools at the Turn of the Century* (New Haven: Yale University Press, 1964), 74–75.

2. *Proceedings of the International Congress on Education of the World's Columbian Exposition, Report of the Committee of Arrangements, National Education Association, on the International Congress of Education*, by Honorable William T. Harris (New York, 1895).

3. The year before his Chicago address, Gilman observed that while there remained a consensus on the importance of "liberal education," there was now disagreement regarding the "agencies by which it may served." The "old fashioned conception of liberal education," he argued, was being abandoned and replaced by one that included education in science and technology. See Daniel C. Gilman, "Is It Worth While to Uphold Any Longer the Idea of Liberal Education?" *Educational Review* 2 (February 1892): 105–13.

4. "Higher Education in America," in *University Problems in the United States*, by Daniel Coit Gilman (New York: Century, 1898), 289–312. The full text of Gilman's address appeared originally in Harris's widely circulated edition of the conference *Proceedings*, 97–104.

5. Broadly speaking, two rather different stories have been told about the university's efforts to "professionalize" American cultural and intellectual life. The first, dating back to Thorstein Veblen, tells a story of betrayal: disinterested inquiry ultimately displaced by a self-seeking tactic designed to enhance occupational status. See Burton Bledstein, *The Culture of Professionalism: The Middle Class and the Development of Higher Education in America* (New York: W. W. Norton, 1978). The other tells of hard-won success: the emergence of a new class of professional academics who launched specialized disciplinary associations and was housed in universities and colleges that provided a safe haven for its essentially scholarly activities. See Thomas L. Haskell, *The Emergence of Professional Social Science: The American Social Science Association and the Nineteenth-Century Crisis of Authority* (Urbana: University of Illinois Press, 1977). The onset of industrialization also played a central yet again contrasting role in both narratives, that of a corrupting taskmaster in the first and a revolutionary force interpreted and tamed in the second.

6. As Gerald Graff has put it, it was one thing to professionalize already existing careers in business, law, and medicine and another to professionalize new careers in the social sciences and literary studies. And while many patterns carried over from one sphere to the other, there was no perfectly homologous relationship between the two. Gerald Graff, *Professing Literature: An Institutional History* (Chicago: University of Chicago Press, 1987), 64.

7. Jürgen Habermas, *The Structural Transformation of the Public Sphere: An Inquiry into a Category of Bourgeois Society,* trans. Thomas Burger (1962; reprint, Cambridge, Mass: MIT Press, 1989). Also see Stefan Collini, "Before Another Tribunal: The Idea of the 'Non-Specialist Public,'" in *English Pasts: Essays in History and Culture* (Oxford: Oxford University Press, 1999), 318–21. Where Collini speaks of "the academic public sphere" as a late-twentieth-century development, I argue here that the emergence of the American university in fact represented the first instance of the cultural phenomenon he sketches in this provocative essay. Also see Collini's "Their Title to Be Heard: Professionalization and Its Discontents," in *Public Moralists: Political Thought and Intellectual Life in Britain* (Oxford: Oxford University Press, 1991), 199–250. Collini makes several points about the role of universities in the professionalization of late-nineteenth-century British intellectual life that I think hold true for American universities in this period, and I repeat some of them here.

8. See Joseph Kett, *The Pursuit of Knowledge under Difficulties: From Self-Improvement to Adult Education in America, 1750–1950* (Stanford, Calif.: Stanford University Press, 1994), 184–85.

9. My account of the expansion and institutional reorganization of American higher education in this section draws from Lawrence Veysey, *The Emergence of the American University* (Chicago: University of Chicago Press, 1965) and essays in Alexandra Oleson and John Voss, eds., *The Organization of Knowledge in Modern America, 1860–1920* (Baltimore: Johns Hopkins University Press, 1979).

10. Eliot, as quoted in Richard Hofstadter and Walter P. Metzger, *The Development of Academic Freedom in the United States* (New York: Columbia University Press, 1955), 302.

11. In his two most popular lectures in the 1890s—"On a Certain Blindness in Human Beings" and "What Makes a Life Significant"—James projected himself, sometimes self-mockingly, as "your college professor" and a member of "the highly educated classes (so-called)." See William James, *Talks to Teachers of Psychology* (1899) (Cambridge: Harvard University Press, 1983), 163, 156. A recurring theme in several talks on what James called "the use of college training" was his effort to define its "preeminent spiritual" purpose as opposed to training for a trade or a profession. See "The True Harvard" (1903) and "The Social Value of the College Bred" (1907) in William James, *Essays, Comments, and Reviews* (Cambridge: Harvard University Press, 1987), 106, 75.

12. As William James remarked in 1903, America was "a nation rapidly drifting towards a state of things in which no man of science or letters will be accounted respectable unless some kind of badge or diploma is stamped upon him." James condemned this development as a "decidedly grotesque tendency."

But the steps he recommended for keeping it in check did not question the notion that a purely academic career, with its own criteria for appointment and advancement, represented a new and reputable professional vocation. "The Ph.D. Octopus," in *Memories and Studies,* by William James (New York: Longmans, Green, 1911), 334.

13. As quoted in Thomas L. Haskell, *The Emergence of Professional Social Science,* 184n38.

14. My account of Ely and the founding of the AEA draws from Haskell, *Emergence of Professional Social Science,* chap. 7; Benjamin D. Rader, *The Influence of Richard T. Ely in American Life* (Lexington: University of Kentucky Press, 1966); A. W. Coats, "The First Two Decades of the American Economic Association," *American Economic Review* 50, no. 4 (September 1960): 555–74; A. W. Coats, "The Educational Revolution and the Professionalization of Economics," in *Breaking the Academic Mold: Economists and Higher Learning in the Nineteenth Century,* ed. William J. Barber (Middletown, Conn.: Wesleyan University Press, 1988), 340–75; and William J. Barber, "Political Economy in the Flagship of Postgraduate Studies," in *Breaking the Academic Mold,* 203–24.

15. During late 1880s and early 1890s, Ely closely identified himself with the Social Gospel movement and campaigned to increase their numbers in the AEA. See Coats, "Educational Revolution," 358–360. Questions were also raised about the preference Ely showed to works by his Johns Hopkins students in the AEA Publication series.

16. Ely's reformist zeal probably had something to do with his leaving Johns Hopkins for the University of Wisconsin in 1890, after he failed to persuade Gilman to give him a tenured position and to fund additional positions in economics. Gilman was aware of a widespread negative view of Ely's competence among mainstream academic economists at the time. See Barber, "Political Economy," 217–24.

17. Patten, as quoted in Steven A. Sass, "An Uneasy Relationship: The Business Community and Academic Economists at the University of Pennsylvania," in *Breaking the Academic Mold,* 236.

18. Dunbar, as quoted in Byrd L. Jones, "A Quest for National Leadership: Economics at Harvard," in *Breaking the Academic Mold,* 113; Robert L. Church, "The Economists Study Society: Sociology at Harvard, 1891–1902," in *Social Sciences at Harvard, 1860–1920,* ed. Paul Buck (Cambridge: Harvard University Press, 1965), 24–27.

19. There was another important source of continuing disagreement within the community of American economists at this time: the emergence of a distinctive regional pattern of opinion regarding economic and social problems. The essays collected in *Breaking the Academic Mold* provide an invaluable overview. Professional training of economists provided by state universities of the middle and far West was conspicuously more service-oriented than that provided by private universities in the East. See Coats, "Professionalization of Economics," 363–64.

20. During the summer of 1896, while teaching at the University of Chicago, Ross publicly supported the presidential candidacy of William Jennings Bryan.

He also wrote a series of articles defending free coinage of silver for the *Chicago Record*. These articles, gathered together under the title *Honest Dollars*, were reprinted and widely circulated as a campaign pamphlet by the Democratic National Committee.

21. In her letter ordering Ross's dismissal, Mrs. Stanford told Jordan she found his views incendiary and dangerous, and with good reason. These were the closing lines of Ross's lecture as reported in the May 8 *San Francisco Call:* "And should worst come to worst, it would be better for us if we were to turn our guns on every vessel bringing Japanese and Chinese labor to our shores rather than to permit them to land."

22. My account of the Ross case draws from Orrin Leslie Elliot, *Stanford University: The First Thirty-Five Years* (Stanford, Calif.: Stanford University Press, 1937), 326–78; James C. Mohr, "Academic Turmoil and Public Opinion: The Ross Case at Stanford," *Pacific Historical Review* 39 (1970): 39–61; Mary E. Cookingham, "Political Economy in the Far West: The University of California and Stanford University," in *Breaking the Academic Mold*, 266–89; and Thomas L. Haskell, "Justifying Academic Freedom in the Era of Power/Knowledge," in *Objectivity Is Not Neutrality: Explanatory Schemes in History* (Baltimore: Johns Hopkins University Press, 1998), 174–233.

23. Haskell, "Justifying Academic Freedom," 185.

24. As with Ross, it is misleading to characterize Andrews simply as a "martyr" to the cause of academic freedom. Andrews resigned as president of Brown in July 1897, shortly after its corporation had instructed him to cease public presentation of what they took to be his controversial economic views. (Andrews had been a professor of political economy at Cornell before becoming Brown's president in 1889.) While the AEA (of which he was then a member) remained silent, the machinery of American publicity quickly seized on and fed the controversy that followed in the wake of Andrew's resignation. Newspapers in Boston, New York, and Chicago provided continuous coverage and commentary. By the end of the summer, the post office and telegraph also had helped to produce two petitions urging Brown's trustees to ask Andrews to withdraw his resignation: an alumni petition containing six hundred names, including graduates of every class since 1838, and a more general petition that bore seventy-six names from twenty-six colleges and universities, among which were those of eleven college or university presidents, including Gilman, Eliot, and Seth Low of Columbia. In the face of widespread public protest, Brown's trustees relented. Andrews agreed to return for a year and then left voluntarily for Nebraska. See Elizabeth Donnan, "A Nineteenth-Century Academic Cause Celebre," *New England Quarterly* (March 1952): 23–46.

25. It is worth noting that Ross's dismissal also exposed what Mary O. Furner has identified as "a fundamental strain" in the new social sciences professions. While every Stanford professor in the social sciences who could afford the gesture resigned in protest (thereby virtually expunging Stanford's departments of history and economics), Jordan quickly filled two vacancies in the history department by hiring newly minted Ph.D.'s from Harvard who accepted their appointments with encouragement from senior Harvard historians. The

"fundamental strain" here, as Furner puts it, was that while "uniform training and experience" were fostering common role definitions and cooperative approaches to opposing interests, "loyalty to different universities and competition for available positions" in choice locations also promoted disunity among new academic professionals. See Mary O. Furner, *Advocacy and Objectivity: A Crisis in the Professionalization of Social Science, 1865–1905* (Lexington: University of Kentucky Press, 1975), 251.

26. The Stanford University Archives contains clippings of some two thousand columns of newspaper articles on the Ross affair from all over the United States and Europe. The clippings may be found in the Stanford University Archives, *University Clippings,* Special Volume (November 14, 1900, to March 1, 1901) and volume 19 (March 1, 1901, to June 30, 1901). The Ross case also rekindled anti-Stanford sentiment in the local and national press. Doubtless the fact that Ross's opponent was a woman, as well as a wealthy capitalist, made her a particularly easy target in some circles.

27. My account of the history of literary studies in this section draws from Michael Warner, "Professionalization and the Rewards of Literature, 1875–1900," *Criticism* 17 (Winter 1985); Graff, *Professing Literature,* chaps. 4–7; Kermit Vanderbilt, *American Literature in the Academy: The Roots, Growth, and Maturity of a Profession* (Philadelphia: University of Pennsylvania Press, 1986); and Gerald Graff and Michael Warner, eds., *The Origins of Literary Studies in America* (New York: Routledge, 1989).

28. Elliot, as quoted in Warner, "Professionalization and the Rewards of Literature," 3.

29. Magill, as quoted in Graff, *Professing Literature,* 77.

30. *English in American Universities, by Professors in the English Departments of Twenty Representative Institutions,* ed., with introduction by William Morton Payne (Boston: D. C. Heath, 1895), 11.

31. *English in American Universities,* 45–48 .

32. Chief editor at Houghton Mifflin, and later editor of the *Atlantic Monthly,* Scudder conceived and produced the Riverside Literature series and thereby was primarily responsible for recreating the New England literary classics as texts for the schools. See Richard Broadhead, *The School of Hawthorne* (New York: Oxford University Press, 1986), 58–59.

33. Burt L. Dunmire's "The Development of American Literature Textbooks Used in the United States from 1870 to 1952" (Ph.D. diss., University of Pittsburgh, 1954) reports that before 1930 only two of sixty-six American Literature texts he examines were written by high school English teachers; from 1930 to 1952, one-third were so authored.

34. See Nina Baym, "Early Histories of American Literature: A Chapter in the Institution of New England," *American Literary History* 1 (Fall 1989): 459–88.

35. My account of the Committee of Ten follows Sizer, *Secondary Schools at the Turn of the Century.*

36. My account of the university extension movement in the 1880s and 1890s follows Kett, *Pursuit of Knowledge under Difficulties,* 183–89. It is worth noting that, during his years at Stanford, Edward Ross frequently gave "extension

lectures" in San Francisco and Oakland. His controversial May 8, 1900, remarks about "coolie" labor were made during an extension lecture at the Unitarian Church of Oakland

37. See Merle E. Curti, *The University of Wisconsin: A History* (Madison: University of Wisconsin Press, 1949).

38. Daniel Coit Gilman founded Johns Hopkins University Press in 1878.
Other university presidents later followed suit, beginning with William Rainey
Harper, who founded the University of Chicago Press in 1891. The University
of California and Columbia University both opened presses in 1893. Oxford
University Press also opened an office in New York to publish American editions of books originally published in England but soon developed an independent list of publications for the American market.

39. The volume James was working on at the time of his death, *Some Problems of Philosophy* (1911), was intended as both a textbook and a summation of
his philosophical ideas.

40. On Dewey's academic career in the 1880s and 1890s, see Neil Coughlan,
Young John Dewey: An Essay in American Intellectual History (Chicago: University of Chicago Press, 1975).

41. It is worth noting that when Ely returned to the United States in 1880
after completing his graduate training at the University of Heidelberg, he had
no immediate job prospects. So he began writing for newspapers and magazines, including the *New York Tribune* and the *Banker's Magazine*. After he was
appointed the sole professor of political economy at Johns Hopkins in 1881, Ely
briefly also held office as state tax commissioner. See Joseph Dorfman, *The
Economic Mind of American Civilization, Volume Three: 1865–1918* (New York:
Viking Press, 1949), 162.

42. Ethelbert D. Warfield, "The Expansion of Our Great Universities,"
McClure's Magazine 8 (August 1901): 24.

43. During 1893 and 1894, the *Educational Review*, then the most respected
journal of its kind in America, published several articles on the various educational exhibits and congresses at the Columbian Exposition. Among the more
interesting of these was George Santayana, "The Spirit and Ideas of Harvard,"
Educational Review 4 (April 1894): 313–25. Santayana observed that visitors
confronted with the motley array of items Harvard had chosen to put on display would carry away "the conviction that Harvard was scientific, that it was
complex, and that it was reserved."

44. Among the most interesting ventures in this arena was the idea for a "*Cosmopolitan* University." Promoted over many months during the late 1890s by the
magazine's founder and editor, John Brisbane Walker, *Cosmopolitan* announced
in August 1897 it would fund a correspondence school with a distinguished
advisory board and an assortment of leading university faculty. Students would
be allowed to attend free of charge. Some twenty-one thousand had applied for
admission by December 1899, before Walker abandoned the idea because his
financial resources were not adequate for the constantly expanding project.
See Matthew Schneirov, *The Dream of a New Social Order: Popular Magazines
in America, 1893–1914* (New York: Columbia University Press, 1994), 108–10.

45. See Steven J. Diner, *A City and Its Universities: Public Policy in Chicago, 1892–1919* (Chapel Hill: University of North Carolina Press, 1980).

46. Like Ely and James, during his academic career Wilson wrote in several different veins, producing a steady stream of newspaper and magazine articles as well as several textbooks that addressed various topics in both history and politics. And he too was in constant demand as a popular lecturer. See Henry Wilkinson Bragdon, *Woodrow Wilson: The Academic Years* (Cambridge: Harvard University Press, 1967); and W. Barksdale Maynard, *Woodrow Wilson: Princeton to Presidency* (New Haven: Yale University Press, 2008). On William James as a public moralist, see George Cotkin, *William James, Public Philosopher* (Baltimore: Johns Hopkins University Press, 1990.)

47. Thomas Bender, *Intellect and Public Life: Essays on the Social History of Academic Intellectuals in the United States* (Baltimore: Johns Hopkins University Press, 1993), 141–45.

Chapter Five: Race and Academic Culture in 1903

This inquiry was carried out at the invitation of my colleague Martyn P. Thompson, who organized the January 9–11, 2004, Conference for the Study of Political Thought Annual International Conference on the "Sciences of Politics." Cosponsored by the Murphy Institute at Tulane University, the conference commemorated the one hundredth anniversary of the founding of the APSA. A brief excerpt of this piece appeared originally in the *Tulanian* (Spring 2004): 26–33. This complete version has been strengthened by the suggestions of Frederick Bradley, Ted DeLaney, and Thomas Langston.

1. As Thomas Bender has pointed out, because this sequence of events reversed the pattern in the natural sciences, it suggests that the professionalization of the social sciences was, by comparison, more deeply embedded in late-nineteenth- and early-twentieth-century historical events. But one's answer to the question of which historical events provide the proper context for understanding the significance of the APSA's founding depends greatly on how one chooses to tell the story of the rise and spread of American academic culture. In the existing scholarly literature, the "social question" created by industrialization has served as the primary historical context for understanding the APSA's founding. The more obvious question I ask here—why did it happen in the Jim Crow South?—has inadvertently been ignored. See Thomas Bender, *Intellect and Public Life: Essays on the Social History of Academic Intellectuals in the United States* (Baltimore: Johns Hopkins University Press, 1993), ix–xvii.

2. My account of the "Twin Conventions" draws mostly from extensive coverage in daily editions of the New Orleans *Daily Picayune* and *Times-Democrat* published between December 28, 1903, and January 2, 1904; Charles H. Haskins, "Report of the Proceedings of the Nineteenth Annual Meeting of the American Historical Association," *Annual Report of the American Historical Association for 1903* (Washington, D.C.: GPO, 1904); and W. W. Willoughby, "The Organization of the American Political Science Association," *Proceedings*

of the American Political Science Association (Lancaster, Pa.: Wickersham Press, 1905), 5–17.

3. Edwin Alderman's role in the development of American academic culture has not been as carefully studied as it deserves to be. There are various reasons for this relative neglect, although two stand out if we restrict our focus to his years as president of the University of North Carolina (1897–1900) and Tulane University (1901–4). First, there is the meager record on the university movement in the South. Second, historians who have studied Alderman's early career treat him primarily as a promoter of popular education in the South, presenting his North Carolina and Tulane presidencies essentially as platforms that allowed him to pursue what he viewed as the more urgent work of modernizing public education at the elementary and secondary levels. But such an approach, while correctly emphasizing Alderman's intense interest in public education, greatly oversimplifies things. As this chapter should make clear, Alderman was at once a university president, a progressive educational reformer, and a nationally prominent spokesman for the New South and for sectional reunion, and he did not distinguish among these roles as sharply as modern historians do. Although dated in many respects, Dumas Malone, *Edwin A. Alderman: A Biography* (New York: Doubleday, Doran, 1940) remains a useful starting place. Also see Michael Dennis, *Lessons in Progress: State Universities and Progressivism in the New South, 1880–1920* (Urbana: University of Illinois Press, 2001), chap. 8.

4. On Rhodes, see David W. Blight, *Race and Reunion: The Civil War in American Memory* (Cambridge: Belknap Press of Harvard University Press, 2001), 357–59.

5. Edwin Anderson Alderman, *The Value of Southern Idealism: A Brief Address of Welcome to the American Historical Association and the American Economic Association on the evening of December 29, 1903* (New Orleans, 1903), 6–8.

6. In this respect, the Twin Conventions clearly also can be taken as another example of the emergence of an "academic public sphere," which I discussed in the previous chapter.

7. On the university movement in the South, see Dennis, *Lessons in Progress;* Dewey W. Grantham, *Southern Progressivism: The Reconciliation of Progress and Tradition* (Knoxville: University of Tennessee Press, 1983), chap. 8; and John Egerton, *Speak Now Against the Day: The Generation Before the Civil Rights Movement* (New York: Alfred A. Knopf, 1994), chap. 3.

8. Henry E. Bourne, "North Carolina Meeting of the American Historical Association," *American Historical Review* 35, no. 3 (April 1930): 481. Also see David D. Van Tassell, "The American Historical Association and the South, 1884–1913," *Journal of Southern History* 28 (August 1957): 465–82.

9. See Nicolas Patler, *Jim Crow and the Wilson and Administration* (Boulder: University of Colorado Press, 2004). It also is worth noting that Johns Hopkins University, now remembered as the flagship of the American university movement in the late nineteenth century, at the time was considered a southern institution and was the wellspring of many professors and administrators who pursued their careers at segregated southern universities.

10. *New Orleans Times-Democrat,* December 29, 1903. On the triumph of a new national culture of reunion, and its accommodation of southern racism, see Blight, *Racism and Reunion.* It is worth noting that the National Education Association was holding its annual meeting in Atlanta at the same time as the AHA and AEA met in New Orleans. Doubtless it also played itself out in part as a sectional reunion event.

11. Alderman, "Value of Southern Idealism," 10–11.

12. *New Orleans Times-Democrat,* January 2, 1904.

13. *New Orleans Times-Democrat,* December 31, 1903. On a "mammy craze" that swept through the South and the entire nation between the 1890s and 1920s, see Grace Elizabeth Hale, *Making Whiteness: The Culture of Segregation in the South, 1890–1940* (New York: Vintage Books, 1998), 98–104. New Orleans had two African American newspapers at the time of the Twin Conventions, the *Republican Courier* and the *Southwestern Christian Advocate.* I have been unable to find evidence suggesting either paper took any interest in the gathering.

14. James McPherson, *The Abolitionist Legacy: From Reconstruction to NAACP* (Princeton: Princeton University Press, 1975), 368–93; also see Ralph E. Luker, *The Social Gospel in Black and White: American Racial Reform, 1885–1912* (Chapel Hill: University of North Carolina Press) 1991), 203–30.

15. The General Education Board continued to operate as an independent identity until 1960, when its programs were subsumed in the Rockefeller Foundation.

16. My account of the workings of the new GEB-style philanthropy draws from several secondary sources: Grantham, *Southern Progressivism,* chaps. 8 and 9; James D. Anderson, *The Education of Blacks in the South, 1860–1935* (Chapel Hill: University of North Carolina Press, 1988), chaps. 3 and 7; David Levering Lewis, *W. E. B. DuBois: Biography of a Race, 1869–1919* (New York: Henry Holt, 1993), 266–72; Eric Anderson and Alfred A. Moss Jr., *Dangerous Donations: Northern Philanthropy and Southern Black Education, 1902–1930* (Columbia: University of Missouri Press, 1999); and Michael Dennis, *Lessons in Progress: State Universities and Progressivism in the New South, 1880–1920* (Urbana: University of Illinois Press, 2001).

17. General Education Board, *Annual Report, 1918–19,* 68–70, as cited in Anderson and Moss, *Dangerous Donations,* 220.

18. By 1915, total northern philanthropic appropriations to black industrial schools in the South vastly outweighed those made to black colleges and universities. That year Hampton Institute's endowment stood at $2.7 million; Tuskegee at $1.9 million. Cumulatively these funds accounted for more than half the total endowment of private black colleges and universities in the United States. By comparison, the most generously funded black liberal arts institution of the period, Lincoln University in Pennsylvania, had only $700,000 in its endowment.

19. One of Ogden's guests at the 1901 Conference on Education was John D. Rockefeller Jr., whose family had contributed in earlier years to black education in the South. After visits to Hampton and Tuskegee Institutes and conversations with other northern philanthropists and educational reformers, the

young Rockefeller was impressed enough to urge his father to make a contribution to the southern educational reform movement.

20. Alderman to Robert Ogden, February 12, 1903, Edwin Alderman Papers, Tulane University Archives; Ogden to H. B. Frissell, April 13,1903, as quoted in Anderson and Moss, *Dangerous Donations,* 48; and Buttrick, as quoted in Anderson and Moss, *Dangerous Donations,* 51.

21. Alderman's speech was later revised and published as an article in the *Independent,* November 7, 1901, 247–49.

22. Walter Bernard Hill, "Negro Education in the South," *Proceedings of the Conference for Education in the South, Sixth Session, Richmond, Virginia, and the University of Virginia* (New York: Committee on Publications, 1903), 206–17. Hill's address was reprinted in *Annals of the American Academy of Political and Social Science* 22 (July–December 1903): 320–29.

23. For a more detailed breakdown of GEB disbursements, see *The General Education Board: An Account of its Activities: 1902–1914* (New York: General Education Board, 1915), 156–57. It is worth noting that the GEB identified Johns Hopkins University as a southern university. Johns Hopkins and the George Peabody College for Teacher in Tennessee each received endowment gifts of $250,000 during this period, which was the largest gift GEB gave to any southern institution.

24. J. M. Stephen Peeps, "Northern Philanthropy and the Emergence of Black Higher Education: Do-Gooders, Compromisers or Co-Conspirators?," *Journal of Negro Education* 5 (Summer 1981): 261–63.

25. "Stirring Up the Fires of Race Antipathy," *South Atlantic Quarterly* 2 (October 1903), reprinted in William B. Hamilton, *Fifty Years of the South Atlantic Quarterly* (Durham, N.C.: Duke University Press, 1952), 53–61. My account of the Basset case draws from several secondary sources: Earl W. Porter, *Trinity and Duke, 1892–1924* (Durham, N.C.: Duke University Press, 1964), 96–139; Bruce Cayton, *The Savage Ideal: Intolerance and Intellectual Leadership in the South* (Baltimore: Johns Hopkins University Press, 1972), 9–10, 84–103; Joel Williamson, *The Crucible of Race: Black-White Relations in the American South Since Emancipation* (New York: Oxford University Press, 1984), 261–71; Luker, *Social Gospel in Black and White,* 224–27; and Fred Arthur Bailey, *William Edward Dodd: The South's Yeoman Scholar* (Charlottesville: University of Virginia Press, 1997), 37–38, 40–42.

26. Exactly how much of a toll events took on Bassett remains an open question, mostly because there is a gap from September 1903 to March 1904 in his private correspondence in the John Spencer Bassett Papers held in the Library Congress. Eight years after the storm created by his 1903 *South Atlantic Quarterly* article had passed, Bassett told Charles Francis Adams that he considered the whole controversy "to some extent artificial." He explained that while the controversy raged he had "received many letters from men of prominence in the State which showed they did not approve" of the campaign Josephus Daniels had launched against him. In Bassett's view Daniels's failure to have him removed showed that it was "unwise to press the spirit of intolerance too far to the front" (John Spencer Bassett to Charles Francis Adams, November 3,

1911). It seems highly unlikely, however, that the "old spirit of intolerance" failed to take a heavy toll on Bassett as the storm played itself out. Bassett's son later recalled that his mother "picked up handfuls of threatening notes every morning, written probably by farmers in the neighborhood and delivered at night. They advised my father to get out of town, spoke of tar-and-feathering, and in one instance threatened his children" (Richard Bassett to Terry Sanford, March 15, 1984). The reason for the gap in Bassett's private correspondence from September 1903 to March 1904 is unclear. The correspondence for these months is also missing from Bassett papers held in the Duke University Archives.

27. Alderman, "Value of Southern Idealism," 12. The entire text of Alderman's address was reprinted in the December 30, 1903, *New Orleans Daily Picayune* as well as in *Publications of the American Economic Association,* 3rd ser., 5, no. 1 (February 1904): 74–78. The December 31, 1903, *New Orleans Times-Democrat* reported Bassett's absence, explaining that he had taken ill just a day or two before the Twin Conventions began.

28. After the Trinity Board announced its decision, it instructed Bassett to publish its statement in the *South Atlantic Quarterly,* along with a memorial the Trinity faculty had presented to the board in advance of its meeting and an editorial from the Trinity student newspaper. The trustees statement began with an unqualified disavowal of Bassett's opinions, stressing that "neither this board nor the college can be held to have approved or countenanced them, or to be in any degree responsible for them." The Trinity faculty also made it clear it did not endorse Bassett's opinion or have any interest in defending them. Similarly the student editorial emphasized that Trinity undergraduates did not share any of Bassett's views and that his article represented a "grave but not unpardonable blunder." See "Trinity College and Academic Liberty," *South Atlantic Quarterly* 3 (June 1904): 62–72.

29. On the Ross case, see James C. Mohr, "Academic Turmoil and Public Opinion: The Ross Case at Stanford," *Pacific Historical Review* 29 (February 1970): 39–62; and my discussion in chapter 4. It is worth noting that one of the two African American newspapers published in New Orleans took notice the Bassett Affair, praising Bassett for writing an article "touching on the relation of races in this country that marks him one of the wisest and bravest men of his time." *Southwestern Christian Advocate,* December 10, 1903, p. 2.

30. On the intellectual foundations of academic racism, see I. A. Newby, *Jim Crow's Defense: Anti-Negro Thought in America, 1900–1930* (Baton Rouge: Louisiana State University Press, 1965), and McPherson, *Abolitionist Legacy,* chap. 18. I am not sure there is much left to say about the intellectual foundations of academic racism. In any case, what I do in this paper is to shift attention to its arguably more important institutional manifestations. On objective racist acts as the primary substance of racism, see Barbara J. Fields, "Origins of the New South and the Negro Question," *Journal of Southern History* 67 (November 2001): 811–26.

31. Malone, *Edwin Alderman,* 147–51. Under Alderman's sponsorship, Washington traveled to New Orleans in the fall of 1902 to address an all-day meeting of black teachers.

32. See, for example, Kim Townsend's overview of Harvard faculty views on race in *Manhood at Harvard: William James and Others* (New York: W. W. Norton, 1996), 230–35, 238–39, 247–48. Townsend observes that on the question of race, President Charles Eliot maintained a standard higher than that of most of his faculty. Yet Eliot also defended the state of Kentucky in 1907, when it forced the previously integrated Berea College—the last of its kind in the Jim Crow South at that time—to establish a separate branch for its black students.

33. On silence as the disciplinary heritage of political science when dealing with race, see Hanes Walton, Cheryl M. Miller, and Joseph P. McCormick, "Race and Political Science: The Dual Traditions of Race Relations Politics and African American Politics," in *Political Science in History: Research Programs and Political Traditions,* ed. James Farr, John S. Dryzek, and Stephen L. Leonard (Cambridge: Cambridge University Press 1995).

34. *New Orleans Times-Democrat,* January 2, 1904.

35. On the gradual shift from a biological understanding of race to a cultural one, see Edward H. Beardsley, "The American as Social Activist: Franz Boas, Burt G. Wilder, and the Cause of Racial Justice," *Isis* 64, no.1 (November 1973): 50–66.

36. W. E. B. DuBois, *The Souls of Black Folk,* 1903 ed., with an introduction by Henry Louis Gates Jr. (New York: Bantam Books, 1989), xxxi. On DuBois and the American university movement, and his challenge to Booker T. Washington, see Lewis, *W. E. B. DuBois,* chaps. 11–13; and Adolph L. Reed Jr., *W. E. B. DuBois and American Political Thought: Fabianism and the Color Line* (New York: Oxford University Press, 1997), chaps. 2–5.

37. DuBois, *The Souls of Black Folk,* 75.

38. See "Two Negro Leaders," *South Atlantic Quarterly* 3 (July 1903): 267–72. Bassett's support for black higher education in the South proved short lived and might be considered another casualty of the storm his October article would trigger.

39. DuBois, *The Souls of Black Folk,* 67–68. It is worth noting that also on display here was DuBois's acceptance of the hierarchical assumptions of academic racial thinking at the turn century.

40. Ibid., 75. DuBois can be read of as a champion of the university movement in the South, although again along strictly segregated lines. In chapter 5, "Of the Wings of Atalanta," one of the five new chapters in *The Souls of Black Folks,* he wrote, "Let us build the Southern university—William and Mary, Trinity, Georgia, Texas, Tulane, Vanderbilt, and others—fit to live; let us build, too, the Negro universities—Fisk, whose foundation was ever broad; Howard, at the heart of the Nation; Atlanta at Atlanta, whose ideal of scholarship has been held above the temptation of numbers" (60).

41. It is worth noting that chapter 6 reprinted a slightly revised version of an essay with the same name that had appeared in the *Atlantic Monthly,* September 1902, 287–97. It seems certain that both Washington and the leadership of the GEB and the SEB were familiar with the argument of this piece before finding it again in *The Souls of Black Folks.*

42. We have no systematic scholarly account of how DuBois's contemporaries actually viewed *The Souls of Black Folk*. But Herbert Aptheker, *The Literary Legacy of W. E. B. DuBois* (White Plains, N.Y.: Kraus International, 1989), 41–86, remains a useful starting place. A sober review of the early publishing history of *The Souls of Black Folks* suggests it was hardly an immediate commercial success. It took five years to sell 9,959 copies of the first edition. Total sales between 1903 and 1946 amounted to a modest 20,000 copies. Also worth noting here is that it was not quite three weeks after the first edition of *The Souls of Black Folks* appeared that Andrew Carnegie contributed $600,000 in U.S. Steel bonds to the Tuskegee endowment fund—of which $150,000 was set aside for the personal use of Booker T. Washington and his family—and overnight Tuskegee joined the ranks of the wealthiest American colleges and universities

43. *General Education Board*, 209. By comparison, during the same period, the GEB made appropriations of $138,000 to the Hampton Institute and $135,483 to Tuskegee.

44. DuBois to Andrew Carnegie, May 22, 1906, in *Correspondence of W. E. B. DuBois*, vol. 1, ed. Herbert Aptheker (Amherst: University of Massachusetts Press, 1973), 121–22.

45. My account of the exchange with Jameson follows Lewis, *W. E. B. DuBois*, 385.

46. Only after World War I did the GEB begin to downplay its efforts to promote industrial education in public schools and gradually overcome its hostility to black higher education. The change stemmed in part from a tour of the South in 1919 that persuaded Wallace Buttrick, now president and secretary, that earlier GEB thinking had been a mistaken on both counts. He then proposed that the GEB spend larger sums on black colleges and universities. It would take another three years, however, for GEB trustees to confirm Buttrick's recommended change in policy. And even with more generous GEB funding for black universities such as Atlanta and Fisk, GEB's goal remained providing support for a conservative black leadership that would cooperate with rather than challenge the Jim Crow system. See Anderson, *Education of Blacks*, 276. DuBois worked for the NAACP and as editor of the *Crisis* until 1934, when he resigned to return to Atlanta University, where he devoted the next ten years to teaching and scholarship.

Afterword

1. I am indebted to Thomas Haskell for drawing my attention to the open-ended practical implications of "self-culture."

2. For an example of what I have in mind here, see the illuminating discussion of the prolonged effort to desegregate Tulane University in Clarence L. Mohr and Joseph E. Gordon, *Tulane: The Emergence of a Modern University, 1954–1980* (Baton Rouge: Louisiana State University Press, 2001), chaps. 3 and 4. In 1963 Tulane became one of the last of the South's two leading private research universities to desegregate—Rice University was the other—thanks

largely to its board's policy of delay and inaction. Mohr and Gordon note that from 1951 onward, the Tulane Board of Administrators routinely referred all segregation questions to its Law Committee, bypassing its arguably more appropriate Educational Affairs Committee. The upshot was a procedure that diminished the importance of then more liberal faculty opinion in shaping university policy and resulted in " a cycle of vacillating indecision that at time resembled administrative paralysis" (139).

3. For a recent account of how modern universities continue to occupy a central place in the cultural life of modern societies, see Stefan Collini's "Before Another Tribunal: The Idea of the 'Non-Specialist Public,'" in *English Pasts: Essays in History and Culture,* by Stefan Collini (Oxford: Oxford University Press, 1999), 305–25.

4. Here I echo points Leslie Butler makes at the conclusion of her fine study of George William Curtis, Thomas Wentworth Higginson, James Russell Lowell, and Charles Eliot Norton, all of whom were important figures in an earlier generation of native-born American champions of "self-culture." See Leslie Butler, *Critical Americans: Victorian Intellectuals and Transatlantic Reform* (Chapel Hill: University of North Carolina Press, 2008), 260.

INDEX

Page numbers for illustrations are given in *italic* type.